ACKNOWLEDGEMENTS

Ideas are not private discoveries, and books are not private property. The individual thinker builds upon the insights of others to achieve a new level of understanding, upon which still others build further. I wish to acknowledge many people whose previous work has helped me in the writing of this book:

Larry Agran, Gar Alperovitz, Richard Barnet, Wendell Berry, Fred Branfman, Jerry Brown, Cesar Chavez, Alexander Cockburn and James Ridgeway, Barry Commoner, Judy and Michael Corbett, Ron Dellums, Samuel Epstein, Marilyn Ferguson, William Domhoff, Richard Flacks, Jane Fonda, Mark Green, Michael Harrington, Hazel Henderson, Sam Hurst, Frances Moore Lappe, Amory Lovins, John Maher, Ken Msemaji, Ralph Nader, Jeremy Rifkin, Kirkpatrick Sale, Peter Schwartz, Derek Shearer, Mimi Silbert, Gloria Steinem, William Irwin Thompson, Alvin Toffler, William Appleman Williams, Leonard Weinglass, Daniel Yergin, and Howard Zinn.

Numerous others have influenced my feelings and thoughts by their example, committment, and their deeds rather than words. In particular, I wish to thank the activists of the Campaign for Economic Democracy for their tireless demonstration that our vision is possible to achieve.

I want to thank South End Press, and particularly Michael Albert, for their help in discussing, editing and producing the book, and for their unique and democratic approach to all sides of the publishing process. Appreciation also goes to my assistant, Cass Levison, for help in organizing the Appendix and in emergency typing and editing.

I have always found writing to be painful personally, for it draws the individual into a necessary isolation and inwardness that conflicts with the social nature of life. In fact, since having a family and, hopefully, becoming a more whole person as a result, I find that I have written less frequently, and with greater pain, over the years. I wish to thank my family and friends, therefore, for understanding the short period of absence and alienation writing this book required.

THE AMERICAN FUTURE

THE AMERICAN FUTURE

NEW VISIONS BEYOND OLD FRONTIERS

BY TOM HAYDEN

SOUTH END PRESS   BOSTON MA.

Cover Design by Michael Prokosch

South End Press Box 68 Astor Station Boston, Ma. 02123

 C-417

CONTENTS

It has been the feeling of pushing back frontiers, be they land frontiers in the West or space frontiers in the skies, that has ignited the spirit of the nation and set it apart from other nations. The drive toward expansion and growth has defined the United States during its 200 year history, and the new efforts to cut back, lower expectations, and retreat into the self go against the grain of the people.

—Business Week

The great convenience of the future as a context of behavior is that nobody knows anything about it. No rational person can *see* how using up the topsoil or the fossil fuels as quickly as possible can provide greater security for the future; but if enough wealth and power can conjure up the audacity to *say* that it can, then sheer fantasy is given the force of truth; the future becomes reckonable as even the past has never been. It is as if the future is a newly discovered continent which the corporations are colonizing. They have made "redskins" of our descendants, holding them subject to alien values, while their land is plundered of anything that can be shipped home and sold.

—Wendell Berry
The Unsettling of America

INTRODUCTION

Just beyond the pleasures and monotonies of everyday life, America seems caught in the coils of a catastrophe whose very obscurity makes it difficult to name and, therefore, to confront and solve. Our former power in the world is collapsing, and with it our economic security and sense of purpose. We ride the constant roller-coaster of inflation and recession, never quite leaving either. The energy sources we once thought were reliable are found seriously wanting, and ever more expensive. Our own health reflects the crisis, with one in four Americans expected to die of cancer. And despite our weaponry, we are unable to rescue 53 hostages held by unknown students in Iran. Talk of war with Iran, or over the Persian Gulf oilfields, has become commonplace among most Americans.

It seems to be one of those times in American history, like the Revolution, the Civil War, or the Great Depression, when a change in the system itself is necessary. But as in the years preceding American independence, the Emancipation Proclamation, and the New Deal, the possible solutions are too controversial, too uncertain, or simply not in sight for a majority of Americans. The 20th century has discredited all utopias. The resulting decline in idealism, in social imagination, leaves many people wondering if the most noble of proposals will only create new problems in practise. "You can't buck the system" and "you can't fight city hall" have become the accepted wisdom for millions of people in the 1970s.

1

But it is also true that the 1970s have not been silent. The questioning of the quality of life, which emerged and erupted in the 1960s, expanded through the nooks and crannies of society in the last decade. A majority of people blamed the oil companies for the energy crisis. Nuclear power plants were questioned for the first time, and a whole industry thrown into crisis. Alternative energy sources, like solar, became newly and widely attractive. A series of populist movements, concentrating on domestic economic issues, began to emerge for the first time since the 1930s: mineworkers went on long wildcat strikes, rent control was won by the tenants of California, taxpayers' "revolts" stirred the country, angry farmers ringed the U.S. Congress with tractors and neighborhood activists organized against speculators, and, in 1980, the smoldering silence of the black community exploded in Miami violence. At the same time, movements for social equality continued to grow. The women's movement held the largest convention in a century, and expanded on local levels everywhere. Unprecedented movements for gay rights arose, becoming the focus of fierce nationwide dispute. Senior citizens by the thousands turned into Gray Panthers. The disabled began to demand, and win, equal rights and access. A majority of students, faced with the military draft, said they would either refuse to fight in the Middle East, or felt grave uncertainties.

As in previous times prior to upheaval and change, these stirrings were everywhere, contradictory, and volatile. There was no longer a center that held together American life, only an anxious groping to find a new direction. By 1980, it had been 20 years since Americans had even experienced a stable, two term Presidency. The once unifying banners of New Deal liberalism and Cold War anticommunism were tattered and limp, but as yet replaced by nothing new and constructive. Voices of the past, nevertheless, were working hard to restore or maintain the way things were, not recognizing or accepting the changes of the 1960s and 1970s.

If there was a turning point, an irreversible breakdown of the system, it happened in the mid-1970s. Defeat in Vietnam, OPEC oil embargo, Watergate: these were shattering blows to American complacency but also metaphors of a world that was changing. The rest of humanity was no longer second-class, their world no longer our backyard. They were demanding, and winning, a more equal footing in the distribution of power and resources. For an American psychology based on being Number One, it was a hammerblow. For an American economy based on cheap energy and vast open markets, it was a fundamental challenge. The long path of the frontier was over. The American future would be shaped either by those who were determined to restore the past at whatever cost, or by those who forged a new vision of American purpose beyond frontier and empire. As with oil supplies, America would not have an unlimited supply of time to make the choice. If the nation procrastinated, further crisis, even war and depression, were just around the corner of the decade.

This book represents an effort to clear the confusion and outline an alternative. Written as the crises of Iran, Mideast oil, inflation and racial identity deepened in 1980, the essays contained here also come from a five-year process of reflection and social action. Like many other Americans, the mid-1970s were a personal turning point for myself. When the Vietnam War ended, I looked up from a 12 year experience of protest, wondering what the future held next. I had learned from the student movement of the 1960s and from the long anti-war struggle, that my particular vocation was educating and organizing people to have greater control over the decisions affecting their lives. I knew that after the war the country would obviously turn inward to its economic and energy problems, and that a new populism would probably arise. But I was less certain of the possible answers to the emerging crisis.

With other friends and allies from the anti-war movement I plunged into the search for *democratic* answers to the problems of inflation, unemployment, energy and above all, the structure of political and economic decision-making which was so clearly in the hands of corporate executives and long-time government bureaucrats. Since their decisions were causing our problems, I reasoned, most certainly their proposed "solutions" would only create more.

And so in 1976, I ran for the U.S. Senate, primarily as a challenge to a tired establishment and to create an opportunity for citizens to focus on alternative democratic solutions to the problems of energy and economics. While our campaign proposed some answers—solar energy, conservation, equitable health care, a shift of priorities from warfare to human needs, greater democratic control over corporate decision-making—its more fundamental assertion was that citizens themselves would find new answers by realizing that they were able to, and that the ruling "experts" were actually bankrupt of fresh ideas.

The campaign did not win a Senate seat, but it received 1.2 million votes, perhaps the largest protest vote for an "alternative" candidate in this century. More important, it triggered a grass-roots movement of citizens who wanted to continue the struggle for alternatives at the community, statewide, and national levels. In 1977, that network became the Campaign for Economic Democracy, a California-based citizens movement working for a transition to solar energy, renters' rights and affordable housing, the end of cancer-causing pollution, equal pay for equal work, investment of private and public capital in job-creating areas of social need, and numerous other programs reflecting the interests of working people, consumers, minorities, and small business. The CED effort took many forms, from running candidates for local office, to lobbying the state Legislature, to involvement in government commissions, to demonstrating against nuclear power and South African apartheid.

Through this grass-roots participation in the new stirrings of the 1970s, we began to research, discuss and formulate more comprehensive answers to the problems we confronted everyday. This book is my own individual attempt to construct a vision out of this collective effort of several years.

The first chapter surveys our nation's history and introduces a main theme of the book: the conflict between a now outdated and destructive "frontier mentality" and a new, more inward-looking consciousness suited to the crises we now face. The next three chapters are case studies of inflation and employment, solar energy development, and the cancer epidemic spreading through our country. They each point toward a need for basic changes in the commercial values and system under which we live. Then as the focal section of the book, chapter five addresses this system, discusses its history, and elaborates an alternative vision which we call "economic democracy." Chapter six continues by applying the principles of economic democracy to envision a new kind of foreign policy, one suited to the preservation of peace rather than empire.

Finally, in the last chapter, the book surveys the shape of things to come in America in the eighties. With the decline of the New Deal coalition, it becomes clear that a "new center" will be the object of political debate and struggle in the years ahead. A rationalization of our economy is likely in the face of energy shortages and foreign competition. Will this rationalization occur from the top down via corporate and government planning and attempt to preserve and extend old privileges and institutions? Or will it be from the bottom up, through citizens initiatives leading to a safer energy and economic future? In this historic confrontation of possible futures for our society, a new coalition within the existing party system flanked by a broad popular citizens movement for change can exert decisive influence in the decade ahead. But only with a new vision will it be possible to ignite and hold together a new majority coalition for progressive and democratic change. The stakes are as high as they have ever been in our history, and citizens will have to break the grips of apathy and become personally responsible for solving the crisis ahead.

The changes will not come easily, and they are only dimly perceived today. But that was also true of ideas like Independence, Union, and Suffrage, in centuries past. In the 1980s, the effort will be to lift the confusion and find a new vision summarized in words like Renewable Resources, Social Responsibility, Stewardship, Economic Democracy. Surely it can be done. The history of our country is that of constant tension between the forces of order, authority, privilege and elite rule, and the rebellious, iconoclastic forces of change, progress, pluralism, and self-determination. In the long run, the side of democracy has always prevailed. In the crisis of the 1980s it will have to prevail again, but sooner and more quickly and thoroughly than many now think.

Tom Hayden
Santa Monica
June 15 1980

ONE
AMERICAN IDENTITY: THE
FRONTIERS OF CUSTER AND THOREAU

I confess I am not charmed with the idea of life held out
by those who think that the normal state of human beings
is struggling to get on; that the trampling, crushing,
elbowing and treading on each other's heels which form
the existing type of social life, are the most desirable lot
of human kind, or anything but the disagreeable symptoms of one of the phases of industrial progress.... It is
scarcely necessary to remark that a stationary condition
of capital and population implies no stationary state of
human improvement. There would be as much scope as
ever for all kinds of mental, cultural, moral and social
progress; as much room for improving the Art of Living,
and much more likelihood of its being improved, when
minds ceased to be engrossed by the art of getting on.

John Stuart Mill
Principles of Economics
1848

In January 1980 the Ayatollah Khomeini scowled from the
covers of our leading news magazines. He was *Time*'s "Man of the
Year"; *Life* titled its cover story, "Khomeini's Fierce Outcry
Against America." Both told the widely-accepted tale of a
"Muslim fanatic" who wanted to turn back the clock of Modern-
ism to the 7th century, and who had already turned Iran into "the
only major nation that is ruled by a mystic philosopher-king sitting
cross-legged on the floor of a bare room in a dusty provincial
town."[1]

7

These editorials were intelligent but uncomprehending, reflecting a failure of the nation's leadership to understand the dynamics of Iran, a failure that is based on a dangerously outmoded way of seeing the world and, above all, on materialistic values that blind America to a central truth of the 20th Century: that human beings wish to "bake their own bread" and desire independence and freedom as well.

The gap between Khomeini and his editorial questioners occurred most dramatically when the Ayatollah declared that "the U.S. Government has no idea what martyrdom is." There followed this exchange:

> (Question) You have not studied seriously economics, international political relations. Your education is primarily theological. Doesn't this raise doubts in your mind that there might be factors in this equation that you don't grasp?

> (Answer) We have discarded equations and social and political terms of reference so far used for assessing all the world's problems. We have built a new framework of values standing up for justice and fighting injustice... You may name this value system whatever you like. We are laying the foundation of this value system, which, we hope, will one day replace—in the UN, the Security Council, and other world bodies—the influence of the capitalists and the great powers that can now condemn out of hand anybody they want to. *Yes, with your criteria, I understand nothing—and I am better off for it.*[2]

Whether Khomeini is indeed "better off for it" remains to be seen. His revolution has yet to demonstrate how far its human concern extends, and there is real reason to fear an irrationality and inhumanity at its very core. Yet in Khomeini's disregard for some Western ways, there is certainly wisdom. These collisions between older imperialisms and rising revolutions, and the perceptual American blindness they create, have been constantly repeated in our time. The Khomeini-US conflict, for instance, is a direct descendant of an earlier one in 1952 between the British, who dominated the Iranian oil fields, and a new Prime Minister,

Mohammed Mossadeq. According to one historian, "to the British public and the press this wild old man (Mossadeq) wearing pajamas and perpetually weeping appeared so ridiculous, so fanatical and unashamedly emotional that he represented the defiance of all reason."[3] U.S. Secretary of State Acheson referred to Mossadeq's forces as "a group of wild men in Iran who proposed to despoil Britain."[4] Mossadeq's crime? He nationalized British Petroleum's oil fields, a deed for which he was overthrown by the American CIA and replaced by the Shah. Twenty-five years later, the followers of Mossadeq—including Khomeini—overthrew the same Shah, recaptured the same oil fields, and were portrayed in the American press as "the defiance of all reason" once again. Is it surprising that the Iranians hold our government accountable? Is it surprising that they were afraid of CIA plots that might reimpose the Shah or otherwise interfere with the future course of their country? No doubt the tactics of the militant students holding our embassy personnel hostage were extreme and criminal. But was our country's intervention against Mossadeq less extreme? The Iranians are retaliating against people they consider complicit in great crimes against their population by holding fifty suspected "spies" (in their view) hostage. We, in retaliation to the holding of fifty of our citizens, talk of war or the withholding of food to starve a population as viable avenues of retaliation. Who is more extreme and less reasoned?

One wonders if during the past 25 years the American government has learned anything. It would seem we should have, after the experiences of Cuba in 1959 and Vietnam from 1961 to 1975. Nevertheless, President Carter and wife Rosalynn spent their 1977 New Year's at the Teheran palace of the Shah, apparently swept up in traditional illusions. According to the President's own account, he had asked Rosalynn, "With whom would you like to spend New Year's Eve?," and she replied, "Above all others, with the Shah and Empress Farah."[5] And that was not all in this Presidential fairy tale. During their visit to Iran, President Carter congratulated the Shah for making the country an "island of stability in one of the more troubled areas of the world," noted that "we have no other nation on earth who is closer to us in planning for our mutual military security," and commented blissfully on the hospitality of the Iranian people for having taken 30,000 American personnel "to heart and made them feel at home." All this was only *one year* before the uprisings that overthrew the Shah's dictatorship and mighty armed forces, installed Khomeini and unleashed a process including the seizure of American hostages by the "hospitable" Iranians.

How did this happen? Could bad intelligence have led Carter to confuse the opulence and weapons of the Shah for real strength, to totally under-estimate the hostility just below the surface of society, to remain utterly blind to the mounting force of the exiled Ayatollah?

The blindness was rooted more deeply than in a CIA cubicle. It came more from a set of assumptions used by one administration after another. Never quite formulated officially, the assumptions can be drawn from both statements and policies declared since the very settling of the United States. They are, roughly,

1. That economically under-developed people are backward in cultural, educational and social terms as well, less civilized than ourselves;

2. that revolution is either a "hangover" of the past or a "disease" of the development process,[6] in the words of Vietnam planner W. W. Rostow, a sinister force composed of demagogues, preying on the backward instincts and irrational resentments of people looking for scapegoats to blame for their impoverishment;

3. that conservative, dictatorial regimes are sometimes justifiable in the under-developed world as necessary evils for the control of unrest and the maintenance of an economy suitable for American-style "development";

4. Economic development, to be successful, must be on the Western model, under the auspices of multinational corporations and World Bank-type investment authorities, aimed at building a free enterprise economy integrated into a larger world system pulling it towards progress; *

5. Revolutionary sentiment will be dissipated by the channeling of people towards an urban, materialistic, consumer

---

*According to *Business Week*'s editors: "Aswarm with arms salesmen and other purveyors of high technology, *Tehran under the Shah had become a virtual Mecca for the multinational corporations.*" (Business Week Team, *The Decline of U.S. Power*, p. 144.)

culture, a model of society which will both develop and meet their "true" needs.

But these assumptions of the American economic frontier are false. History shows that industrialization and cultural wisdom do not necessarily go hand in hand. Revolution was at the base of the development of our own society and of those in Europe as well—it is no more nor less sinister as practiced elsewhere. Sometimes revolution is progressive, sometimes not. Corrupt and brutal dictatorships like those in Paraguay and Pakistan, Chile and the Phillipines should no more be morally justified or militarily subsidized on the grounds of their benefitting U.S. (corporate) interests than should the Soviets justify intervention in Czechoslovakia on similar grounds. And whether we like it or not, history shows that development under the auspices of the World Bank and multinationals is not development at all, but stagnation. The productive efforts of the people of countries like Jamaica, Liberia, and Thailand (and their natural resources as well) benefit not their own economies but those of the countries who dominate the World Bank and sponsor the multinationals, principally the U.S. And finally, the idea that citizens of countries such as Iran will put aside their militance in pursuit of personal materialism seems an equally hopeless notion. It fails to recognize the moral, cultural and national motivations at work.

The same American world view has mistaken misery and injustice as inevitable, supported dictators as lesser evils, and left the American people with an isolated philosophy of materialism in a world where a near-majority earn less than enough to stay alive. Most importantly, it is a philosophy that can only bring about a decline of ethical fiber among Americans themselves, trading vision for consumer comfort, and abandoning such virtues as discipline, sacrifice and will-power to the new nationalisms of the world.

The fact that should jar Americans is not so much the rise of a Khomeini, but that we have less to offer as a philosophy to oppressed people than Khomeini does. In fact, we lack any clear philosophy that can inspire a majority of Americans to any endeavor requiring personal sacrifice for a larger purpose.

By returning for a moment to the January 1980 editions of *Time* and *Life*, we can obtain a glimpse of the competing moral reply which America makes to Khomeini. The reader of *Time* will plow through 33 pages before finding and finishing the interview with the Ayatollah; the *Life* reader will scan 30 pages. Of these 66 total pages, one half (33) are covered by advertisements. Ten of the ads promote cancer-causing, mind-dulling cigarettes and liquor; six are temptations to buy the latest gas-guzzling high-obsolescence automobiles; the rest of the miscellaneous consumer enticements include a full-page closeup of a Big Mac, and a camera modelled by Cheryl Teigs.

Consumption as an ethic cannot compete with national freedom. All it can do is bloat the American society with selfish resentment against an increasingly restless world we once thought we inspired. Consumption, moreover, is not a realistic ethic for American society itself in a world of inflation, energy shortages, and closing frontiers.

The Closing Frontier: Confronting Limits

The end of the frontier is the crucial fact for the next generation of Americans. We are going to have to understand the poverty of the assumptions listed earlier, realize that they were held only to rationalize behavior that must now change, and finally reassess and develop a new way of thinking to fit a new world. In the past decade our country has been slapped three times with the news: 1) the loss in Vietnam showed we were not the policeman of the world, 2) devaluation of the dollar showed we were not the banker of the world and 3) the OPEC cartel showed we could not continue to consume energy with no attention to the effects on others. That we live in an era of limits and restraints is becoming clear through episodes like the seizing of our hostages in Iran. Within the industrialized capitalist world, the U.S. is no longer economically superior to Japan or Germany. We face rising competition from the Soviet bloc. The developing world is becoming more powerful and demanding.

What is less understood is the crisis which is just around the corner of history for an America that is five percent of the world's people but consumes 30-40 percent of the world's resources, while in the Third World, 70 percent of the world's population consumes only 16 percent of the world's resources. At current levels of consumption, the U.S. will need to *double* its energy intake in the next 20 years. If our energy use were to expand in this way it could only be by denying others even a level of resources necessary for survival. Is this the ethic we want for the future? Do we wish to become a fortress of gluttony amidst a sea of starvation, two sides of the same coin? Is that the relation we wish to have toward others? We take their means of life and sustenance and build a military to keep them at bay. This is the imperialist logic of our current ethos and one we are badly in need of changing. Yet even if we don't see the moral desirability of change, history is about to compel us.

World supplies of oil are expected to be surpassed by world demand within the same period.[7] For the U.S. will soon be dependent on foreign imports for half our supply of nine (out of 13) vital raw materials located in the Third World—bauxite, chromium, cobalt, manganese, natural rubber, nickel, tin, tungsten and zinc).[8] And even if the US could secure control of all these raw materials over the short run—an immoral vision, to be sure—the earth is running out of virtually every non-renewable resource vital to industrial society. The very eco-structure itself, according to Lester Brown, is being threatened by population increase and resource overuse. World population is now doubling every fifteen years, at exponential and terrifying rates. It took an estimated 2 million years to reach a population level of one billion earthlings; only 100 years to achieve a second billion; 30 years to create a third billion; and only 15 years to reach a fourth.[9] The earth's population is rising at a net increase of 73 million people per year. The planetary limit is being reached. Forest productivity, the fishing potential, cropland, and grassland yields have all fallen or peaked since the 1960s. A White House report concludes that "overcrowding, poverty and hunger will haunt the globe in the year 2000," "food and energy prices will continue to spiral," 20 percent of the earth's plant and animal species will become extinct, "the gap between the richest and the poorest will increase," and "life for most people on earth will be more precarious in 2000 than it is now."[10] Never in American history has there been a gloomier official prognosis of the future.

While resources at the beginning of the frontier were cheap and plentiful, it is obvious that they become increasingly scarce and expensive as time and exploration go on. That is why crash programs for synthetic fuels, nuclear power, ocean mining and space production all threaten to consume as much capital and energy as their proponents project creating—and, at any rate, are incapable of meeting our energy needs in the crucial time-frame of the next decade.

But for those who want to face reality, the burning issue is to discover a new American ethic that can captivate and energize the American people, without war and imperialism, in a time of collapsing empire. There is no inevitability in the decline of societies, and no reason that America after two centuries should accept that its greatness lies buried in the past. Reduced to the lives of individuals, the same viewpoint would mean bringing children into the world only to inform them that the best times of living already are over. It is contrary to the spirit of life to accept such fatalism. But if we are to project an alternative we must replace the basis of improving life by economic expansion with something different and more suited to the reality of our times.

The root of the frontier worldview is based on the material progress claimed by the expansion of capitalism, first in its free-enterprise and later its large-scale bureaucratic forms. This concept of progress has justified exploration and expansion, investment and profit, science and technology virtually for their own sakes. The supreme philospher of self-interest, John Locke, wrote that "land that is left wholly to nature is called, as indeed it is, *waste.*"

One corollary of this tradition is the idea of frontiers without limit, suggesting that freedom is not secure without an American capacity to control and expand a constantly outward push. Being Number One on every material level is a national goal and by now even a psychic need. A further corollary is that wealthy corporations are creators of an ever-greater "pie," or Gross National Product, which gradually allows more people to share in at least some benefits. The GNP—the total sum of goods and services produced—is a purely material measurement of achievement, and encourages planned obsolescence as a management strategy, conspicuous consumption as the accepted fashion, and "growth" as an all-purpose buzzword for a way of life. Moreover, focusing only on quantities of wealth and product fails to notice their unequal

distribution—the fact that under two percent of the U.S. population has control of around 32 percent of all privately controlled
wealth, that about one third of one percent of the U.S. population
own 20 percent of all personal wealth and that the top ten percent
own fifty percent of all personal wealth—and the poor quality of
much of our material abundance (the cars that break down, the
clothes which fall apart so quickly), the by-products accompanying
our high productivity (from auto deaths, industrial accidents, alienation at work, and black lung, to pollution and resource depletion), and the qualitative failings of our society. For example,
we are the 15th in infant mortality, most of our artists are employed in the creation of mindless commercials, many of our scientists create weaponry, wife beating and violence against women
generally is on the rise, pornography is a bigger industry than
movies and recording together, racism is still a part of the national
fabric, crime is rampant and, not surprising, mental illness is
epidemic.[11]

This set of materialist visions which dominate our lives is a
hangover from an earlier phase of American history, when the
Protestant ethic met the abundant frontier of the New World. The
chemistry of the relationship gave birth to an expansionist
America. The ethic fortified generations of settlers, pioneers and
entrepreneurs in the face of the adversities standing between them
and Wealth. Brutal imperial wars against the Indians, Mexicans
and other European powers were rationalized by this ethic of
destiny. The necessary sacrifices were made to save and invest in
the future. Max Weber, in his *Protestant Ethic and the Spirit of
Capitalism,* pointed out that Calvinism required "the idea of the
necessity of proving one's faith in worldly activity."[12] The
proof God required was amply given; the American economy
became the richest and most industrially advanced in the world.

California always was the pinnacle of the expansionist dream,
beginning with a Spanish romantic novel by Garcia Ordonez de
Montalvo in 1542, describing the place as a plentiful island "very
close to the Terrestrial Paradise," abundant with gold, silver and
fertile lands and inhabited by beautiful Amazon women. That this
was a figment of the imagination rarely occurred to the later con-
querers, adventurers, explorers and wandering lunatics who found
their way West in subsequent centuries. "For one of the most per-

sistent themes of the Judeo-Christian heritage of the Western World was the existence of an earthly paradise... The quest for the seven cities of Cibola, the legend of El Dorado where gold had been gathered for years, and even the belief of Ponce de Leon that there existed a fountain capable of restoring youth, are all part of the European dream... To many migrants who made their difficult and hazardous way to California in the 19th century, California was the land of abundance which man had sought for centuries." [13]

This dream, in its time, had at least a connection to reality. Gold, after all, was discovered, and "in California... all the dreaming after gold that had built empires, started wars, deposed kings and annihilated whole peoples was distilled into an incandescent ray of hope... the call to California was a clarion of opportunity, of possibility, of new beginnings, and great expectations." [14]

After Gold came railroads, oil fields and then land fever in southern California promoted by the Los Angeles *Times* in editorial oratory like this: "Better than the Utopias of the ancients is this modern Utopia of the Pacific. Better than the Gardens of Hesperides, with their golden fruits, the gardens of this sunset land." [15] For the 30-40,000 monthly immigrants to southern California in the 1880s, everything seemed free as the air.

A critical historian of the American frontier, William Appleman Williams, points out that expansionism was supported by an American majority. "Beginning with the rise of Jacksonian Democracy during the 1820s... Americans steadily deepened their commitment to the idea that democracy was inextricably connected with individualism, private property and a capitalist marketplace economy. [16] Farmers, workers and businessmen were won to the frontier approach, at home and abroad, for a mix of reasons. Some identified with the 1845 editorial in *Democratic Review*, justifying the taking of Mexico and California, by claiming a "manifest destiny to overspread the continent allotted by Providence for the free development of our yearly multiplying millions." [17]

In these optimistic circumstances, the "work ethic" was an often voluntary form of behavior, not a pious demand of self-serving employers upon alienated workers. Of course, it took a promise to the worker of a stake from business and government—the hope for land, opportunity, a better life. However, the motivation of the migrants who built the canals and railroads had to be more than material blessing alone. To leave homes and farms in the East or Midwest, to cross the plains, mountains and deserts, to endure the weather and the isolation, all this took dedication to a dream which can hardly be compared to anything in the experience of contemporary Americans. Those earlier generations had a cause beyond themselves, the individual interest and the whole were connected in a common pursuit of achievement and expansion. As a US officer told the Indians upon declaring California a Republic:

> We come to prepare this magnificent region for the use of other men, for the population of the world demands more room, and here is room enough for many millions, who will hereafter occupy and till the soil.[18]

A crucial subtheme of the frontier philosophy has been the idea that Americans are expanding freedom in a world of savage totalitarianism. From the very settling of the country down to the present, the foreign enemy has changed in identity, language, skin-color, and continent of origin, but his inhuman and diabolical ways were the same, and they served the same American domestic purpose: to satisfy Americans that this country had a civilizing and freedom-spreading mission in the world. From the first Indian to the last Vietnamese, this racist myth has created an innocent moral defense for the most sordid of conquests.

But of course all these views are quite false. The Iroquis, for example, in their political federation provided the model for the U.S. Constitution which was soon considered Western white man's chief contribution to world civilization, conveniently forgetting that it was the Native Americans who employed the political forms first (more equitably) and curiously for centuries before they were adopted by the "superior race." It seems also reasonable to conclude that Native American attitudes to wealth and nature were also not primitive, but actually superior to the less ecological materialism of the invading Europeans. Similarly, of course the Japanese were at least equal to we westerners in cultural heritage and technology when *we* dropped (a sign of superiority?) nuclear bombs on their cities. And as to Ho Chi Minh and the

Vietnamese it seems most unlikely that history's scales will be kinder to Johnson, Kissinger, and Nixon.*

The roots of our world view lie in the creation of America itself. It was a rather righteous, ruthless and ambitious breed who braved the seas to conquer, settle and open the West. Amerigo Vespucci, for whom the United States is named, condemned in his diaries the "barbarous" natives he encountered for being "contented with what nature gives them. The wealth which we affect in this our Europe and elsewhere, such as gold, jewels, pearls and other riches, they hold of no value at all."[24]

These "savages" had to be either annihilated or subdued into "civilization," and so they were, from the Atlantic to the Pacific in a blood-letting process that is still not over after four centuries. Along the way of expanding the frontier there were also several major wars abroad, only one of which was triggered by a direct attack on U.S. territory (Pearl Harbor). "From the Halls of Montezuma to the shores of Tripoli," generations of Americans fought to preserve an expanding system from the external threat.*

The most important aspect of this rather uniquely American experience is the tendency it creates in us to find fault and danger in the *outer*, rather than the *inner* world. Such a moral worldview makes oneself both superior towards those who are the Others and also towards one's own internal contradictions and moral weaknesses. It creates a purposeful righteousness, a destiny that the truly and obviously "manifest" are those blessed enough to be American. And it creates a way to endure life's shortcomings by offering at least a positive comparison with the plight of others. It works, to a point, if the only measure of success is growth. But it provides a poor base for self-improvement or the development of wisdom about ourselves and others.

---

*Andrew Jackson on the Indians: "(They may) cast off their savage habits and become an interesting, civilized, and Christian community."[19] Woodrow Wilson on World War I: "(It is an American) duty toward people living in bararism to see that they are freed from their chains, and we can free them only by destroying barbarism itself... peace cannot be had until the civilized nations have expanded in some shape over the barbarous nations"[20] (1912) *Time* magazine on the Japanese: "The ordinary unreasoning Jap is ignorant. Perhaps he is human. Nothing indicates it."[21] (1944) *Time* on Vietnam's Ho Chi Minh: "A Mongoloid Trotskyite."[22] Lyndon Johnson on Indochina: "We cannot be blackmailed by any yellow dwarf with a knife."[23]

The fact that slavery existed at the foundation of American society makes the point well. It took an extreme sense of moral self-righteousness to ransack the African continent, uproot and transport tens of millions of people in the subhuman holds of ships, sell them as commodities to the highest bidder, control them with whip and chain, and rationalize the entire degrading process as morally progressive. Even today the record of slavery tends to be minimized by most Americans as a mere "chapter" of U.S. history rather than a fundamental infection of the national character.

Slavery was not the only case where moral justifications have been used to cloak economic interests. Whatever its impact on our consciousness, the moral idea of Manifest Destiny, for example, was closely connected with an economic fact of enormous consequence: given the arrangement of our economy, depression and social strife would be the domestic result of not having new frontiers and markets abroad. Tobacco and cotton farmers needed foreign markets from the very beginning of the U.S., and food producers followed by the 1830s. Then came manufacturing. As the journal *Iron Age* stated in 1877, "As our manufacturing capacity largely exceeds the wants of home consumption, we shall either have to curtail the same by shutting up a great many establishments or we shall have to create a fresh outlet through export."[25] A State Department document in the McKinley era officially declared that, "...every year we shall be confronted with an increasing surplus of manufactured goods for sale in foreign markets if American operatives and artisans are to be kept employed the year around."[26]

The famous 1893 "frontier thesis" of Frederick Jackson Turner was the most celebrated effort to provide a rationale for America's imperial drives. Connecting expansion to prosperity, Turner made significant reference to the frontier as a "gate of escape."[27] By this he meant that Americans were blessed with a safety valve like few other nations, an ability through expansion to overcome the build-up of domestic contradictions faced by European powers.

Appleman Williams convincingly traces this economic motive through American history beginning with the "imperial anti-colonialism" of 1812 which secured American ambitions west of the Mississippi; the Louisiana Purchase of 1803 by which France "conceded without a fight a huge strip of real estate extending from the Gulf of Mexico to the Pacific Ocean"; the Monroe Doctrine of 1823 in which "Americans boldly asserted their claim to predominance throughout the entire Western Hemisphere"; the 1890 massacre at Wounded Knee which eerily coincided with the official U.S. declaration that the internal frontier was closed; the Open Door foreign policy of Woodrow Wilson who said in 1907 that "the doors of the nations which are closed must be battered down"; the "Pax Americana" dream of Charles Evans Hughes in 1924; and the modern Cold War doctrines in which the freedom of American corporate investment is equated with the national interest in freedom and progress and secured by immense military exports and, when need be, interventions.[28]

It is Williams' further implication that the *domestic* consumer society is a kind of "supplementary frontier" which helps keep material production—and therefore prosperity and employment —at acceptable levels. Critics like Williams have long forecast a profound American crisis if and when these two frontiers— domestic consumption and foreign markets—become saturated and limited and the economy is not transformed to bear the change, as has been the case in the past decade.

In addition to the moral philosophy of "manifest destiny" and the economic imperative of maintaining growth in production, there has also been a *political* rationale for the frontier as central to American progress. This argument has been that democracy itself can only flourish under conditions of national expansion.

The *Federalist Papers* contained the political, and earliest constitutional, arguments linking a frontier with democracy. America's founding philosophers sought to rebut the argument of the French philosopher Montesqieu that democracy could only be viable in small states. The Montesqieu thesis implied that size and growth, not to mention empire, were the enemies of a democratic society, and that there was an inherent link between limits of scale and opportunities for effective citizenship.[29]

It was Madison's worry in the *Federalist Papers* that democracy would lead to a dangerous factionalizing, even what he called a "majority faction." While the newly-founded American state clearly had broader popular support—from urban workers and small farmers—than any other comparable government at the end of the 18th century, it was plagued by internal dangers needing a philosophical and structural solution. There were, after all, 18 uprisings aimed at overthrowing colonial governments between 1760 and the American revolution, an additional half-dozen slave rebellions, and another 40 riots of one sort or another recorded. The Revolutionary War was fought by a freezing, suffering, largely propertyless army starkly different than the 10 percent of Americans who owned half the nation's new wealth and were to benefit most from independence.[30]

In these conditions, Madison wrote of his worries that the continental soldiers might develop "a rage for paper money, for an abolition of debts, and equal division of property, or for any other *improper and wicked project.*" Such elements together could become a "majority faction," Madison wrote, since factions arose from "the various and unequal distribution of property," and "those who hold and those who are without property have ever formed distinct interests in society."[31]

Madison's solution was to submerge a potential "majority faction" within a representative government. The key was the frontier. By creating "an extensive Republic," Madison believed "it will be more difficult for all who feel it to discover their own strength, and act in unison with each other." He wrote confidently that "the influence of factious leaders may kindle a flame within their particular states, but will be unable to spread a general conflagration through other states."[32]

Madison's defense of the 18th century elite, it should be noted, also "worked" for the common man. In conjunction with the Manifest Destiny morality and the opportunities of the frontier, the Constitution brought a new enfranchisement that seemed an historic guarantee against either political or economic tyranny. That franchise would, after time and struggle, be extended to millions of other Americans initially denied its benefits. The key to the successful enlargement of this freedom was the existence of the frontier at home and overseas. For with a frontier, the "improper and wicked" demand for an "equal division of property" would never be channeled into a political struggle of the have-nots against the rich at home. It could be rechanneled into a conquest of California or a war, in Woodrow Wilson's words, "to make the world safe for democracy."

Custer Vs. Thoreau: A Choice of World Views

General George Armstrong Custer was the archetype 19th century *Man* of the American West, reaching a stature in fantasy only obtained by John Wayne in this century. The youngest general in the U.S. Army, Custer established himself early as the valorous symbol of the frontier spirit. He was, according to one biography, spreading a "contagion of faith and fortitude," a "creature of Glory, tilting at windmills and breaking down the gates of hell." [33] The death of this "epic hero," the biography continues, "inspired more fabulous paintings than any other military event" in history. For this blond, long-haired young general, one of Custer's associates observed, "fighting and fornicating are incompatible. When he feels the need for a woman, he leads a wild cavalry charge and stampedes the old Adam out of his system." [34] After service in the Civil War, where he helped turn the tide at Gettysburg (though losing 250 men), Custer led the 7th Cavalry into the Great Plains, fast becoming the best-known and most glamorous Indian fighter. The Black Hills Treaty of 1868 had prohibited entry by whites into the region without Indian permission. But Custer, who already had surprised and massacred a Cheyenne tribe, had no intention of leaving the Black Hills and Yellowstone to the Sioux. His reports that the hills were filled with gold "from the grass roots down" helped turn settlers into "summer locusts, crazy to begin panning and digging." [35] It also increased the clamour for U.S. troops to protect the railroad's invasion of the sacred buffalo lands. But in the end, Custer's own greed and arrogance led him to a state of military over-extendedness. Wanting everything, he led his troops into Yellowstone County where, by the banks of the Little Bighorn, they were surprised and overrun. In death, however, his legend had begun, one of civilization versus savagery, the conquering spirit mortally endangered by evil, his mythical romantic heroism covering over the true racist venality and avarice that led to his humiliating destruction.

There were, even then, voices of warning along the path of expansion, dissenters who stood against the grain. Their cries sounded to most Americans like an antique crusade of traditionalists against the modern world. As Wendell Berry writes, these other voices represented an alternative path not taken, "the tendency to stay put, to say, 'No farther. This is the place.' "[36] One origin of this vision was among the native Americans, of whom Bernard de Voto has written, "The first belt-knife given by a European to an Indian was a portent as great as the cloud that mushroomed over Hiroshima... (The Indian) both began to live better and he began to die."[37]

The typical Indian worldview rejected the new materialism and emphasized instead the spirit, the community and the sacred unity of all living things. A classic disclaimer from the white settler worldview was given, for example, by Chief Luther Standing Bear, who announced with bemusement that "the Great Chief in Washington says that he wishes to buy our land." Commenting on Washington ethics, the Chief said,

> One portion of the land is the same to him as the next, for he is a stanger who comes in the night and takes whatever he needs. The earth is not his brother but his enemy, and when he conquers it he moves on.
> The whites too shall pass—perhaps sooner than other tribes. Continue to contaminate your own bed and one night you will suffer in your own waste.
> When the buffalo are all slaughtered, the wild horses all tamed, the secret corners of the forest heavy with the scent of many men, and the view of the ripe hills blotted by the talking wires, where is the thicket? Gone. Where is the eagle? Gone. And what is it to say goodbye to the swift and the hunt? *The end of living and the beginning of survival.*[38]

If the Indian voice was silenced in the violence of industrialization and acquisition, dissenting voices in the majority culture were more often isolated. The incentive of the expanding frontier was more powerful than the warnings of philosophical skeptics. "The spirit of gain is always on the stretch," de Tocqueville wrote in 1835. "(The Americans) strain their faculties to the utmost to achieve paltry results and this cannot fail speedily to limit their range of view, and to circumscribe their powers. They might be much poorer and still be greater."[39]

Perhaps the most radical and articulate of the critics was Henry David Thoreau, the opposite of Custer, who denounced both the corporate-industrial age from Walden Pond and the Mexican War from a prison cell.

Thoreau was the key articulator, if not the father, of a mode of thinking which haunted but could not subvert the dominant institutions. Born of the Transcendentalist movement, his philosophy questioned the very value of the age of industrial expansion and Protestant Ethic. The worker, he complained, had "no time to be anything but a machine"; they had "become tools of their tools"; led "lives of quiet desperation"; spent "the best part of life earning money in order to enjoy a questionable liberty during the least valuable part of it." Thoreau questioned the Irish railroad workers for building an "improved means to an unimproved end." To Thoreau, the railroad was yet another escape from staying in place, living in the here and now, slowing down and simplifying daily existence so the important issues of life could be faced. "We do not ride on the railroad," he said, "it rides upon us."[40]

California was the other end of the frontier civilization from Walden Pond, but even there there were voices questioning whether the state was becoming Paradise Lost. In 1868, as the Gold Rush led to boom town corruption, violence and massive land speculation, leaving a growing gap between rich and poor, Henry George analyzed the contradictions of Growth:

> The new era into which our state is about entering... is without doubt an era of steady, rapid, and substantial growth, of great addition to population and massive increase in the totals of the Assessor's lists.[41]

On the other hand, George pointed to what Robert Louis Stevenson earlier had called the "banquet of consequences" which all people must eventually sit down to:

> We cannot hope to escape the *great law of compensation which exacts some loss for every gain*... Let us not imagine ourselves in a fool's paradise where the golden apples will drop into our mouths; let us not think that

after the stormy seas and head gales of all the ages *our* ship has at last struck the trade winds of time. The future of our state looks fair and bright—perhaps the future looked so to the philosophers who once sat in the porches of Athens.[42]

Lord James Bryce raised much the same question a generation later at the height of southern California's population boom. "What will happen," Bryce asked in a 1909 Berkeley speech,

when California is filled by 50 millions of people, and its valuation is five times what it is now, and the wealth will be so great that you will find it difficult to know what to do with it? The day will, after all, have only 24 hours. Each man will have only one mouth, one pair of eyes, and one pair of ears. There will be more people—as many perhaps as the country can support—and *the real question will not be about making more wealth or having more people but whether the people will then be happier or better.*[43]

What these philosophers shared was a totally different concept of people's relationship to the environment, technology and economic enterprise than the prevailing trend. They stood for the quite literal meaning of that passage in Genesis which placed Man in a steward or caretaker role between the Creator and all living things, the land, water and air; whereas the dominant view had transformed the idea of man's "dominion" into "domination." With respect to technology the dissenters suspected the inventions of science unless they truly served human needs; the prevailing view worshipped science and technology as roads of escape from the apparent restrictions of the natural environment. Science and technology in the majority view, became the means of making an altogether new physical and social landscape. As for economic enterprise, the dissenters rooted themselves in the earlier nineteenth century realities of small farms, dependency on wood and other sources of renewable energy, and face-to-face community life built on self-reliance. Corporations were created and chartered in those times by state governments for only limited purposes and in the "public interest." In the new age of capitalist growth, these traditions were undermined and the values associated with them dismissed as romantic. Industrialization became the key trend, coal and non-renewable resources the underpinning, cities the center of population, distribution and communications, and corporations became federally-chartered as virtually permanent and unlimited enterprises.

Because the new system "worked," it made possible the achievement of prosperity, or at least a realizable dream of it, for a majority of the immigrants streaming into America. "It is striking," writes economic historian Robert Heilbroner, "that without exception it was the Protestant countries with their 'Puritan streak' of work and thrift which forged ahead in the economic race."[44] And because it worked alternative visions were eclipsed, ignored or crushed. Most Americans threw themselves into hard work, mindful of past European tyrannies they had fled, and swept up in the freedom to strike it rich on the Western Frontier. Like embers in a fire, the critics of the corporate growth ethic would have to await a different breeze before their slower-burning qualities could be nurtured and cherished. The apparent infinity of the frontier would have to encounter what Henry George had called "the great law of compensation" before an alternative vision would become a possibility for most Americans.

The New Priorities: Redefining Success

In the 1970s and 1980s, the "great law of compensation" has begun. With energy shortages, rampant inflation, continuing discrimination, corporate scandal, environmental disaster and military debacle, a new questioning has arisen in the very mainstream of American Society. If Thoreau were to return today, he would find that Walden Pond has likely become a Love Canal. He would also find a majority audience open to proposals for a new way to survive and live.

With the 1960s, a new generation of Americans began to look *inward* for their worldview. Despite official summons to yet another "new frontier," more and more Americans were questioning the home front. In the frontlines were those minorities who had been arbitrarily barred from the consumer dream but who had suffered disproportionately on military frontiers abroad. When

Cassius Clay rejected the draft, declaring "No Vietcong ever called me a nigger," he was rejecting the entire tradition of focussing on foreign enemies. The real war, he was saying, was still at home.

Children of affluence, looking for something more challenging than suburban life, soon joined the blacks in defining the quality of life at home as the real frontier to be conquered. The pretense, hypocrisy and emptiness of the affluent society was expressed first in books—J.D. Salinger's *Catcher in the Rye* (1957), John Kenneth Galbraith's *The Affluent Society* (1959), Michael Harrington's *The Other America* (1960), James Baldwin's *The Fire Next Time* (1961), Betty Friedan's *The Feminine Mystique* (1963), Rachel Carson's *Silent Spring* (1962), and Ralph Nader's *Unsafe at Any Speed* (1963). Then came a multiplying series of citizen's movements for student and civil rights, peace, consumer protection, women's rights and environmentalism. The enemy was no longer seen as a foreign conspiracy, although several Administrations tried to paint a fearful image of Cuba and Vietnam as Russian and/or Chinese puppets, and critics of the Vietnam war as treasonous un-Americans. For the first time since the early 1930s, millions of Americans identified their enemies as being *within* the values, technical drift, social policies and major economic institutions of America itself. The broad disenchantment began to be felt not simply on the campuses, but in the military, in factories and offices. Where Americans were willing to accept hundreds of thousands of casualties in World War II, as well as major economic sacrifices, the Vietnam generation was unwilling to accept a far-smaller body count or pay increased taxes for the war. Where an earlier generation fought for democracy abroad, the Vietnam generation realized it was fighting for democracy at home. The threat to American freedom was not coming from the Kremlin so much as from the spies operating out of the White House, CIA and FBI.

The 1970s became a fast downhill slide for America's empire and sense of national self-confidence. "The American Century" proclaimed by *Time* in the 1940s had led instead to a world of Khomeinis. Our former competitors, Japan and Germany, were re-emerging from the ashes of World War II to out-perform us in the international marketplace. Our economy developed simultaneous tendencies to recession and inflation. Real disposable income began to sink for the first time in anyone's memory. The gap between black and white began to widen once again and racial strife grew as a "new right" developed. Watergate and Koreagate disgraced the political profession and helped drive voter participation down to all-time lows. Our vaunted science and technology was producing Pintos, DC-10s, faulty nuclear reactors and a poisonous threat to air, land and water. Continued political assassinations and unexplainable catastrophes like Jonestown pushed the country towards its worst stereotype of a banana republic. We drifted towards a service rather than an industrial manufacturing economy, with more people swept up in the self-indulgences of consumption and fewer and fewer—with the ironic exception of illegal immigrants—in the traditional self-sacrifice of production. The harder one worked or saved, the less security one seemed to have. The younger generation, in Michael Harrington's phrase, began to experience the rags-to-riches, Horatio Alger myth from upside down. They were becoming the first generation in American history facing the possibility of doing less well than their parents. Worst of all, instead of an abundant frontier, it appeared that we were running out of every resource, beginning with oil, that we had depended on for our way of life.

By continuing the frontier ethic, America could become an international Custer in a world of Sitting Bulls, 5 percent of the world's people defending its control of 30-40 percent of world resources.

Or rather than following Custer's path, an America of the post-frontier era can undertake an examination as sweeping as that which founded the nation itself, searching for a philosophy appropriate to the new age. A moral, economic and political vision equivalent to the Federalist Papers could be an imperative for survival in sanity and beyond survival for a new and more rewarding way of life. At the center of any re-examination would be the question of the frontier, which has provided a transcendant vision, a base for economic growth and a catchall allowing political stability for two centuries.

If the old frontier was a "gate of escape" to Frederick Jackson Turner, the gate is now closed and the only remaining frontier lies in the human imagination.

The frontier that we have been trying to escape, and which

now must be faced, is *within*. There are limits to outer expansion, but no limits to improving the quality of life, the integrity of our character, the breadth of our knowledge, the sensitivity of our feelings, the capacity to find purpose in a life that is too quickly over. Americans will need what Appleman Williams calls "the kind of quiet confidence that comes with and from accepting limits, and a concurring understanding that accepting limits does not mean the end of existence itself, or of the possibility of a creative life."[45]

The reason it will be difficult to make this necessary transition is that in the process, the very identity and character of the American people will necessarily be challenged to change. The pursuit of the outer frontier has created a set of attitudes embedded deeply in the personality of people. In E.F. Schumacher's imagery, the frontier types are the "people of the forward stampede," as opposed to the "home-comers" who, like himself, explore the inner frontier.[46] The "forward stampede" in behalf of a controlled, standardized global marketplace engenders a personality focussed on outer appearances and things. The pursuit of consumer goods has become "the most basic expression of life style, indeed of identity itself," in the words of *Fortune* magazine.[47] The doctrine of consumption "sets men and women clamoring after material goods long after they have accumulated enough to satisfy their physical needs (for) when worthiness is measured by possession, no one can own enough."[48]

There is a basic insecurity created by what Mark Twain called the "limitless multiplication of unnecessary necessaries."[49] As Schumacher pointed out, the very pursuit of "more" creates an anxious dependence on remote and distant forces over which control becomes more difficult, even impossible. Where this insecurity does not lead to war, it at least creates a drive for a standardized, homogenized, predictable world. The corporation becomes a new kind of fortress, or enclave, on the world frontier, creating a protective support framework for those facing a hostile world. Variety, creativity and caring are the victims. The idea that "nice guys finish last"—true enough in a hostile competitive setting—is the victor. The obvious lesson is that we should become mean in order to prosper. We forget that it is within our power to alter our institutional setting so that prosperity and morality will no longer be incompatible.

On the frontier, identity was bound up with *conquest* of both the environment and other people. From the experience with technology arose a belief in the superiority of the machine over any human factor, a belief which has been central to the production of everything from the Three Mile Island nuclear reactor to the Sikorsky helicopters used in the Iran "rescue mission". There was a kernel of truth in this attitude from the beginning; the Colt .45 and other firearms did overpower the Indians, and the railroads did expand commerce. But after two centuries of essentially unfettered machine development, many have concluded with Galbraith "that we are the servants in thought, as in action, of the machines we have created to serve us."[47] The frontiersman doing for himself with the barest of tools has become the "urban cowboy" driving a half-empty truck through the night. The attitude remains but the conditions are reversed: the modern cowboy has been conquered by technology in the form of CB radios, stereos, off-road vehicles, campers and bass boats which become a more and more expensive escape and burden.

The second aspect of the legacy of conquest is personal, a psychic need to subdue and control which infects human relationships from home to the job.* Michael Maccoby's portrait of the corporate "gamesman," based on interviews with 250 executives, defines the continuance of the frontier ethic into corporate and government offices. No less a gamesman than Henry Kissinger once compared himself to "the cowboy entering a city or village alone on his horse."[51] The "macho" spirit of constant games, of seeing life as a daily contest, of seeking victory for victory's sake, of identifying corporate achievement with personal success, takes a personal toll. Maccoby found that most corporate managers "were not neurotic, but were underdeveloped." A high percentage were college athletes and military men before entering the business

---

*"For most managers it is more exciting to govern a large empire than a small one —and more enriching as well. Samuel Richardson Reed, who has conducted the most comprehensive merger studies, concluded in a 1968 book that 'Managers' personal and group goals of security, power, prestige, increased personal income and advancement within the firm may well be identified more with firm growth ... than with classic profit maximization.' " (Mark Green, "The Road to Monopoly" in *The Big Business Reader*, p. 499)

world, pursuing lives of constant embattlement. Maccoby found that they fear "feeling trapped," that they want "an illusion of limitless options." But this external orientation limits their "capacity for personal intimacy and social commitment." The gamesman attitude limits deep friendship and intimacy, and throttles the development of inner strengths "so that he might gain satisfaction from understanding (science) or creating (invention, art)." While concluding that there is nothing worse than an aging gamesman, imagine, they in fact run our country—Maccoby also discovered that "there are seventy year old *craftsmen* whose goal in life is not winning, but making something better, and who are still energetic and interested in new ideas, although retired from the corporation." [52]

The conquering impulse also damages personal life by separating sex and love, physical affection from genuine feeling. Sexual "conquests" are increasingly experienced as empty and negative acts of compulsion little different than the games of conquest that infect bureaucracies both private and public. These short-term and superficial ego gratifications are substitutes for fuller personal development. Hazel Henderson has noted an even deeper "masculine" quality to the conquering urge. "The masculine psyche does seem more attuned (either biologically or by cultural conditioning) to manipulating external things and objects, while the female psyche by contrast seems more attuned to 'software,' i.e., interpersonal and social relationships and arrangements." [53] The policy implications of this mindset are blatant but little discussed. Energy expert Daniel Yergin, for example, was once told by a high Department of Energy official that solar energy is "too feminine," but that giant synthetic fuel plants had a "macho" sex appeal. [54]

The emphasis on outer appearances involve a physical role model for both men and women, who must look a narrow, pre-scribed way to qualify as "attractive." The psychological anguish which this limited notion of beauty and status creates is hard to measure. But its unreality is not. We live in a society, for example, where the largest minority are the *disabled*. Because of the cowboy definitions of the "perfect specimen," America ignores or limits hundreds of thousands of military veterans and Americans in wheelchairs, 14 million deaf or hearing impaired people, 7 million

blind or vision-impaired people, and millions of elderly people
with disabling illnesses of all kinds. These are human beings whose
lives are as important as any other, whose perspectives on life can
only be enriching to others, yet who are treated as the rejects or
waste of a "productive" society. When one considers that half the
population is either disabled, or related to someone disabled, and
that the "able-bodied" may at any moment become "handi-
capped," the flight from reality towards the "playboy" image is
truly fantastic.

The psychological reason for refusing to explore inner frontiers is the fear of self-knowledge. We tend, writes Abraham
Maslow, "to be afraid of any knowledge that could cause us to
despise ourselves or make us feel inferior, weak, worthless, shameful. We protect ourselves and our ideal image of ourselves by
repression." In the same process, of course, we tragically repress
the positive and necessary experience of human growth, denying
or dulling our potential creativity.[55]

Thus the conquering spirit comes to encounter its final
"enemy": the inner tendency to desire love, warmth, art, craft,
community, knowledge. The drive to suppress and make secondary these human tendencies results in massive casualties in the
form of personal breakdown, death and addiction. The President's own Commission on Mental Health has found that fully
one-fourth of the US population—60 million people—suffers
"severe emotional distress,"[56] And the numbers have been rising
for 20 years.

"Perhaps it will be sufficient," Hazel Henderson has written,
"to alter the goals and symbols of success so that our narcissism
is expressed in self-actualization and in reintegrating our self-
images, so that competition may be rechanneled into enhancement
of physical fitness and well-being, and acquisitiveness may re-
emerge as striving for knowledge and higher levels of consciousness."[57] There is little doubt that such a "rechanneling" would be
benign for the planet in the short run. But to assume that the paradigm of American social character is permanently fixed flies in the
face of theories of evolution and adaptation. If *survival* requires
fundamental changes in both institutions and culture, such
changes are definitely a possibility. This is certainly one of those
moments when human survival requires rapid adaptation, some-

thing more than a rechanneling of greed into athletics.

Others claim that there is a new frontier in outer space, a new safety valve for channeling the world's tensions without war. But there is no possibility of this "high frontier" being available in the coming decade to large numbers of people. Space will hopefully and at most be "staked out" for civilian research and development rather than a Soviet-American "star wars." Instead of reviving the frontier ethic, the lesson of space should be that human beings are far from suited to be masters or conquerors. We are discovering instead that we are specks of life on a lovely, fragile and obscure planet somewhere in a boundless universe. Momentary beings on a perishing planet, we may try to extend our ethics of exploitation and pollution into the galaxy, but more likely the universe will impose its own laws on us. As Karl Jung once wrote, "Space flights are merely an escape, a fleeing away from oneself, because it is easier to go to Mars or to the moon than it is to penetrate one's own being." [58]

The New Ethic: From Quantity to Quality

The new era needs a new morality in the same sense that the Protestant Ethic served the rise of expansionist capitalism. In his powerful analysis of that earlier historical connection, R.H. Tawney identified the moral void created in the wake of capitalist growth. "Economic ambitions are good servants," Tawney noted, but "they are bad masters." The very self-interest that promoted the exploitation of others for profit had a negative side. It ignored the whole human being, reducing the person to a one-dimensional material creature. However, Tawney wrote, "since even quite common men have souls, no increase in material wealth will compensate them for arrangements which insult their self-respect and impair their freedom. A reasonable estimate of economic organization must allow for the fact that, unless industry is to be paralysed by recurrent revolts on the part of outraged human nature, it must satisfy criteria which are not purely economic." [59] Though not addressed here, this change will require basic reforms of the school system so that we can "educate for the uncertainty of freedom beyond frontiers," in the apt phrase of Marilyn Ferguson. [60]

The emerging morality will begin by recognizing an ancient truth—that the great moral and religious philosophers throughout history have tended to promote inner, rather than outer, rewards, modesty rather than status hunger, love rather than domination. Rarely has personal profit been defined as the goal of life.

In the frontier framework, however, the accumulation of profit was seen as crucial to the process of reinvestment and over-all growth. The personal motive—material enrichment—was assumed to coincide with the general good. Because of the incredible abundance of the frontier, this synthesis was possible. But in an era of limits, an edict of Jesus—"it is easier for a camel to pass through the eye of a needle than for a rich man to enter heaven"—may take on a special relevence for an over-consuming America in an underfed world. The factor of greed may have been a spark of progress in the time of material expansion and industrialization, but in a finite-resource world it can be the destroyer of the future. Millions of individual selfish, private decisions can no longer be assumed to add up to the public interest.

Another fairly obvious moral imperative will be the spread of environmentalism into a worldwide creed. The frontier age has nearly stripped or destroyed the earth's most precious resources. The throwaway mentality of past generations regarded the environment as a bottomless dumping ground for hazardous, often toxic wastes capable of poisoning future generations. When one considers the hypothesis that the entire genetic inheritance of the human race is less than a teardrop,[61] or that what distinguishes the fertile earth from the barren moon is a severely-threatened eight inches of topsoil and equally threatened and fragile atmosphere, it is clear that there must be a shift to the ethic of stewardship. It is instructive that the word "steward" is traceable to the Greek root "oikonomos," or "housekeeper." The Greek word, in turn, is the basis of the English word "economy," which once meant keeping a house in order. We have departed from this original notion to define economy as simply the exploitation of given resources for a means of production. Instead of the modern mechanistic view, which implies a science of economy, we should return to the concept that implies preserving, nurturing and caring for the home of humanity.

The significance of technology will be sharply reconsidered in the new era as well. Nuclear power is perhaps the key symbol of a past generation's willingness to create things which cannot be controlled. This ability to make machines which then in effect control their makers has fostered a secular religion of science and technology in both the U.S. and the Soviet Union. But uncontrolled technology is a menace in an era of limited and fragile resources. So is the easy assumption that it is "progressive" to automate more and more of agriculture, industry and services. A high-technology, capital-intensive and often dehumanized process replaces the quality work that only human beings can do.

Technology is sometimes described as "neutral," and science "objective," as if it is primarily the values and priorities of the users which determines the ill effect on society. This argument is made by those economistic socialists, for example, who believe that nuclear power can be made safe if only the profit motive is eliminated from production. While it is true that the drive for profit tends to minimize expensive safety considerations, it is also true that nuclear technology has a life of its own, that it is more than a neutral means to an end, that it becomes an end through its impact on social structure (centralizing it), and culture (mass dependency on technological elites).

This is why "appropriate" and "alternative" have been used to describe the best technology of the new era. It is not a choice between the present technology or none at all, nor is it a simple question of using existing technology for different purposes. It is a matter of developing technologies that are both controllable and carefully matched to human ends.

In our factories for example, it is not true that technologies are neutral or scientifically fixed. There are many ways to make cars. It does not necessarily follow that the most profitable way for the owners is also most efficient in resources use much less best for the workers or people of the community adjacent to the plant.

In terms of its cultural values, American society will have to travel from the era of "conspicuous consumption," as Thorsten Veblen called it, to an era of conspicuous austerity and simplicity.[62] American society annually throws away 11 million tons of iron and steel, 800,000 tons of aluminum, 400,000 tons of other metals, 13 million tons of glass, 60 million tons of paper, 17 billion cans, 38 billion bottles and jars, 7.6 million TV sets, and 7 million automobiles.[63]

The excessive status orientation of American society—driven by the objective need to produce ever more goods—needs to be replaced by an ethic which asserts the importance of the quality of life over the quantity of possessions. This does not imply that the poor should be content with less, nor that the unequal distribution of wealth should be ignored as unimportant from a spiritual standpoint. While the drive for equality should continue, however, the possibility of a materialistic middle class life style—by 1975 standards—for all Americans, not to mention the world's people, will become more and more remote because of objective limits. Those with the greatest privilege should be asked to make the greatest sacrifices, while everyone pares down their material expectations to what they really need. But at the same time, of course, the quality and pleasure of all our lives must be improved. This simultaneous loss in GNP and gain in quality is possible because in an altered social setting, commodities will not be the basis of status or dignity, self-respect nor the aquisition of skill, and these "goods" as well as the potential for friendship, caring, and creativity will be enhanced for all.

The new ethic will combine a simple, self-determined lifestyle with an enrichment of the meaning of labor. The clutter of life must be overthrown to concentrate on experiences of true value. As Thoreau warned, there is too much time spent in "preparing" for life and too little spent living it. For millions of Americans this is because work itself is a stifling routine which is accepted primarily to earn enough money to get away from it. After taxes there is usually just enough money left over to "enjoy life" from Friday to Sunday and perhaps during two weeks vacation each year. Most working people are employed for 40 of their most vital years in return for an equivalent of 15 years free time parcelled out in weekends. (For many not even that since they *must* work 2 jobs or overtime shifts.)

Some propose automation, shorter work weeks and early retirement as alternatives to the tedium of work. Others even project a future in which leisure becomes a major dilemma as the need for human labor is radically reduced by machines. These notions misunderstand both human and social needs. I believe that people have a *basic need for real work*. It is a crucial way we express ourselves, develop our skills and awareness, meet our needs, and reproduce our own existence.

The call for less work is understandably based on the alienation and mediocre wages now prevalent on the job. But it does not mean there is a real decline of work that needs to be done. In fact, there is a mounting agenda of work that American society needs to do. Some of it is rote, socially-necessary drudge work that should be more equally shared, for it does not enhance our lives or increase our skill or knowledge as we do it, and so no one group should have to carry the whole burden for others. Beyond drudgery, there is *socially-valuable labor* which can be meaningful to millions of people because it can link their personal efforts to a larger cause. Here we must distinguish between unnecessary goods and services—which have only a luxury value to society—and the kind of work which is useful because it improves society, the economy, the culture, the quality of existence, and enhances the well being of the people doing the labor.

In my parents' generation, there were two instructive examples—the public works programs of the New Deal, and the defense production effort for World War II. In both cases, the work was intrinsically very hard. But most Americans threw themselves into it willingly and with satisfaction. There was a connection between their individual labor and social good. We were not producing unnecessary consumer gadgets. We were creating the projects, services, equipment and technology which would lead to economic recovery and victory in the war. Only during such a process can people begin to feel whole, an integration of their personal, economic, and citizenship roles.

Therefore the new era needs not only a new morality, but a new economy, a new discovery of the dignity of work. The new economic order cannot be based on unlimited expansion or profligate use of scarce and expensive resources. It cannot be built on planned obsolescence and profitable waste. And it must offer more than "lives of quiet desperation" to those who work or else invite alienation and ever-declining productivity.

There are three priorities in creating the structure and technology for life beyond the frontier. First, every American and every person on earth must obtain a minimum of food, shelter, education and health care to lead a human existence. Second, there must be a transition to renewable resources, mainly the new technologies of solar, wind, hydro, geothermal and biomass energy. Conservation and recycling and building things that last will have to replace the grab-and-throwaway ethics of the expansionist economy. Third, the world must be knitted together by the spread of information technology—television, satellites, computers, etc—in as decentralized and widespread way as possible. This democratizing of information is the only alternative to the runaway technology and centralized priesthoods of the current age based on fossil fuels and nuclear power. Past generations used technology to exploit, divide and often conquer the world. We must use technology—particularly in communications and transportation—to bring the planet together.

This triple economic agenda—making basic necessities available, producing renewable energy resources, making a world information network—is clearly an agenda of work which provides the same connection between personal labor and larger mission which inspired the 19th century immigrants and the later generation of the Depression and second World War.

The Global Vision: Sharing the Planet

The foreign policy of the frontier age was expanding the frontier. A new foreign policy will be based on an economy where the excessive need to produce, and therefore dispose of surpluses, will decline. A new ethic of lessened consumption at home will create an increased interim supply of grain and resources for the world's billions of underfed and improverished people. The longer-term need is for an acceptance of the limits of military power or economic imperialism, and a transformation towards moral and political solidarity with other races, nations and cultures as the primary means of a durable national defense. This, of course, will not prevent the emergence of violent contradictions in the world, nor the rise of irrational forces, but it will defuse a globalized frontier crisis in which the U.S. might become an isolated nuclear fortress surrounded by violent forces of change. And instead of representing little more than the image of a consumer society in a starving world, America will be able to connect with the positive aspirations of billions of people for a sharing of not only the resources, but the cultural and scientific heritage of the planet.

Racism and ethnocentrism could be the most explosive triggering issue for America if the Custer mentality prevails. Not only are volcanic explosions like that in the Miami ghetto (ironically named "Liberty City") inevitable, but whole regions of America will come to resemble the Third World in the next decade. California, for example, may have a non-white majority by 1990, and other states will follow—there is no escape, no suburban enclave, no wall of police, which can hold back a resolution of the issue of race, the ultimate way in which American identity is defined in contrast to a feared Other.

The new era will also need a new form of politics and citizen participation. The proprietors of the existing order have largely maintained the Madisonian notion of limited democracy. Nevertheless, voting rights have been expanded, as have the rights of labor, local communities, women and minorities after long and intense struggles. To preserve the economic status quo there will be increased pressures to restrain democracy. Presidential advisor Samuel Huntington, for example, condemns the 1960s for having been a time of "an excess of democracy." Too much protest and citizen participation, he believes, prevented the American government from achieving "the national interest" in Vietnam. More ominous are the recent calls by national economic leaders for a lowering of the standard of living of a majority of Americans in order to "fight inflation." As the editors of *Business Week* commented in 1974, "it will be a hard pill for the American people to swallow, the idea of doing with less so that big business can have more."[64] This philosophy of continued privileges for the few combined with forced austerity for the many can only be achieved by suppressing and reducing the democratic process.

But democracy must not be a casualty of the current crisis. That would mean a freezing of all possibility to make a sane passage to a new era. The shift ahead from *quantity* to *quality* must involve an expansion of the citizen's role as an active participant in history. Otherwise there can be neither personal growth nor improvement in the texture of society. The "inner frontier" can only be enriched by an expansion of democracy.

To intensify the democratic process means allowing people to make direct input into decisions that affect their lives. The trend should be towards a fuller, more inclusive democracy in which all institutions are made accessible and accountable. The major structures that will feel the pressure of democratic reforms are undoubtedly the large corporations, the media and the political party system. An inevitable awakening of the disenfranchised will transform a monolithic cultural framework into a richer pluralism.

To return to the Federalist Papers debate of the 18th century, it can be concluded that Madison was wrong in asserting that "an extensive Republic" was indispensible to democracy. In fact the "extensive frontier" of the past century has seen the growth of huge, impersonal and global institutions which have made the citizen feel more and more irrelevant. Montesquieu was more correct in asserting a linkage between democracy and smaller states—or decentralization into more self-sufficient communities. His view went back to Aristotle who said, "The good life depends on intimacy and small numbers" and "A state ought to be large enough to be more-or-less self-sufficing, but not too large for constitutional government. It ought to be small enough for citizens to know each other's characters, otherwise right will not be done in elections and lawsuits."[65] The choice is between empire and democracy.

These, in short, are the choices before the next generation of Americans as the old frontiers decline. The 1979-80 crisis in Iran, coming in the wake of Vietnam and world oil shortages, should serve warning that the world familiar to most Americans will never again be the same. The crisis in Iran may be the turning point, or it may take another shock—a cutoff of Saudi oil, a wave of black violence in inner cities, a nuclear meltdown in a populated area, a prolonged depression—before the lesson is driven home.

The issue can be stated simply:

An attempted preservation of the *old frontiers* will mean fossil fuel energy shortages, massive inflation, chronic underemployment, centralized economic and political power, increasing racial injustice, environmental and human health catastrophes, leading to the brink and perhaps to the actual beginning of a World War III over energy and other resources.

The vision of an *inner frontier* means turning to conservation and renewable resources, which in turn will stabilize prices, open up meaningful work, protect the physical and human environment, make possible a democratic and decentralized set of economic institutions, and pull our over-consumptive country back from the edge of war.

On a personal level, the choice is whether to accept the status of what C. Wright Mills once called "cheerful robots," or whether to melt our armoured personalities and realize that there is a human *spirit* that cannot be valued on the stock market or quantified in a laboratory, but which exists if we let it, and which contains the powers of intuition and creative discovery that make us finally different and unique. With this spirit, we can become self-reliant citizens of the world, sons and daughters of Thoreau instead of Custer.

TWO
ECONOMY: HUMAN SOLUTIONS
TO INFLATION AND RECESSION

YEAR OF HARD TIMES: NO REMEDIES

With chilling and rare candor, President Carter's new budget outlines a coming year of economic misery for most Americans—recession, double-digit inflation, rising unemployment and higher interest rates.

—LA Times, Jan. 29, 1980

US ECONOMIC EMERGENCY PREDICTED

The US economy is "lurching towards a national economic emergency" and there is "nothing in income, fiscal or monetary policies to suggest a way out," Henry Kaufman, an influential Wall Street economist declared yesterday.

His remarks, made in Los Angeles to an American Bankers Association conference, helped trigger a broad decline in bond prices and added impetus to tumbling stock prices as well.

—Washington Post, Feb. 1, 1980

At the beginning of the 1980s, inflation and unemployment symbolize a dominant fact in American economic thinking: the sense that things are out of control. After 40 years of confidence that government could "manage" the ups and downs of the economy, the very tools of government management seem to have broken down. Yet a bitter impasse remains: Traditional liberals see the solution as more New Deal measures; traditional conservatives see the opportunity to take revenge on the legacy of Keynes and Roosevelt. Both sides of the liberal-conservative debate are unwilling to even consider that their ideologies may be obsolete. The conservative solution is to create unemployment perhaps for ten million Americans by the end of 1980. The liberal solutions all

43

seem to create more inflation. Lacking any alternative economic philosophy, the nation seems paralysed, even disintegrating, under the onslaught of rising prices, unemployment, global economic and energy crises. The obvious fact that things are out of control means that more than tinkering or a return to the past will be needed to restore a feeling of confidence to the American people. Only a new vision and program of action, based on the realities of a new era, will fulfill the broad desire to "get America moving again."

The Failure of Traditional Remedies

The liberal versus conservative face off about how to manage inflation and unemployment began with the Roosevelt-Hoover confrontation in the 1930's and has continued in much the same form through every subsequent Presidential debate. Since it has been 50 years since the Wall Street Crash precipitating that economic debate, it is no wonder that the rhetoric has become stale on both sides. The decline of the old frontier, and the consequent decline of cheap American growth, have created a crisis for both sets of political assumptions.

The conservative has argued that government is the enemy because of its policies of tax and spend, and its budgetary deficits, all of which create greater consumer demand than there is supply of goods and services, which in turn pushes prices upwards. The solution to inflation, in this view, is the cruel necessity of unemployment and high interest rates. By throwing people out of work and increasing the difficulty of borrowing, consumer spending and demand will be reduced, which in turn will bring prices down again.

There are glaring moral and practical problems with this conservative prescription. First, it imposes a painful inequality on a majority of citizens who are asked to believe that their suffering— unemployment, cuts in services, disruptions of family life—is an inevitability that is good for them in the long run. For all the references to "national" recessions, there is never an unemployment line for the rich, but only for the minorities, women and working people in general. To pass this off as "inevitable"— that only the poor should lose—is a crime against common sense.

Second, the conservative prescription does not work. It is based on a free-market model of competition which has long since been replaced by a structure of corporate oligopoly and government income-maintenance programs. The result is that (even during recessions) corporations have the power to maintain or even increase already high prices. At the same time, the presence of labor, minimum wage, unemployment insurance and welfare laws denies the corporations the classic ability to bring prices down by lowering wages, again hurting anyone but themselves. These forces of corporate oligopoly and government protection have become institutionalized in the economy since the 1930's and they make the free market model obsolete. They create instead the phenomenon of so-called "stagflation," the simultaneous existence of inflation and recession.

The liberal, New Deal alternative has been to see government in the positive role of stimulating demand to "produce our way out of hard times." From the 1930's to the 1970's, the liberals did not see inflation as a problem nearly as serious as unemployment, and they were generally right by any reading of the Consumer Price Index. Theirs was the economics of stimulus, believing that by employment policies which put money in people's pockets, and by sufficient consumer advertising, rising purchasing power would itself push corporations to invest more, which in turn would create more jobs, more wages, more purchasing power, more investment.

The problem with the liberal model is also moral and practical. It is based on an ethic of consumption for consumption's sake. There is, from the viewpoint of economic result, little difference between making a bomb or a bicycle, a television set or a wheelchair. The Gross National Product can be expanded by building cars with maximum safety features or cars that turn into fireballs upon collision. And in fact, the latter, requiring faster replacement, are actually a superior spur to economic growth. It's all for the greater production of goods and services.

Whatever the concommitant moral decay and human loss, there is also a practical problem with the traditional liberal model; it assumes constancy of the costs of production. That is, the liberals assume purchasing power can be exerted without creating inflation because the cost to corporations of producing goods and services will remain roughly the same. This view underestimated the skyrocketing "production costs" of the Vietnam War—approximately $2 billion per month in 1968, without any tax increases to pay for it—which set off the chronic inflation of the past 12 years. And it continues to ignore the progressively-increasing cost of conventional sources of energy—oil, gas, coal, synthetics, nuclear—as old fields decline in output and new resources become scarcer. In these contexts, increasing purchasing power merely increases wasteful consumption and the investment of profits in ever-more capital-intensive sectors of the economy, resulting in higher prices and fewer jobs per dollar invested. The ensuing inflation wrecks havoc upon the well being of all those living on fixed incomes, especially the elderly, and also acts to redistribute wealth in general from those who work for a wage to those who make money from ownership. Thus if wages lag behind prices real wages decline, and even if wages catch up eventually, there is an interim period during which there was a defacto pay cut with the money saved going over into the column marked "corporate profits."

Jimmy Carter, like every U.S. President since Roosevelt, has represented a mixture of the liberal and conservative doctrines in national economic policy. If both viewpoints were practical, whichever way one might judge the moral issues, the President might be able to create a synthesis of the doctrines that would at least be workable. But when both liberal and conservative ideologies are in shambles, the President's policy only draws on the worst of two worlds.

Carter has tilted towards more conservativism in his "economic mix" than any Democratic president since the 1930's. He increased interest rates to an all-time high of 19%, promoted the doubling of energy price increases through decontrol in one year, proposed to increase the military budget $15 billion in 1980, and recommended slashes in social programs ranging from CETA to food stamps. But he also responded to the pressures of minorities and unions to "enlarge a handful of politically sensitive social programs" for unemployed youth and moderate-income housing. The result is a budget more tilted to guns than butter, but which satisfies neither conservatives (since it projects a deficit of $15 billion) nor liberals (since it puts Pentagon priorities above social needs.)[1] The central point is that the Carter budget, like a raft in an ocean storm, will have little effect on either inflation or recession. Of the two economic crises, Carter has clearly chosen to focus first on inflation and intends therefore to launch a recession while making it appear inevitable. For example, the prestigious economist Otto Eckstein, president of Data Resources, Inc. declared that "the U.S. economy got into a situation where a recession is the only way out."[2] But while the recession "will be far worse than almost anyone had predicted,"[3] it will have only a moderate impact on the long-term problem of inflation it is intended to combat. And it can be predicted that the "counter-recession" program which is sure to follow within a year will do only a little to relieve the unemployment problem it will claim to attack. In the several U.S. recessions since the second world war, there is a persistent pattern of the unemployment rate after "recovery" being slightly higher than after the previous recession.

Since our economic experts are on the whole intelligent and capable people, it is hard to believe that there are new causes of inflation and recession that they have yet to discover. And yet this is the wishful attitude taken by Americans of all kinds. Leave the world of economic policy to the experts. They alone know the answers, or where to look for them; they are qualified, they understand the obscure words, they possess the computers to do the measuring. Nothing in American life is delegated more to "experts" than the matter of economics. Furthermore, economics is assumed to unfold with a historical inevitability, earning the profession the unpleasant titles of a "dismal science" or a "black art." With these assumptions about the inexorable nature of the economy, those who speak of "equity" or of the "human factor" are seen as militants or bleeding hearts lacking any and all sense of realism.

But what if the reality is the other way around? What if the emperors of economic thinking have no clothes? What if their assumptions are so wrong about the world that their intelligence can only take them in directions that worsen the problems they claim to be resolving? What if American economic thinking, in the caustic phrase of Hazel Henderson, is "a form of brain damage"?[4] It would mean that Americans would have to begin to overthrow the reign of experts and approach economics from the vantage point of self-interest and common sense. There can be no economic democracy until a majority of Americans begin to take responsibility for finding their own alternatives to the coming decade of distress.

In traditional economic discourse, the concepts of supply and demand are almost permanent in character, fixed in history, measurable by any forecaster. However, the larger themes of this book—the decline of the frontier, a menacing energy crisis, and concentrated corporate power—shed light on certain new realities that cannot fit the theoretical supply and demand model. The concept of "supply" is not as obvious as an infinite pot of gold. Supply of resources, for example, is declining, or being contaminated and therefore made more costly, or cartelized and therefore withheld until prices rise. The traditional notion of supply also ignores as immeasurable the role of *human* energy which, by *labor*-intensive processes, could alter the very meaning of supply itself from a quantitative to a qualitative concept. For example, labor can be substituted for high-technology processes to conserve depleting resources.

Demand is equally ambiguous when carefully defined. Is a market survey a real measure of "genuine" demand when billions are spent each year on advertising to stimulate over-consumption? Does a demand for more goods and services have a higher moral value than a demand for less?

So we can begin to see that economics is not an abstract science whose sovereign rules determine life, but a *reflection of values, power relations, and the distribution of resources among people.* It is true that economic "laws" exist because absolute limits exist, and a given use of society's resources will create a corresponding denial of those resources for other purposes. But within this fixed boundary, we are led to conclude that *economics involves a matter of choice in the way available resources are valued and allocated.*

In this chapter we are going to spend most of our effort understanding the dynamics of inflation, but before getting deeply into that subject it will be useful to consider the causes, impact and a possible long-term cure for unemployment as well. For while it is the continuing inflation which is a new and unique phenomenon, the problem of unemployment is not only painfully chronic but a supposed "necessity" if prices are to be kept down. As long as unemployment is seen as the "cure" to inflation, Americans will be trapped between cruelties that yield no positive hope.

Unemployment: Causes and Cures

The closing of the old frontier also brings to a close the main avenue of employment opportunity in American history. Millions of immigrants could find work—or its promise—because of economic expansion. The mere unfolding of the frontier, of course, did not mean equal economic opportunity for women, blacks, Hispanics or Asian-Americans. But it did create the economic conditions for a relative prosperity, an enlarging "pie" which all could hope to share.

The disappearance of the frontier, or the shrinking of the pie, eliminates a key factor in job creation and signals a coming social crisis of vast proportions. Any society where more and more people must compete for fewer and fewer jobs is doomed to instability. But America could be plunged from there to chaos, not only because of the unique role the frontier has played, but also because of the explosive relationships of class, race and sex in the American economy. The largely white immigrant generations have gained a foothold in the economy over several decades, but their security is being reduced by inflation, declining wages and unemployment. They are perched just above a volcanic basin of unrest. The cutoff of the ladder of upward mobility at just the moment of rising expectations among minorities (with "boat people" and illegal immigrants lining up behind them) will have an incalculable effect on the possibilities of social peace. Just as surely, a society which decides to either lay off women workers first in recessions or, alternatively, trap them in second-class economic slots, at just the moment that the idea of *social* equality for those women is widely and irreversibly accepted, is heading for a disaster.

Even during frontier expansion, of course, America had cycles of depression and times of massive unemployment. But now with the frontier cushion gone, and the traditional cycles threatening to become more intense, government and corporate officials seem inclined towards a blithe politics of acceptance with regard to unemployment. In each decade since World War II, the level of unemployment deemed "acceptable" has risen. In the 1950s, for example, the 4.3 percent rate was seen as far too high, and policy was directed to bringing unemployment down to 2 percent, then considered to be the "frictional" amount of joblessness due to workers shifting between jobs. By the 1980s, in contrast, the official full employment goal had become 4 percent, a figure that was thought to be only a remote ideal.[5] In addition, the statistical measuring is designed to minimize the problem by excluding from the count workers who have given up the search, part-time workers unable to find full-time jobs, and many women who would like to work but are at home for want of opportunities. By these warped definitions, one could theoretically solve the unemployment crisis by discouraging enough workers from looking for jobs, a sorry kind of academic calculus that will do little to repay the indignity and hunger of those who are nonetheless out of work.[6] Statistics, of course, are no escape. Unemployment is not inevitable, but a chosen course, benefitting some and penalizing others. What

Percent of Civilian Labor Force Unemployed

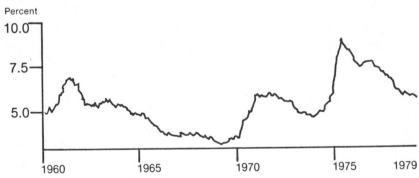

Source: *Employment and Earnings*, April, 1979.

must be addressed are the underlying dynamics that make unemployment necessary to the American economy.

Number unemployed (millions)

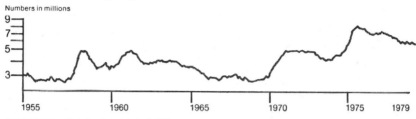

Numbers in millions

Source: *Business Cycle Developments*, April, 1979.

Why must our economy throw people out of work instead of making the best possible use of every last producer? What causes unemployment to recur, as if it serves a desirable purpose?

Anyone who has worked for a living knows that life on the job is very different depending upon the unemployment rate. Life can be quite relaxed when jobs are plentiful. One works, but not in fear; one can take a little more time to socialize with other workers; one can avoid dangerous tasks and speed-ups. But when unemployment is high, everything turns around. The foreman becomes threatening. The pace of work is faster. The power relationship with management has changed. The greater the unemployment, the more likely labor will settle for last year's wages. Management becomes tougher on everything from wages to benefits to expenditures for safety.[7]

In general, there is a correlation between profits and unemployment in an economy like ours. Stating it simply, as unemployment rises, so do the profit rates, and when unemployment falls, profits do likewise. When unemployment and profits are both up,

Youth, Minority, and Female Unemployment

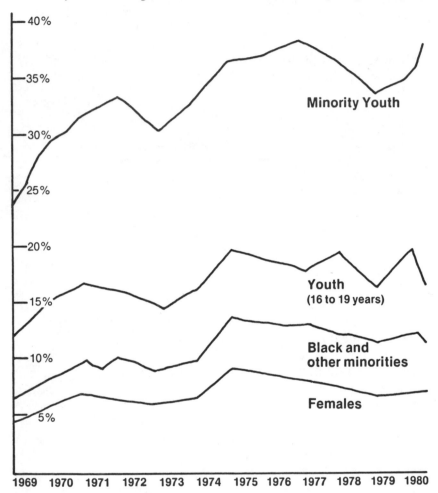

Source: Bureau of Labor Statistics.

the owners of firms tend to increase their investments to take advantage of the promised high returns. These investments in turn create new jobs and slowly deplete the unemployment rolls. But then workers become stronger at the bargaining table, and the owners must expend more money on wages, benefits and improved working conditions. Moreover, they become unable to compel workers to produce as much as they could under the threat of unemployment. Profit margins decrease, and investment follows —and so again the economy heads towards stagnation and recession.[8] The colder economists term this process a necessary "wringing out" of the system; the more political economic advisors have called it "zapping labor."[9]

In recent years, each new recovery peak in the cycle has left more people out of work than before, so shrinking definitions of "full employment" allow for a permanent and growing pool of discouraged or part-time workers.[10] The causes of this trend appear to lie in corporate investment which is turning away from dependence on the current labor force which made the investors rich in the first place, and toward more profitable alternatives.

One of these investment alternatives is in "labor-saving" devices. The economy is moving toward dependence on machines instead of human labor as a means of producing goods in each plant, and towards high-technology, capital-intensive industries in place of older, established craft—or labor-intensive processes. As this "progress" rolls on, fewer and fewer jobs are created per dollar invested. Each recovery from recession involves a greater investment of capital in expensive, high-tech industry, and this in turn makes greater unemployment a growing likelihood.[11] The machines have another value which enhances their profitability. In the words of one California agricultural specialist, "machines don't strike," a quality of obedience missing among California's farmworkers.

The other corporate policy trend that results in unemployment is investment into states or countries which are attractive for their cheap labor, lower taxes, and weak environmental and health regulations. In this wicked game of corporate blackmail, jobs are the reward to regions which will sacrifice union rights, clean air, and local autonomy to the corporations, and unemployment is the penalty for regions where wages are good, unions are respected and local officials are tough defenders of clean water and air.

To seriously address the unemployment crisis, then, requires abandoning the preposterous but deeply-embedded notion that recessions are inevitable. We must instead argue that corporations should invest their rising profits in new jobs. It is necessary to reconsider the links between unemployment, profitability and investment. While unemployment may now narrowly benefit the profit margins of certain employers, the social and economic costs overall are crippling to everyone else. Aside from the psychological anguish, the racial tension, and the rising needs for police and social workers which unemployment causes, direct economic costs in lost tax revenue and production are shocking. Dr. Steven Sheffrin of the University of California calculated these losses for the twenty year period 1956-76. He found that the failure to maintain the Eisenhower era unemployment rate of 4.1 percent cost the nation $2.3 trillion in lost production overall. The 1976 loss was equivalent to 17 percent of all goods and services produced that year. In addition, if unemployment rates had remained at Eisenhower era levels or lower, there would have been an additional $750 billion in federal tax revenues. To measure the magnitude of loss, $100 billion in 1976 dollars would have paid for the elimination of poverty (estimated to cost $16 billion), increased anti-pollution spending to clean up the environment by 1985 ($18 billion per year), and created full national health insurance ($64 billion).[12]

Unemployment as a permanent feature of life will not be solved without changes in the criteria for making investment decisions, and in whose voice is considered in those decisions. The right to work should not depend on the cycles of the economy, or on the blackmailing of people to sacrifice their lungs for a job. It should not be necessary for productivity to only rise under the threatening lash of unemployment, nor should the bargaining power of workers over matters affecting their lives be tied to fluctuations in employment levels.

Therefore, there will have to be criteria more human and responsible than "the bottom line" built into investment decisions, criteria that protect jobs even in times of weakened profits. The incentive to lay off workers will diminish only if corporations operate by new rules and responsibilities that promote decent employment as an economic right and a social necessity.

If unemployment is to be seriously challenged, the freedom of corporations to arbitrarily close their doors in one location only to re-open in cheap labor havens elsewhere will need to be curbed as well. Only through arriving at national and international standards of corporate behavior, including uniform labor and environmental laws, can the long-run tendency towards the "runaway shop" be reversed. But in the near term, any measures which include the voice and needs of the employee and the community in corporate decision-making are steps which will impede the wanton sacrifice of jobs for profits.

Investment criteria, in both the private and public sectors, will have to mandate a greater interest in the quality and quantity of employment as a goal equal to what is actually produced. The military and petrochemical pre-occupations of American society guarantee a capital-intensive, as opposed to labor-intensive, strategy of investment, with the implication that somehow "national security" can be achieved in spite of long unemployment lines. What this perspective so easily forgets are the scores of urban insurrections which resulted from the misplaced priorities of the Vietnam War, the simple fact that more New York City residents die of drug addiction each year than their whole state lost in Vietnam at the peak of the fighting, and the lesson that President Eisenhower himself once drew:

> Every gun that is made, every warship launched, every rocket fired, signifies, in the final sense, a theft from those who hunger and are not fed, those who are cold and are not clothed... The world in arms is not spending money alone. It is spending the sweat of its laborers, the genius of its scientists, and the hopes of its children.[13]

Another example of irresponsible investment decisions is the use of pension funds, which cumulatively constitute the largest single pool of capital in America, up to $500 billion by some estimates. Whether the funds are public or private, their investment is usually entrusted to "experts" who care little about the social effect of their decisions or the actual interests of the working people who "own" the capital. Thus, machinists, steelworkers and other unionists have discovered their pension capital invested in corporations engaged in anti-union activity, and public employees have uncovered the use of their pensions to prop up

Capital Investment Per Job

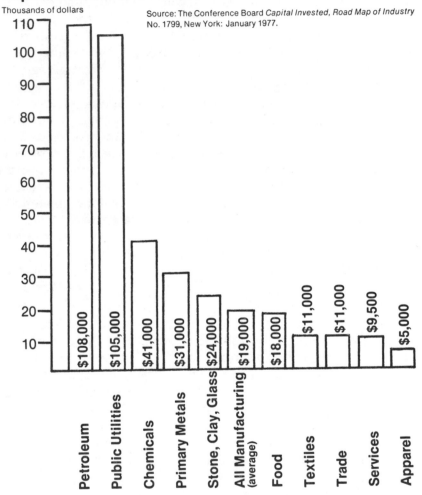

Thousands of dollars

Source: The Conference Board *Capital Invested, Road Map of Industry* No. 1799, New York: January 1977.

Industry	Capital Investment
Petroleum	$108,000
Public Utilities	$105,000
Chemicals	$41,000
Primary Metals	$31,000
Stone, Clay, Glass	$24,000
All Manufacturing (average)	$19,000
Food	$18,000
Textiles	$11,000
Trade	$11,000
Services	$9,500
Apparel	$5,000

nuclear power plants at home and corporations in South Africa abroad.[14] Many of the investment policies have been so disgraceful from even a self-interest viewpoint—gambling on the slumping stockmarket, for instance—that studies have found a better rate of return could have been achieved merely by leaving the pension money in an ordinary passbook savings account. If the pensions were invested in the home mortgage market, or in mass transit and conservation, the "overall return" would do far more for the economic security of today's workers than policies which squander funds in less productive areas. If recovery from recession, without massive tax increases, is going to be possible, it certainly will require a greater control of pension funds in the public interest.*

In short, full employment in desirable working conditions has to be seen as a good and necessary investment. Its prospect, however, has never seemed dimmer. The continuing obstacle in its way, growing to ever stormier proportions in the 1960s and 1970s, is the rise of inflation. The current economic wisdom and popular consciousness of the American people are shaped to believe that the curse of inflation can only be lifted by occasional spells of joblessness. That myth will have to be broken, and the real causes of inflation understood, before the jobs of workers are no longer threatened in the battle against high prices.

The Global Causes of Inflation

Understanding modern inflation, and why liberal and conservative remedies do not work, requires beginning with the *global*

---

*Two of the finest analyses of how pension funds can be used to improve housing, small business, new energy programs, family farms and community economic health are by George Williams and Nathan Gardels, "A Response to Fiscal Crisis and the Tax Revolt: Toward Public Control of Capital and Credit," (School of Architecture and Urban Planning, University of California, Los Angeles, November 21, 1978) and by John Hagelberg, "Public Capital and Community Needs: Los Angeles City and County Public Investments," (Los Angeles: Center for New Corporate Priorities, 1979). These activists of the Campaign for Economic Democracy, joined by church and labor groups, were able to achieve an Executive Order by Governor Brown on January 30, 1980 creating a Public Investment Task Force.

environment. Stated most clearly by Robert Fuller of the Worldwatch Institute, inflation is "the rising cost of living on a small planet."[15] The growth of population, from 3 to 4 billion in the last generation, means a massive rise in world demand, while the rapacious environmental policies of nation states and powerful corporations have contributed to a decline in the supply of resources. Demand will continue to escalate while the resource supply rapidly becomes thinner, requiring more elaborate technical recovery processes, and thereby becoming progressively more expensive to obtain.

According to Richard Barnet, "In the first twenty-five years after the surrender of Germany and Japan the industrial world used more petroleum and non fuel minerals than had been consumed in all previous human history." As each barrel or cubic foot of gas becomes more difficult to procure, the productivity of capital declines. Projected synthetic fuel plants, to take only one example, will be larger than any energy facilities ever built in the U.S. Water desalination projects, 300 foot smoke stacks for coal, LNG supertankers, drilling rigs for the North Sea, and nuclear breeder reactors are all monuments of a world straining to stretch out the supply of receding energy resources. Rising costs are built into the very attempt to wrest more out of an overtaxed environment. Moreover, costs are driven up by the fact that the world is no longer America's backyard, as it was between 1945 and 1970— "the longest period of growth that capitalism had ever experienced" in the words of Robert Heilbroner—but is now a place of pluralistic power centers in which other nations can and will charge more for the sale of their resources.

The Worldwatch Institute has documented the depletion of other vital resources in addition to oil. Their findings show it is steadily becoming more costly to obtain food, to extract ores, to find fresh water, or to obtain enough grassland, cropland and wood supplies. There is little ability to expand supply, for instance by irrigating arid lands or using fertilizer to improve yields, without incurring soaring costs and further strains on the environment. Exactly these "technical fixes" were tried after the physical frontier of the U.S. closed in the 1890's; by the 1940's and 1950's, American agricultural productivity was increased by chemical

U.S. Consumer Price Index, 1800-1979

(1967 = 100)
Log Scale

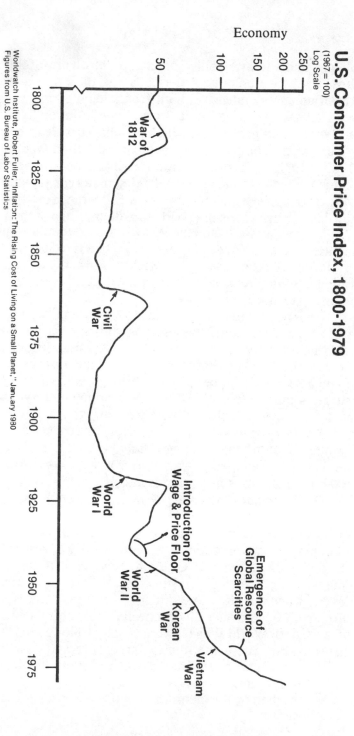

Worldwatch Institute, Robert Fuller, "Inflation: The Rising Cost of Living on a Small Planet," January 1980
Figures from U.S. Bureau of Labor Statistics

technologies and the availability of cheap petroleum products. Now those fixes are presenting Americans with their true costs, in the form of an energy-intensive, high-technology, overprocessed and over-packaged system of agriculture. Food inflation has risen more and more, and packaging, which is indispensable to corporate agriculture, may be becoming more expensive than food itself. From 1963 to 1971, food consumption rose by 2.3 percent on a per capita basis while the tonnage of packaging materials jumped by nearly 40 percent. Everything points to a re-appearance of "the law of diminishing returns" which David Ricardo outlined in the 19th century. That law, reasserted by the Worldwatch studies, is simply that increases in the amount of labor applied to a fixed acreage do not proportionally increase the yield. Rather, there are diminishing marginal returns that invariably set in as the earth's natural limits are approached.

Inflation is not confined to capitalist countries, but appears in the Soviet Union, China and other nations whose planned socialist economies include price controls. The Worldwatch study indicates price increases of 30-40 percent in Eastern Europe during the late 1970's, and a 33 percent jump in many food costs in China. This again suggests that certain of inflation's fundamental dynamics are not manageable simply by re-organizing the institutional balance from the private to the public sector, or vice versa.

It is also worth noting that on a global basis the budget for armaments, most often used in wars over control of resources, is over $500 billion, an investment that is massively inflationary and wasteful. *The more nations spend for defense, the less they get.* The president of Ling-Tempco-Voght (LTV) has explained the inevitable paradox of capital-intensive defense systems: "... The unit cost of new aerospace products has consistently increased by a factor of four every ten years... One can show that in the case of a fixed defense budget, if this trend persists, we are only 62 years from the day when our Navy and Air Force will each consist of a single airplane."[22] Wars have always been closely correlated with inflation and, until World War II, were usually followed by deflation. But since the rise of the nuclear arms race and peacetime military establishments, a permanent war economy has been a major contributor to inflation. When more money is spent on the world's weapons than on the incomes of half the world's people—

as is presently the case—the international order is surely out of control and heading into a combination of bankruptcy and violence.

This means a challenge to both conservatism and liberalism with their common emphasis on expansion and consumption. Conservatives cannot simply maintain wishful rhetoric about "leaving the free market to do its work" when it is apparent that our own ecological systems are being taxed beyond their carrying capacity by forces of institutional greed. And liberals cannot speak of "stimulating demand" in a world where there already is not enough to go around.

Conservation along with a de-militarization of the world's nation-states would certainly begin to reverse the menacing encroachment of today's demand on tomorrow's depletable resources. Put another way, the global solution to inflation lies in creating an equitable distribution of wealth within the context of a stable and sustainable environment.

The Corporate Causes of Inflation

In a pure system of supply and demand, or in a more concentrated economic system with a plentiful frontier, inflation can be minimized and controlled. Today we have neither a free market nor such a frontier; instead there is a system of relatively centralized corporate power whose growth is limited by scarce and costly resources. This is a basic institutional reason for contemporary inflation. Capital tends to be perpetually "over-invested" as a result of policies ranging from tax treatment of capital gains to narrow notions of efficiency that promote mechanization of labor. The dangerous paradox is that *inflation is profitable while at the same time it self-destructively drains the economy to death.*

In 1977, Leslie Ellen Nulty wrote an academic study for the Exploratory Project for Economic Alternatives, which provided powerful evidence for the view that corporate power is a central factor in inflation. Though few were sympathetic on official levels to her analysis (one meeting of her organization with President Carter resulted in little more than a thank-you letter), it marked an important moment in the political thinking of the American left: the first significant shift of emphasis to the problem of inflation, an issue which until then had been monopolized by Republicans. A Coalition Opposed to Inflation in the Necessities (COIN) soon emerged, with a composition ranging from civil rights organizations to environmentalists, nutritionists to building trades leaders.

Nulty's conclusions were refreshingly simple by comparison to most economic discourse on "stagflation." First, she found that about seventy cents of every consumer dollar is spent on four needs—food, housing, medical care, and energy bills. These four items she described as "basic necessities of life." The annual rate of inflation of the four necessities between 1970 and 1976 was 44 percent greater than the annual inflation rate for non-necessities. "If inflation had been concentrated on air fares, electric toothbrushes, and yachts, or even spread evenly, it would not have put such a powerful squeeze on the budgets of most Americans and might never have become the major issue it is today." To the fact of inflation in the necessities, the COIN project added the observation that profits had risen steadily for agribusiness, the oil industry, the medical lobby and real estate speculators. This combination—goods and services that people must have, provided only by powerful economic interests—explained in almost classical supply-demand terms the emergence of chronic inflation in the heart of the economy. Case by case, here is what the COIN project found:

1. *Food.* Compared to a 41 percent inflation rate among non-necessities over the period 1970-77, food costs soared by 67 percent. Little of the increase went to farmers or agricultural workers. The average farmer obtained only three cents from every consumer dollar spent on bread, and the hourly wages of food industry workers didn't keep up with their own rising food bills. On the other hand, the profits of food processors, grain dealers and corporate middlemen rose handsomely. After-tax profits in food marketing rose by 150 percent from 1970 to 1977.[26] Monopoly in the food industry includes four firms controlling 75 percent of bread and flour, three firms controlling 82 percent of breakfast cereals, and one firm controlling 90 percent of all soups. Vertical integration of agricultural corporations is replacing the family farm, with 97 of chicken farming, 85 percent of citrus, and 90 percent of sugar production under such control.

Comparative Inflation Rates
Necessities vs. Non-Necessities

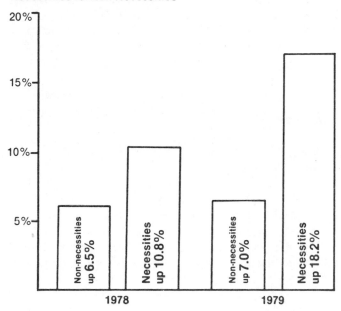

Price Increases in the Necessities
October 1978 to April 1979

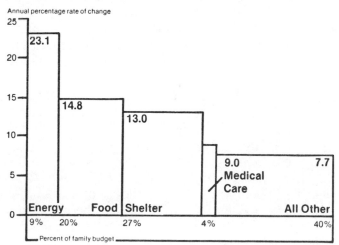

Source: Bureau of Labor Statistics.

2. *Medical Care.* Costs in medicine rose by virtually the same rate as those for food, 68 percent. Again, the wages of nurses and hospital workers were not to blame; they barely kept up with the cost of living and, from 1955 to 1975, the share of consumer hospital bills going to labor costs dropped by 14 percent. On the other hand, the average doctor made $63,000 in 1976; and profits for the larger drug companies registered at 18.2 percent during the same period. Insurance companies, in COIN's phrase, continued to be "collection agencies for the doctors and hospitals," looking the other way while as much as $4-5 billion was spent for unnecessary surgery and 150,000 hospital beds were empty symbols of the excesses of the the medical industry.

3. *Housing.* Home ownership came to be a vanishing American dream in the 1970s as prices rose by over 100 percent, more than twice as fast as costs of non-necessities. Monthly costs alone for the first-time home owner went up 73 percent between 1970 and 1976. The key causes of housing inflation were interest rates and land speculation, which increased by a third as components of new home costs. In 1977 they were 27 percent of the cost; by 1977, they had risen to 36 percent. At the same time, the labor share of the cost of building a new home actually declined by 8 percent.[28] The result was that home ownership rapidly became affordable only for the affluent. In 1965-66, the bottom one-third of American families by income level bought 17 percent of the new homes that were sold, while the top 25 percent purchased 31 percent of them; by 1975-76, the bottom third bought only 4 percent of all new homes, while the top 25 percent increased their share of purchases to 58 percent.[29] More and more wealthy Americans bought second homes while working people settled for mobile homes. The tax laws encouraged the spiral of speculation further by allowing almost indefinite postponement of taxes on capital gains from home sales as long as those gains were invested in purchasing an even more expensive home.

4. *Energy.* From 1970 to 1977, energy prices rose 99 percent, twice as fast as the prices of non-necessities.[30] As a result, one in every five older Americans was forced to choose between buying their usual groceries or paying their utility bills, "between eating and heating,"[31] and the U.S. Government in 1979 actually published a pamphlet instructing Americans how to stay warm by

wrapping themselves in newspapers. Energy costs are of course a driving force throughout the entire economy, pushing up the price of such things as shipping, fertilizer, clothing, phonograph records and automobile dashboards. To the claim that environmental regulations are responsible for increased costs, the answer is that *all* federal anti-pollution requirements only increased the cost-of-living by one-half of one percent in 1977 (a calculation that did not include the lower medical bills that surely come from cleaner water and air).[32] And to the claim that OPEC is responsible for increased energy costs, the obvious answer is that it is at least a shared responsibility with the American banks and oil companies. If there is anything deficient in the Nulty and COIN analysis, it has been a tendency to *under*estimate the bearing of energy on inflation by equating it with the three other necessities. The energy impact on inflation is at once more massive and threatening than the other three issues combined. While prices for gas and home-heating oil have risen disastrously for American consumers, the energy crisis has been a vast windfall for oil companies and banks. The huge earnings of the oil industry are reflected in the percentage increase in profits for the first quarter of 1980 in comparison with the previous year. Occidental registered a 236 percent increase, followed by SOHIO with 169 percent, Exxon 120 percent, Getty 109 percent, Conoco with 103 percent, and Texaco with 97 percent (Gulf had a relatively "low" 56 percent hike).[33] The cash flow of the oil industry, which ran between $25 and $30 billion annually in the late 1970's, will be augmented in the next five years by between $50 and $80 billion in additional surplus *after* windfall profits and other taxes.[34] The multinational banks are even bigger beneficiaries of energy inflation. Citicorp and Chase Manhattan alone are interlocked with a dozen oil companies through 27 directors. Along with Morgan Guaranty, Chemical Bank of New York, Bank of America and a few others, these financial institutions are hungry for control of the more than *one trillion dollars* OPEC is expected to invest in countries like the U.S. between 1975 and 1985.[35] Moreover, because the big banks are outside the reach of U.S. regulators, the world money supply is beyond control. The Federal Reserve Board traditionally was able to combat inflation by determining how much money banks could lend and how much would be held in reserve, thus controlling the

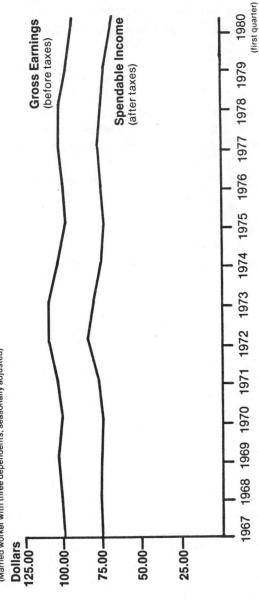

Weekly Earnings in 1967 Dollars
(Married worker with three dependents, seasonally adjusted)

Gross Earnings (before taxes)

Spendable Income (after taxes)

Dollars
125.00
100.00
75.00
50.00
25.00

1967 1968 1969 1970 1971 1972 1973 1974 1975 1976 1977 1978 1979 1980 (first quarter)

Source: U.S. Bureau of Labor Statistics

money supply. The rise of the Eurodollar market changes all that. Now if a bank wants to extend a loan to a debtor nation, or raise new funds for speculative investments, it can simply "create" more money, profiting from its own inflationary policy.

The corporate ideology lays the blame for inflation on high wages, increased government regulation and wasteful spending. Their proposed solutions are higher interest rates, more unemployment, less environmental protection, less social welfare spending. But as Nulty's analysis shows, these solutions don't come to terms with the particular sectoral inflation that devours 70 cents of every dollar. In the basic necessities, wages are rising more slowly than prices. As even the President's Council of Economic Advisors reported on the 1972-75 period when inflation began to soar, "the dominant influence was the rise in fuel and food prices... and the rise in consumer *prices led to efforts by wage earners to recover lost real incomes."*[36] Over the 1970's the purchasing power of the average American worker declined from 1968-69 levels. While in the 1960's real buying power increased *every* year, in the 1970's it frequently fluctuated and, on the average, slightly declined.[37] Therefore, the corporate solution of cutting wages to fight inflation is false in its perception of where the problem lies.

The same false perception is apparent in the corporate attack on regulation. Government rules and regulations, however burdensome or wasteful, are provably marginal to the problem of inflation in the necessities; reducing anti-pollution requirements, for example, by even one-fifth would reduce consumer prices by only one-tenth of one percent, according to Nulty.[38]

Nor are recession and unemployment the answers, as we have already seen, since more unemployment has not necessarily meant less inflation in the 1970s. And while cutting government spending makes sense on its own merits, it will not directly make it easier to afford food, housing, health care or energy. As a matter of fact, major cuts in government spending or regulations might make the costs of these necessities increase.

The view that corporate power is implicated in high prices leads to a different notion of combatting inflation. The real "inflation fighters" would become those people across the country struggling to control corporate costs of daily life,

including;
—renters across California struggling for their share of the benefits from Proposition 13, for rent controls and affordable housing, and the end of rampant speculation;
—health activists fighting for a system of preventive medicine which controls the reckless spewing of cancerous chemicals into the workplace and community, leading to multi-billion dollars worth of long-term health costs;
—small farmers demanding enforcement of acreage-limitation laws which would allow their families to return to farmlands increasingly controlled by absentee corporations and even foreign speculators;
—pioneers in solar energy who seek stable and secure energy prices from a competitive renewable resources industry free of the stranglehold of the oil and nuclear monopolies;
—peace advocates demanding a shift from wasteful weapons systems like the MX Missile to useful public transit systems in American cities.

Seen from this perspective, there are all sorts of programmatic solutions that would reduce inflation and increase jobs, and could be carried out within existing federal and state budget limitations, thus increasing revenues and reducing deficits. They would include in the field of *energy*: regulation of oil and gas prices, and a shift to funding decentralized solar and conservation instead of nuclear and synthetics; in *food*: prevention of grain speculation, crackdowns on middleman profiteering, subsidies to cooperatives and direct marketing ventures, enforcement of reclamation law and new lending practices to make family farms and cooperatives viable entities; in *health*: national health insurance with cost controls and incentives for preventive approaches, health-maintenance organizations where the incentive is to save rather than spend money; in *housing*: credit allocation for affordable housing, tax and other dampening measures against land speculation, greater government investment in housing rehabilitation. This list is both incomplete and imperfect. But it is intended to show a *direction* that is crucial to lessening inflation yet virtually ignored in official economic debates in America. This approach to curing inflation must begin with an awareness of how the declining productivity of capital at the end of the plentiful frontier leads to corporate price increases as a way to generate the level of profit perceived as necessary to maintain an elite lifestyle and system that may have "worked" in the period 1945-55 but is inappropriate in any imaginable future. Our ability to define the value of the world's currency in terms of the dollar, which prevailed from 1945 to 1968 (from victory in World War II to defeat in Vietnam) is clearly at an end. And our ability to command cheap energy resources from our industrial machine is likewise over, due to the sheer cost of technologies like nuclear power and the rising political power of other countries in the world. This means a capital crisis which can only be resolved, from the business point of view, by higher prices extracted from the consumer.

If the free market model on the frontier was inherently capable of reducing prices, the corporate model in the post-frontier era is apparently not. The corporate economy and state in an era of limits are inherently inflationary. In a very real sense, the system itself may become too inflationary in total cost for a majority of Americans to afford.

The Role of the State in Inflation

The impact of government spending and bureaucracy on inflation are real American issues, not just partisan Republican platform planks.

The fever of modern runaway inflation was precipitated by an act of government, not of business, by the application of liberal, New Deal deficit-oriented economics to a critical national issue, not by a special act of corporate arrogance. *Our current inflation began with Lyndon Johnson's way of waging the Vietnam War.*

President Johnson faced a many-sided crisis in 1967-68, trying to fight an unpopular, immoral war which was draining our ethical and economic strength. He chose to continue the war at a cost of *two billion dollars per month* without seeking a tax increase from a hostile Congress. For money he turned instead to the printing press, plunging the nation into a mounting deficit that would not come due until peacetime. Johnson's invented money went through the Pentagon into a) the accounts of capital-intensive, high-technology, monopolistic defense corporations who produced weapons—to be immediately destroyed; and b) the pockets of millions of American soldiers who used them to purchase pre-existing goods and services; and c) from there into the hands of foreign banks and governments who wondered why they were helping finance the Vietnam War by holding U.S. currency that became weaker by the hour.

It was no accident that the Tet Offensive of early 1968, which shattered any international illusions about a U.S. victory, was swiftly followed by the first major post-World War II collapse of dollar confidence, as foreign-held dollars were massively exchanged for gold. Nor is it any accident that 1960's deficit financing of the war triggered the double-digit inflation in the 1970's.

Periods of war and deficit spending are closely correlated with inflation throughout American history, but after each war in the past prices had always come down. Not so with Vietnam. Something historically new occurred. In part the decline of the frontier of cheap resources, and the growth of corporate power bent on expansion into that disappearing frontier were at fault. But another factor was the role of the massive, bureaucratic New Deal (liberal) state into America's political economy.

From 1770 to 1930—that is, to the Great Crash and before the New Deal, *on the average* American prices remained fairly stable, and if there was a chronic problem, it was deflation. It is important to stress "on the average" to take account of the violent boom-and-bust nature of the economic cycle before the New Deal. There was serious inflation only during war, and otherwise the critical problem was falling prices—a 25 percent decline between 1823 and 1848, and a fifty percent drop between 1873 and 1898.[39] This up-and-down rhythm, with a secular tendency towards deflation, seems to have occurred in other capitalist countries as well until the 1930's.

Then came economic collapse and the emergence of the New Deal. The government stabilized the inherent boom-and-bust cycle of the economy by a range of fiscal and monetary policies associated with Lord Keynes. Since that historic intervention, the economy has been sufficiently managed to prevent another crash.

But something equally important has happened: with the containment of the boom-and-bust cycle, prices have only risen and never come down. With the deficit spending of the Keynesians, inflation became institutionalized as a process which could only go one way—up. For a long while this was an insignificant fact because the United States had extremely favorable access to energy supplies and world markets. The annual rate of inflation, while not going down, remained fairly constant between 1.5 percent and 3 percent during the 1950's and 1960's. It crept up to between 5 and 6 percent during the Korean and Vietnam Wars, but went down to less than one percent during the four years after Korea—for virtually the last time. While these figures seem balmy in retrospect, it should still be remembered that even a 2 percent annual inflation rate reduces the value of a dollar to about 84 cents in a decade. Americans noted the disappearance of the nickel Coke and the 25 cent hamburger, but regarded their general economic prospects with optimism.

Those happy days ended in 1965; here are the yearly inflation rates since then;[40]

Year	Percent	Year	Percent	Year	Percent
1965	1.9	1971	3.4	1977	6.9
1966	3.4	1972	3.4	1978	8.0
1967	3.0	1973	8.8	1979	13.3
1968	4.7	1974	12.2	1980	18.0 (as of
1969	6.1	1975	7.0		June)
1970	5.5	1976	4.8		

It is dramatic to note that President Carter's official anti-inflation goal is the reduction of the annual rate to seven percent, one-third of the June 1980 figure, though not including energy prices. And even if that were achieved, it would be a higher peacetime rate than the inflation during Korea and Vietnam, and would double the cost of everything in eleven years.

To understand the connection of government with this inflationary spiral, we have to examine the issue of rising federal budgets. Just as prices averaged out between 1770 and 1930, so did government spending. Except for periods of war, the federal budget remained low and fairly stable. When some of us formed the Students for a Democratic Society in 1962, for example, the federal budget had just passed the $100 billion mark for the first time. As with the issue of prices and inflation, we on the left did not think the issue of government spending was one of scale but rather priorities. We were not trying to lessen the budget in quantity, but merely shift its focus from military to social priorities. And this was correct at the time. The Republican concerns both about inflation and government spending seemed rigid and ideological, mired in the 1920's and out of touch with the realities of 1960.

But then realities began to change. In one decade, the federal budget doubled, the most rapid increase in American history. By 1971, the budget was $211 billion; by 1975, it had tripled the 1960 figure, rising to $362 billion; by 1980, it will be over six times the 1960 figure, reaching beyond $600 billion.[41] At such an accelerating rate of increase, the federal government would spend $3 trillion in 1990.

Our federal debt, the amount of money we owe the banking system for budget deficits incurred, shows a similar tendency to shift from stability to terrifying and uncontrollable levels. The debt remained fairly level between $270 billion and $300 billion from 1946 to 1966, but was skyrocketing towards $900 billion at the end of the 1970's.[42] In 1980, interest on the federal debt was the *third* largest item in the United States budget. The total interest cost was $65 billion, coming to 12 percent of the entire federal budget, with one-third of it going to foreign banks.

The massive debt is the result of deficit financing during two wars, and an 18 year pattern of spending in which the federal budget was balanced only once. The government makes up its negative yearly balance by going to the printing press, expanding the money supply and cheapening the dollar.

Beyond the inflationary effect of deficits, the federal budget in its entirety perpetuates inflation. The key to understanding how spending and inflation connect is through the economic device of "indexing." Incomes and costs in most government programs are indexed to the inflation rate; in this way public employees receive cost-of-living increases, defense contractors obtain cost-plus contracts and so forth. When the inflation rate is low, there is little problem with this method of payments, but when inflation rates go out of control, so too does indexed government spending. The historic liberal-conservative compromise of the New Deal was to finance social programs out of rising real incomes, not out of inflation. The faith of New Dealers was that the tiger of inflation could be ridden rather than killed. Now however, the interaction of indexed government spending with an inherently inflationary corporate sector means that the tiger becomes wild and triumphant.

Almost the entire federal budget is allocated and indexed for warfare or welfare, both of which increase the structural problems of inflation and unemployment. For the fiscal year ending September 30, 1980, the projected budget priorities paint a clear picture of the problem. Of a $531 billion outlay, the top priorities are:[42]

1. military (nearly half of which is for pensions)	$125.8 billion
2. social security	115.7 billion
3. interest on national debt	65 billion
4. medicare and health	53.4 billion
5. public assistance	31.4 billion
6. aid to veterans	20.5 billion

These major programs account for $440 billion, or over 80 percent of the federal budget. One notices at once that there are no investments in energy conservation, mass transit or new technologies near the top of the budget. It seems rather like a budget for a society that wants to defend itself as it retires. What is equally apparent is the thoroughly indexed nature of the expenditures. As inflation rises in energy, the military budget shoots up; as it rises in consumer necessities, it increases military pensions, social security and public assistance; as health costs spiral up, so does the Medicare budget, and so on. If inflation continues at the rate of the past decade, the federal budget will have an *automatic* tendency to skyrocket until some future point of no return.

Only an alternative budgetary process, combined with new national priorities, and a government emphasis on protecting consumers from corporate profiteering, could begin to reduce the inflationary impact of current government spending.

First of all, the nation needs an *honest budget*. Like a product out of *Alice in Wonderland*, nothing in the government budget is as it seems. There is a comprehensive deception about the true cost of most items, that takes several forms. The initial deception is that present costs are considered with no requirement to take long-term inflation into account. Nor are employment impacts required in judging spending priorities. Nor are the actual, integrated costs of priorities required for consideration in decision-making. When the cost of a proposed power plant is examined, for instance, there is no official analysis of the hidden costs of tax subsidies, water which will be consumed, farmlands which will be lost, energy which will be used to create energy, health problems which will be incurred, nor of the relative economic and social merits of alternative energy sources which could provide an equivalent amount of power. All budget decisions should be officially weighed on the basis of *total cost*, not the narrower grounds of "cost-effectiveness."

Second, the nation should be shifting its inflationary military and energy policies toward a conversion program which prepares workers and communities for development of new technology, particularly by investing in alternative energy systems relying on photovoltaic solar cells, wind machines, methane digesters, hydroelectric and geothermal facilities. Coupled with a serious conservation program, this kind of effort would combine productive investment with growth of a labor-intensive industry that would lower energy inflation; exactly the opposite of today's policies which waste capital in ever-more expensive investments employing ever-fewer people. A $20 billion transfer from the military budget to a crash solar energy program would do more for American economic security then the mindless manufacture of a few more missiles and nuclear reactors.

Third, any federal budget-cutter who proposes to fight waste and inflation without taking on the military-industrial complex is a hypocrite. Not only is military spending inherently inflationary and capital intensive, but it devours the capital and technical resources necessary for the growth of more productive and worthwhile civilian industry—it has constituted 10 percent of our GNP for the past 25 years.⁴⁴ At least 70 percent of federal research and development money is devoted to military purposes, gradually robbing America of the ability to develop competitive new technologies. While the US has provided costly military protection to West Germany and Japan since World War II, their scientists have been free to concentrate a far greater effort on developing the technology for consumer goods that are superior to American products.

Of course, America must have a system of effective national defense, not one which weakens the nation economically while overprotecting it militarily. As *Business Week's* editors acknowledge: "It is no longer enough to mindlessly focus on the Soviet Union as a military enemy while the economic heart of the country is being eaten away by other nations."⁴⁵ For security and economic reasons alike, the national defense program must be *spartan* in character, designed to protect carefully-defined and popularly-supported national interests rather than the merely fanciful or profitable. And it must be justified on genuine security needs, instead of the "military Keynesianism" which has resulted in a disproportionate number of military facilities in the political jurisdictions of powerful members of Congress. The military budget is an albatross of waste, tragically reflecting the state of the society it purports to defend. If America defines its national interest as protecting a worldwide empire for the expansion of multi-national corporations, then massive military spending is inevitable, further inflation is inevitable, the decline of the dollar is inevitable, and a collapse into social and economic havoc at home may become irretrievable.

However, it is inadequate to speak of shifting from "military to civilian priorities" if those new priorities are going to contain the same waste and irrationality as the defense sector does. For example, the shift of one defense contractor, Rohr Industries, into civilian mass transit resulted in the incredibly expensive Bay Area Rapid Transit (BART) system in California. The delays and cost overruns in construction, the inadequate quality of service, the shutdowns, accidents and one major fire on the system, have undoubtedly led to overall costs equal or greater than any transportation savings. Another obvious example is the shift of Department of Energy resources to increased solar energy development, which has resulted in a budget emphasizing wasteful "power tower" and "space satellite" programs desired by aerospace contractors at the expense of practical and immediate solar applications.[46] A third such example is the rising expenditure for "health care" which funnels billions of dollars to pharmaceutical companies, high-technology laboratories, and a burgeoning hospital industry without a commensurate decline in illness and cost of treatment.[47]

The government bureaucracy increases the inflationary nature of these spending programs. Like the issues of inflation and spending, liberals have generally allowed the question of bureaucracy to be monopolized by conservatives and Republicans. But like inflation and spending, the problems of bureaucracy should be seen as massive and troubling from *any* ideological perspective. Liberals have perhaps a special place in their hearts for the bureaucracy of government, or the public sector over the private, because it has been government that has acted as the protector of last resort for the poor, the elderly, the disabled, the oppressed, and it has been government—more than industry—which has been responsive to grass-roots pressure and political action. But we are not living any longer in the rosy dawn of the New Deal. That was fifty years ago. Even Eleanor Roosevelt would be shocked at the bureaucratic monstrosity which corporate liberalism has wrought.

Government bureaucracy *is* an obscene burden. There is no reason for Republicans alone to hold this insight. Those of us who confronted the federal government—under two liberal Democrats— during the movements for civil rights and peace in Vietnam should be in the forefront of the struggle against bureaucracy rather than those hypocritical conservative ideologues who attack government with rhetoric while reaping its tax benefits and military contracts. Those of us who know first-hand the hollowness of civil rights enforcement, the stymying of citizen input into government agencies like health services or urban development, ought to be credited for battling bureaucracy rather than the Republican developers who favor politicians with big contributions in return for greasing the wheels of the land-use and planning bureaucracies. At the same time the solution is not to cut essential human programs but the real dead weight within the military budget.

Bureaucratic management in large nation-states seems to be inflationary in some inherent sense. The crucial reason for this could be the sheer, multiplying complexity of coordination itself, on top of the spiralling social and environmental costs which government inherits from the inflationary private sector. It is quite possible that government is becoming what Hazel Henderson describes as an "Entropy State."[48] Originating in physics, the concept of Entropy is part of the law of thermodynamics which says first, that energy is constant and can neither be created nor destroyed, only transferred; and second, that the tranformation of energy creates a permanent decline in the total energy available for use. While the total amount of energy in the universe is constant, its entropy is also constantly increasing.

Translated to an analysis of organization and bureaucracy, the concept of entropy would tend to explain the increasing complexity, specialization, fragmentation and paralysis of systems which seem to both grow steadily yet also collapse of their own weight. What Henderson calls the "transaction costs" of the system begin to offset productivity and grow faster than any new wealth can be created, thus encouraging constant inflation. The government sets rules of bureaucratic conduct for the society which engulf nearly everyone in ever more expensive transaction costs. There are, for example, nearly 150,000 law firms in America engaged in mediating a constantly-rising number of claims. The sheer existence of the legal profession, and the rules by which it operates, tends to *increase* rather than decrease the numbers of cases being handled. The same is true of the medical profession and its rules: as the profession itself grows, so do the number of patients and costs of treatments, though health may even decline.

This tendency to bureaucratic giantism is further fueled by the "social costs" caused by the private sector but left to the government to absorb. The nightmarish and lengthy list of these costs includes unemployment insurance for workers left behind by the multinationals, medical payments for those maimed and hospitalized by unsafe automobiles and assembly lines, air and water clean-up programs for a polluted nation, and police forces to "contain" the unemployed. "The cost of cleaning up the mess," Henderson writes, "mounts ever higher. The proportion of GNP that must be spent in mediating conflicts, controlling crime, protecting consumers and the environment, providing ever-more comprehensive bureaucratic coordination, and generally trying to maintain 'social homeostasis' begins to grow exponentially."[49] The "excessive dependence on professional services" alone, writes Robert Fuller, is a major source of inflation, and "lessening our dependence on 'experts' may be as important in countering inflation as lessening our dependence on foreign oil."[50]

What, then, can be done about bureaucracy's impact on inflation? First of all, the State cannot and should not be radically dismantled as some conservatives and anarchists would prefer. Nor should its partial dismantling, in the form of drastic cuts in government programs, be considered the first step in fighting inflation. That would only impose new burdens on those already disadvantaged by sex, class, age and race discrimination, dredging up a recession as the cure. We have already seen that the growth of the state, while having a dynamic of its own, is inseparable from the growth of corporate power, and solutions must treat both institutions.

The real first step should consist of *returning the responsibility for "social costs" from the state to the corporations which created them.* By *in*ternalizing such "externalities" (as they are presently defined), there could be a major reduction in government bureaucracy and spending. Such a change would require new standards of overall economic and social performance in addition to profit, as a measure of corporate achievement, and a democratic restructuring of the corporate world to include the consumers, employees and community voices that presently bear the "external" results of "internal" decisions now based only on expanding production and profit. Changes such as less stress in the workplace, less pollution of the environment, less chemical exposure in industry, and less promotion of junk food, for example, would lower illness rates and consequently, the size and cost of government health programs.

The second serious step would be to reduce the bloated bureaucracy of the welfare state by *returning major responsibility*

for certain programs and services from the government to society.
A shift from professionalism to voluntarism, from bureaucracy to
self-help would reduce both the size of government and the rate of
inflation.

One example of a voluntary citizen approach to government
rather than an expensive bureaucratic one is the SolarCal Council
in California. Created by Governor Brown in 1978 to accelerate
the public acceptance and commercialization of solar energy, the
Council has 30 citizen-members from business, labor, environmental, minority and public-interest groups, who meet formally
four times per year as well as attending several subcommittee
meetings. The total cost of the Council's work is only $150,000
annually, including an office and several staff—out of a state
budget of $24 billion. The Council takes conscious pride in "doing
more for less" rather than seeking to inflate its bureaucratic
stature. Because it depends on citizen involvement rather than
staff, and because it has real influence, the members have a direct
incentive to take responsibility. The Council has succeeded in its
two-fold mission of creating a popular "solar lobby" and advising
state officials on policy directions. An author of The Harvard
Business School's report, *Energy Future,* called the Solar Cal
Action Plan "the most outstanding solar energy program this
author has yet encountered... worthy of study by every state
energy commission and by the Department of Energy."[51]

The role of voluntarism can be extended even beyond citizen
involvement in government. In the past few years, there has been
an explosion of self-help organizations which can take over many
of the services now performed by official agencies.

By one estimate there may be as many as 500,000 networks
involved in such diverse activity as bartering, flea-marketing, community gardening, birthing, drug and alcoholism programs, varie-
ties of consciousness-raising, nutrition and health, exercise and
meditation, food and medical cooperatives.[52] Some of these new-
type voluntary associations have mixed, even reactionary,
meanings. Corporations or government, for example, will often
try to cut costs by externalizing burdens to the consumer, as in the
cases of "personalized banking," direct long-distance dialing,
self-service gas stations, volunteers in hospitals. The hidden costs

of this kind of voluntarism include dislocated workers and greater unemployment insurance.

But this does not mean that decentralization or technology inevitably has to contain negative repercussions; one of the best ways to reduce the size and cost of government is by *employing communications technology* to provide services and information, create citizen feedback, and build more efficient links between government and the public. By "electronic participation" citizens can save the cost in time, transportation and emotional output that often occurs in going to City Hall; while government, on the other hand, can decentralize many of its programs and services into the neighborhood by the use of two-way television broadcasting of the kind which is already past the experimental stage.

It was Thoreau, not Ronald Reagan, who long ago supported the motto, "That government is best which governs least." By that he surely did not mean a heartless government that cuts services to the poor. "Must the citizen ever for a moment, or in the least degree, resign his conscience to the legislator?" he asked, and answered himself, "Why has every man a conscience then? I think that we should be men first, and subjects afterward."[53] What he meant was that *self-reliance* is a crucial factor in solving social problems and preventing the expensive growth of state bureaucracy.

Alexis de Toqueville made a parallel observation when he cited the vast network of "public associations" as the key to American democracy.[54] Instead of the state bureaucracy absorbing more and more functions once left to the family and the community, and thus increasing the rate of entropy, an actual decentralization of state power might result in more independent communities with people exercising the responsibilities of *self-government*. There may be no way to reduce inflation without a rise of self-sufficiency and healthy grass-roots democracy.

The Cultural Causes of Inflation

Inflation is a byproduct of the collision between the economics of waste and the era of scarcities, between the aspiration for economic justice and the profit priorities of the marketplace, between the tradition of self-reliance and the bureaucratic giantism of the welfare state. In its simplest terms, inflation arises when a society begins to consume more than it produces, when it "steals from the future" in the phrase of Governor Jerry Brown.

The right wing has interpreted this definition to mean that the demand for social justice should be tapered to what society can "afford." Translated into political priorities, this message has meant less welfare, less aid to the disadvantaged, a postponement of national health insurance and other social programs, usually accompanied by appeals to hard work, self-sacrifice, and infinite patience. The hypocrisy of this doctrine can be revealed by one example: if work and sacrifice were really the keys to success, the upper rungs of the American economic ladder would long ago have been scaled and occupied by the black slaves who labored at tasks more backbreaking than those which led Horatio Alger from rags to riches.

Any attack on over-consumption should begin at the top. Why should an aerospace corporation, as happened in 1980, use its investment tax credits to pour money into a canteen, a fast food chain, and a real estate company instead of into a more fuel efficient plane and job-creating public transit vehicles? Why are top executives' salaries often ten and twenty times the wages of those who work for them? Why are certain food and toy corporations allowed free reign in advertising worthless or dangerous junk to children, turning them into the next generation of addicted consumers? Why is our national leadership too often obsessed with opulence as a symbol of achievement? How can a society make a transition to less consumption without leadership? How can a society remain stable if its elites choose to impose austerity on the majority in order to maintain conspicuous consumption for the few?

While the principal offenders are the corporate rich, a majority of Americans continues to be swept up in the consumer lifestyle based on the endless production of more gadgets and junk. The capital-intensive, inflationary industries have managed to convince millions of people that their status is bound up in the possession of gas-guzzling cars, electric typewriters, two television sets per family, heated swimming pools, toilets which flush 100 gallons of water per day, escalators on top of elevators, microwave ovens, plenty of fast foods, and steak dinners twice a week. Many Americans are "hooked" on the habits that support inflation. The fact that they are only pawns in a larger system, or that some are more responsible for waste than others, does not justify their going along with the game of over-consumption. Like resistance to the draft in a time of unjust war, personal resistance to alluring blandishments of corporate advertising helps to change the system. The individual solution to inflation lies in disconnecting from the world of overindulgence and over-consumption

In an era of limits, there is no responsible, human response to inflation except to realize that less *is* more, and the best things in life *are* free. A personal ethic of frugality, which was justified as necessary for capital accumulation and expansion a century ago, now is necessary to share limited resources among billions of people, and to protect the survival of life itself on a restricted planet.

To reverse inflation and simultaneously evolve a full employment economy will involve a major institutional and ideological change. Reforms altering the relation of unemployment to profit, and of profit to investment, making corporations responsible to communities, trimming bureaucracy and fostering a new personal ethic of cooperation instead of consumerism will all play a powerful role. But little will be accomplished unless a solution to the overshadowing spectre of the global energy crisis is also achieved. For continued global dependence on petrochemicals will leave little opportunity for turning back job-denying, inflation-fueling corporate policies. Therefore we must turn to the issue of energy consumption and to the promise of a solar transition.

THREE
ENERGY: TOWARD A SOLAR SOCIETY

It is probable that all the world's governments will be more or less completely totalitarian even before the harnessing of atomic energy; that they will be totalitarian during and after the harnessing seems almost certain. Only a large-scale popular movement towards decentralization and self-help can arrest the present tendency towards statism. At present there is no sign that such a movement will take place.

Aldous Huxley,
Brave New World

The industrial giants of the energy business have always been suspect morally and politically to millions of Americans, but in 1979 they were showing signs of a more serious kind of weakness. They were becoming failures at their basic task of providing affordable, reliable energy.

Two crises of 1979 symbolized this stark new reality. First, in March, the Three Mile Island nuclear power plant came close to a meltdown from a failure which safety engineers, after 20 years of experience, could neither predict nor understand. At the time, the Chairman of the Nuclear Regulatory Commission, Joseph Hendrie, compared himself and the Governor of Pennsylvania to "a couple of blind men staggering around making decisions."[1]

The second crisis occurred in Levittown, Pennsylvania, a suburb that attracted GI's returning from World War II with money in their pockets. Levittown symbolized the expanding, sprawling post-war middle class living in tract housing miles from work. When this suburban bubble burst and gasoline lines formed in Summer 1979, Levittown became the scene of the first middle-class riot against energy shortages, with the National Guard occupying the city for two nights.

83

How Inflation is Driven by Increasingly Inaccessible Oil Supply

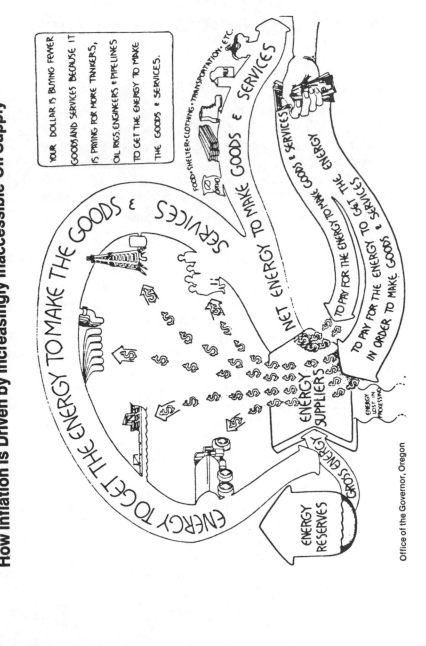

Office of the Governor, Oregon

If Harrisburg and Levittown were representative rather than accidental tragedies, then America had already, unknowingly, entered into a new age of restraints without having made any significant adjustments in an economy and way of life based on expansion.

The only word—in a time when words of warning are wearing out—that can describe this new period is: catastrophic.

We are dependent on multinational oil firms and foreign powers for 9 million barrels of imported oil per day, and on the nuclear industry for as much as one-third of our electricity in places like Chicago, New York and Philadelphia. Imported oil costs have doubled in 1979; home heating oil costs have jumped by one-third and gasoline leapt from 61¢ to $1 per gallon in the same time frame; and nuclear power, which increased seven-fold in cost per kilowatt in the 1970's, is bound to become even more expensive each year.[2]

Americans will be subject to: skyrocketing energy inflation which will spill over to inflate the cost of other necessities like food and shelter as well; capital shortages for cities and social services as more and more dollars are accumulated for the energy industry's new projects; aggravated unemployment rates because of the energy companies' capital-intensive, high-technology nature; cancer hazards and genetic threats from the byproducts of the petrochemical society; further declines of personal and community independence in the face of centralized bureaucratic power; and dangers of brinksmanship or outright war over precious fossil fuel resources in the Middle East.

Time is running out for a crisis-free transition. It is hard to imagine the U.S. government and oil industry weaning itself from a Middle Eastern dependency that has grown since 1973 soon enough to avert one catastrophe or another. The OPEC nations have already decided that they cannot indefinitely feed the American oil habit on American terms while the multinational oil firms as well have powerful vested interests in rising OPEC prices. Therefore the stage is set for further price hikes, pressure on supplies, and possible shortages. In addition, political events in the unstable Middle East—internal crisis within the Saudi state or the Khomeini regime in Iran, or a Palestinian attack on oil tankers in the Straits of Hormuz—could throw the Western world into over-

The Fossil Fuel Age
in the Context of Human History

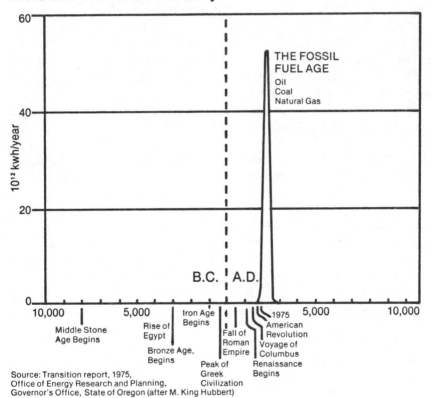

Source: Transition report, 1975,
Office of Energy Research and Planning,
Governor's Office, State of Oregon (after M. King Hubbert)

night chaos and depression. And when the Soviet Union becomes a net oil importer in the next three years, as is predicted by the CIA, all of these threads of danger will swiftly tighten.[3]

The End of the Fossil Fuel Age

And even if these problems do not materialize in a sudden and total Armageddon, there is a more gradual transformation of the energy reality which will change the U.S. and advanced industrial countries permanently. Put simply, we are now running out of affordable fossil fuels. It is estimated that this generation could consume 80 percent of all the oil and gas left on earth. The pinnacle of world oil production will be reached and the downturn will be experienced in these several decades. Denis Hayes points out that such underlying trends alone can determine the rise and fall of great empires. For example, the discovery of America and its mineral wealth enabled Spain to fight wars, survive indebtedness and become a world power in the 16th century. But the subsequent decline in availability of minerals spelled the end of Spanish strength. As Hayes notes, "The industrial nations have been shaped by the availability of cheap, plentiful oil at least as much as Spain was by the flow of gold."[4]

The orthodox reaction to this crisis has been to promote nuclear power, synthetic fuels, and coal with deregulated energy prices to spur development of further oil and gas. But there is one central fact about these conventional sources that controversy and cliche tends to blur: *none of them are serious alternatives for the perilous decade of the 1980's.*

This point has been made in detail by the Harvard authors of the most prestigious energy book in many years, *Energy Future*, by Stobaugh and Yergin.[5] Published in 1979, their book was supplemented by a long *Foreign Affairs* article in January 1980. These authors, and most of their colleagues at the Harvard Business School, happen to *favor* the maximum development of conventional energy sources. But they are pessimistic about an energy policy for the 1980s which *relies* on conventional sources. Their general reason for doubt is quite simple. "Our conventional energy production—oil, gas, coal, and nuclear—may be thought of as *well-explored* producing regions" and therefore any dramatic increases from such sources is unlikely. They cite the specific problems with each conventional source as follows:

1. *Oil and gas.* Even with deregulation of prices, there is "little likelihood of a substantial increase in the domestic production of *oil and gas* to meet anticipated demand. In fact, the United States will be fortunate if it finds enough new oil and gas to keep production at current levels."

2. *Coal.* The "use of coal is increasing, but more slowly than industry expectations." Because of economic cost, environmental and health problems, coal's contribution to energy supplies is forecast to be only one-half of the Carter Administration's expectations.

3. *Nuclear.* In 12 years, the authors predict, nuclear power might provide the equivalent of one-third our present supply of imported oil, but only in the completely unlikely event of continued operation of all existing plants as well as completion of every plant now on order. The improbability of this scenario suggests a "far more limited role for nuclear power under any conceivable scenario than might have been imagined in recent years."

4. *Synthetic fuels.* The authors are especially critical of the president's projected $88 billion syn-fuels program, concocted during the 1979 Camp David "summit," and later cut back to a $20 billion program financed out of the the windfall profits tax. The Harvard authors argue the program would take too long to succeed, would "create tremendous inflationary pressures," and while building plants "as large or larger than the largest industrial plant project ever built at one time in the United States" with an unknown strain on skills and infrastructure to deploy unproven technology, divert "attention and resources from the immediate problems of the 1980's to partial solutions that *might* become available in the 1990's."

More significant to the current crisis is the conclusion Stobaugh and Yergin came to one year after writing *Energy Future.* In their updated article in *Foreign Affairs,* they revealed that even their expertise had not prepared them for the accelerated "telescoping" of the energy crisis. The "energy future" had already become the "energy present."

These impending crises lead the energy industry and the federal government, like two writhing dinosaurs, to increase their pressure for a policy that only amounts to more of the same. The energy industry's 1979 campaign for deregulation of oil and gas prices, for a $100 billion synthetic fuels program, for more nuclear plants, and for a centralized Energy Mobilization Board, are all self-serving attempts to "solve" the energy crisis which will only aggravate it. The total cost of deregulation alone will be higher than that of the whole Vietnam War and the syn-fuels and nuclear program will be as expensive over the coming decade. The proposed government answer to the energy crisis is to increase inflation. Its answer to inflation is recession, and its answer to objections is to override them with a new authoritarian bureaucracy.

Powerful as the energy industry is, it has bred a massive and effective opposition which will be difficult to override. The environmental opposition of the past decade, which began in the late 1960s, has been augmented by a highly effective resistance to nuclear power and, in the past two years, by a new labor militance against the profits and power of Big Oil. Underlying these active forces are the skeptical attitudes of millions of Americans. Recent polls show that two-thirds of the public blames the oil industry for the energy crisis, and one-third favors nationalization.

The combination of economic and political difficulties has largely stalled the energy industry's game plan. Price deregulation of natural gas passed by only one vote in the House of Representatives, oil decontrol was resisted even more fiercely this year and only passed when combined with a massive windfall profits tax, the synthetic fuels program will have major and prolonged opposition, and the nuclear industry has seen a decline of new reactor orders from 36 in 1973 to 4 in 1975 to none at present.[6]

Thus there is a serious energy stalemate emerging. On the one hand, energy conservation and new technologies have not been introduced rapidly enough to offset the continued dependence on imported oil and nuclear energy. On the other hand, fewer and fewer conventional power plants are being built as economic and political opposition rises. There is a parity of political power emerging between those representing oil and nuclear, and those who speak for conservation and renewable resources such as solar.

The stalemate is likely to drag on against the worsening background of steadily rising prices, periodic shortages, entrapment in global crisis, and polarization at home.

We are entering a downward spiral into the ugly politics of blame. Consumer activists, environmentalists and especially the anti-nuclear movement will increasingly be attacked as the obstacle to achieving secure energy supplies. A kind of McCarthyism, perhaps even a severe repression, is certain to be attempted by the energy industry to deflect blame from itself and to pave the way for higher prices, the end of environmental red tape, and a streamlined siting process for new power plants. With sufficient public anxiety, and a federal government dominated by the Republicans a near-term possibility, the chances for a return to the confrontation politics of the 1960s are growing by the day.

Showdown in California

California is a microcosm of the energy stalemate. There is no state with a greater conservation and solar consciousness. We have a governor who is the foremost anti-nuclear, pro-solar advocate on a state level in the country; an Energy Commission dedicated to the same goals; a Legislature which not only passed the strongest nuclear safeguards bill in the U.S., but another which commits the state to the "maximum feasible" solar program in the coming decade. None of this would have been possible, of course, without a profound environmental consciousness cutting across all lines of public opinion.

On the other hand, tangible success in building an energy alternative has been negligible in comparison with the magnitude of the crisis,. As of 1980, for example, there were 60,617 documented solar applications in a state which contains a housing stock of seven million units, and 29,000 of the solar devices were for swimming pools. By comparison, Israel has 3-400,000 solar hot water installations, and Japan nearly 2 million.[7]

The California energy stalemate was described in an alarming but little-noticed memo of May 1979 by Energy Commissioner Emilio Varanini in response to an inquiry from Assembly Speaker

Leo McCarthy's office.[8] "Utilities and energy producers continue to rely heavily on a narrow range of conventional choices," Varanini wrote, "despite the State's encouragement for promising new energy alternatives." To the utilities, "the choice is between the conventional future and nothing, and the conventional future is blocked." The result is a "stalemate which confronts us with energy shortages or a prolonged reliance on those technologies whose economic, environmental, and social costs are viewed with increasing concern by the public."

"Failure to act," Varanini concluded, "will probably allow the conventional technologies to dominate California's energy future." He spells out what that future would mean:

—10-15 new sites for nuclear or coal plants probably in the Sacramento and San Joaquin Valleys and the Southeastern desert,

—a capital cost of at least $75 billion (over three times this year's total state budget),

—water requirements for cooling leaping from the present 37,000 acre-feet per year to 700,000 acre-feet per year, in a future era of predicted water shortages,

—The loss of 20,000 acres of agricultural land, or the crop equivalent of 150,000 acres of alfalfa,

—heavy air pollution and a need for 3,000 acres of disposal sites if the state chooses coal,

—a plutonium economy if the state chooses nuclear,

—continued inflation and unemployment as the state remains dependent on fossil fuels for the bulk of its energy.

Variani's dire prophecy was accompanied by a positive set of alternative recommendations. Calling for an "immediate transition strategy relying on non-conventional technologies to the maximum extent possible," Varanini wrote that "what is needed now is the political will to choose an alternative future and to commit the state to making it happen."

The central features of the Varanini plan were "legislatively-established priorities" to end the drift of energy policy. The legislature would establish a priority ranking among the various options for meeting electricity demand, then direct the utilities and regulatory agencies to meet those priorities on schedule. Varanini listed conservation and solar energy as top priorities, and geothermal, wind, cogeneration, repowering, biomass and fuel cells as the preferred new technologies to develop. Only if those options prove inadequate to meet demand would less desirable technologies, such as conventional coal plants with advanced clean-up systems, be allowed. Nuclear plants, in Varanini's scenario, would have no future except in the unlikely circumstance of solutions to safety, economic and waste disposal problems.

It is no wonder that Varanini's memo was met with little response from the Legislature, for it suggested a mandatory departure from comfortable past assumptions towards an uncharted future. The lobbyists for the status quo are more persuasive than concerns for the unborn in any capital. What, after all, is the realism of a non-nuclear California depending on largely untested, alternative energy resources?

There is no easy answer to such a question, because it depends on factors beyond engineering measurement of technical feasibility. Ultimate values must be considered, as well as the potential of a popular mobilization and willingness to experiment and take risks.

Choosing an energy path is an expression of values and preferences, not just an adjustment to inevitable technical trends. The growth of the oil and gas industry in the last century was an extension of the individualistic, frontier values; of belief in technology as inherently progressive; of the assumption that nature should be exploited for personal gain. The rapid rise of the nuclear industry in the last generation was only a continuation of this same set of preferences, with perhaps an even greater fascination with the potential of science and technology solving human problems. But none of these developments were technically or scientifically inevitable. They were chosen from diverse options because those people with most influence over decisions preferred growth and high-technology to all other possibilities. Our roads and cars, skyscrapers and congested, polluted cities, are monuments to the dictates of profit and power, not inexorable science.

On the other hand, the path of solar and conservation represents a different set of values. Solar lends itself to the search for inner frontiers within outer limits, self-determination and personal self-reliance, respect and stewardship towards the environment, solutions woven into the fabric of life instead of imposed from above and afar.

Any decision to "go solar" partly involves *the choice* of a more democratic, pluralist, creative lifestyle, and a stress on meaningful work, whatever the possible short-term cost in dollars. And any decision to "go nuclear" means leaving destiny to the "experts," placing present comfort over the well-being of tomorrow's children, trading community control for passive consumerism, adopting a macho swashbuckling Wild West commitment to get more energy by whatever means necessary.

The "realism" of going solar also depends on an estimate of the possibilities for a mobilization of popular support. That is, if people are engaging in a crusade, the time gap between vision and reality can be considerably reduced, and there will be a high tolerance for mistakes committed in the pursuit of ideals. On the other hand, if people think of solar as "apple pie," desirable—but only a pleasant dessert after the main course—then there will be greater acceptance of the notion that solar won't be "ready" until the next century, and mistakes will be seen as proof that the technology is still unproven and flaky.

It is our experience in California that a mobilization for solar is possible and leads to real results in terms of acceleration of its timetable. It was mobilization by the Campaign for Economic Democracy and other groups that led to the creation of the Solar-Cal Council, passage of laws requiring "maximum feasible" solarizing of California in the 80s, protection of solar entrepreneurs against monopolies, and local ordinances requiring solar and conservation in new housing construction and in the retrofit market.

Therefore, while risky, it would be fair to assume that a mobilization in behalf of a crash solar program—similar to the space race or a wartime effort—would be supported by a growing number of Californians. Even if the time is not ripe at precisely this moment, the problems of inflation, shortages, and global insecurity are bringing about the opportunity more rapidly than most observers realize.

Finally, in any judgement of how realistic a dramatic energy initiative happens to be, there is the question of how willing are the people of California to accept the risks of experimenting with a new technology. When Governor Brown's home solar system for water heating was shut down for a few days, it was noted with amusement. How many people would feel the same way about relying on an "unproven" technology to deliver electricity to their homes and factories? The answer, obviously, is not many if we live in a society which assumes that a bird in the hand is worth two in the bush. Varanini recognizes this problem. Since there is "no guarantee that an immediate, exclusive reliance upon these options would meet the probable range of expected electricity demand," he argues for a "transitional" strategy in which new technologies are mandated goals while allowing the utilities to pursue conventional and new technologies. But the great virtue of his position is that it speaks to the honest concerns of millions of Californians about whether new energy sources are practical, and protects against a future backlash if an unproven technology happens to go wrong. What this argues for is a *state plan for a transition to new energy sources,* containing fail-safe or fall-back provisions.

Towards a Solar California

The vision of California as the first society based on renewable resources has been explored by a group of energy experts working on a Department of Energy grant to the Lawrence Livermore Laboratories. Their research, concluded in May 1978, was an effort to apply Amory Lovins' "soft path" energy proposals to California.[9] Lovins' pioneering studies propose that the nation develop an energy policy based on certain "soft" criteria, including: sustainable rather than depletable sources, low environmental impact, adaptability to local conditions, likelihood of failing gracefully rather than catastrophically, resistance to accident or sabotage, a matching of quality to end use, and no requirement of massive technological breakthroughs.

Their 350-page report came to the startling (and little-reported) conclusion that:

> From a technical point of view, it does appear feasible for a complex post-industrial society such as California to operate on renewable, largely distributed (decentralized) energy systems, even assuming that California population doubles and economic activity triples in 2025 compared to 1975 figures.[10]

This is a very dramatic conclusion when one realizes how far California is from a self-sufficient state today. In 1975, we received 44 percent of our energy from within the state, 32 percent from other states, and 24 percent from foreign sources.[11]

The authors base their conclusion on the projected massive development of several resources. *Biomass* (organic materials) would contribute one quad (quadrillion BTU's) of needed energy by conversion of municipal and agricultural wastes, as well as "energy farms" devoted to biomass crops on non-commercial forest, brush, grasslands, and perhaps kelp beds in the ocean. Natural rubber from guayule and oil from jojoba are also major desert crop possibilities. This vast energy-producing system would require using 17 percent of the state's land area. A later study, by the California Department of Forestry, concluded that the *wood wastes* in the state's vast timberlands alone could be burned to produce the electrical equivalent of four nuclear plants at half the cost.

Secondly, on-site *solar heating* would provide 1.5 quads of energy for urban and industry demands. Third, a widespread network of *windmills* would generate 0.7 quads of electricity from sites on grazing lands and mountain passes. *Geothermal* energy, primarily from new resources in the Imperial Valley, would generate 0.3 quads in this scenario; *cogeneration* (producing steam and electricity in the same process) 0.2 quads; and *hydro-electric* power 0.1 quads.

The major problem acknowledged by the authors is a short-fall of 0.6 quad of energy needed for liquid fuels for transportation. If California still remains a "car country," using energy for transportation at an 8 percent higher rate than the rest of the U.S., the authors believe there will be a crisis which can only be solved by imported gasohol from biomass, synthetic fuels from coal and oil, the development of hydrogen or new fuels created from unproven sources like kelp.*

*An extremely useful and thorough study done in 1980 by Heather Ball of the Santa Monica Energy Project calculated how conservation in the transportation sector could eliminate California's dependency on foreign oil for 44 percent of its daily travel needs by 1990. Ball estimated that increased fuel efficiency in automobiles could save .53 million barrels per day (mbd), increasing the number of passengers in automobiles to two and getting 10 percent of the workforce into

The degree of conservation measures adopted could change these findings, however. The authors assume electricity growth rates over 2 percent per year (close to current rates, though one-third of the 1960's and early 1970's rates), a figure which could come down further due to either high prices or dramatic conservation measures. And they assume the existing economic and other institutional arrangements to remain the same for the next half century, an assumption which guarantees higher levels of economic waste that would take place in a less profit-and-status oriented society.

The authors assume a conservation program "in which implementation begins almost at once" if the 2025 target date is to be met. In identifying conservation priorities, they find that California's housing stock is "especially poorly insulated" in 2-4 million units; that the state "uses more lighting than the rest of the country per square foot of office space"; the public buildings and schools which could be retrofitted take up 925 million square feet, or one-third of total floor space in the state.[12]

We could assume that the authors' vision is achievable from a technical viewpoint, and that it is up to a citizens movement combined with enlightened planning, to overcome the formidable obstacles blocking the way.

In considering this possibility, it is important to rid ourselves of the notion that we have to change a permanent way of life and venture into the total unknown. We do not. Californians used thousands of solar units to heat household water in 1910; agriculture not so long ago was based on family farming and reliance on the sun and wind. Windmills and hydropower were widespread a few decades ago. It is the age of the Liquified Natural Gas plant for heating water that is new, as is that of the air conditioner, and mechanized, pesticide-oriented agriculture. Whatever has been based on a plentiful supply of cheap fossil fuels— the freeway system, the state water programs, corporate farming— has arisen in a short time—mostly since the 1950's—and can be replaced without catastrophe if planning is undertaken in time.

---

vanpools could save .07 mbd, increased airline efficiency would give .05 mbd, and increased freight sector efficiencies would provide .11 mbd, totalling .76 mbd, more than imported oil provides. Her conclusion: "Our total foreign dependence can be overcome by 1990 with *no* reduction in present mobility."

Take California's nuclear power plants. If one follows the rhetoric of the nuclear industry, it would seem that these plants are everywhere and our lives hopelessly dependent on them. The average citizen certainly is tormented into thinking that nuclear power may be necessary to our survival despite its risks. That this is complete nonsense is testimony to the power of nuclear propaganda. California now has only two operating nuclear plants, at Rancho Seco near Sacramento and San Onofre by San Diego. One at Humboldt is closed for safety reasons, Diablo Canyon is fiercely contested, Sun Desert was killed by Governor Brown in 1978, and one other was rejected by voters in Kern County in the same year. Nuclear provided only 1,400 megawatts of power to the state in 1978, or 1.2 percent of the state's energy.[13] But this small percentage shrinks even further when we realize that a probable third of the power is lost in transmission. Taking this into account, nuclear today provides only one-half of one percent of California's total energy demand. If we cannot free ourselves of such minor levels of nuclear addiction, we lack the moral and political strength to meet any serious challenge.

Another illusion which must be dispelled is the belief in a linkage between *economic growth* and growth of *energy demand*. Industry propagandists foster this idea by predicting mass unemployment and energy shortages if their latest power plant is not approved. The industry philosophy perhaps was best expressed by a Detroit auto executive in the 1950's, who declared that "small cars mean small engines, small windows, small doors, and small profits."[14] Naturally it is true that an energy-intensive, capital-intensive *form* of economy cannot endure massive reductions in energy consumption without its structure and policies changing. But what is false is the claim that our high-energy, high-tech emphasis spurs economic growth. We are, after all, in the midst of the most severe dollar crisis in American history; the longest period of double-digit inflation in the cost of necessities; and, as this is written, entering into the first stage of a recession with unemployment rates 25 percent higher than when President Carter took office. And all this is caused principally by our failure to solve the energy crisis. Dependence on depletable fossil fuels, especially in the hands of cartels, is inherently inflationary; the cost of energy in the mid-1970s rose at 22.5 percent a year.[15] Energy production devours as much as 25 percent of all business capital available for investment. And our energy policy insures unemployment; though oil companies are five of the six largest corporations in California, the oil industry employs only 1.4 percent of workers outside agriculture.[16] Nationally the energy sector employs only ten workers per million dollars invested compared to a median of 27.5 workers per million dollars in all industry.[17]

By contrast, the very policies often stereotyped as "no growth" could lead to an economic *boom*. First of all, investments in renewable resources are generally non-inflationary. The sun, the earth, the rivers and the wind contain an available potential that is difficult to monopolize and almost impossible to deplete. Although materials and equipment for insulation and weatherization, or pumps and collectors may rise in price, the basic resource itself is free and can be counted on. Moreover, the capital outflow required for fossil fuels (billions to Indonesia for LNG and to Saudia Arabia for oil) would be exactly reversed by solar: capital would be invested within this state or country, stimulating domestic businesses and multiplying beyond the energy sector.

Jobs From the Sun

The employment impacts of solar investments would be dramatically more positive than in the present energy industry. The U.S. Council on Environmental Quality (CEQ) reported in April 1978 that "widespread adoption of the various solar technologies would create an enormous number of jobs of many types—from welders to plumbers, from sheet metal workers to electrical engineers, from architects to carpenters."[18] Concentrating just on solar for water and space heating in new residential housing and, where feasible, in already existing housing, the California Public Policy Center has estimated that 375,000 jobs would be created per year in the 1980's, cutting California's official unemployment rate in half.[19] The California Energy Commission found in 1979 that "in producing the same amount of useful energy, solar energy can create 5 to 10 times the number of jobs as coal or nuclear power and at least three times as much as oil-based power plants."[20] And, of course, this does not begin to count the jobs possible from conservation and other forms of solar besides residential space and water heating. More, as presently constituted, energy industry jobs, for example in petrochemical firms and mining uranium, are terribly dangerous. A transition to solar is therefore not only a move to create jobs and to make energy safer, but also to make work itself safer and more rewarding. The truth is that the only possibility of combating inflation, investing productively at home, and creating millions of jobs, lies in a policy stressing the renewable energy path.

It is often asked whether the possibility of a solar society exists only in California and a few other sunny states, thus dooming the rest of the country "realistically" to a nuclear or coal future as fossil fuels diminish. There are already deep regional energy differences in America. Certain industrial states like Illinois, Pennsylvania, New York and Massachusetts depend on nuclear power for 15-30 percent of their electrical power, ten times more than California. These same states are pressured by freezing winters toward greater acceptance of higher prices and more nuclear plants.

However, if understood properly, concepts of solar, renewable resources and conservation provide answers for the colder regions of America as well as the hot zones. The general term "solar" refers to all kinds of *natural* energy sources, and a solar program simply tries to take advantage of this natural energy to the maximum extent possible. To give a very simple example, the traditional barn in the colder regions of America has been painted red, a color that absorbs sunlight. Hay or barley was stacked on the side away from the sun, and snowdrifts allowed to pile up, creating a "double wall" of natural insulation. Often the roof facing the wind was long and sloping, not only to prevent roof stress, but to keep building up the snow break for insulation.

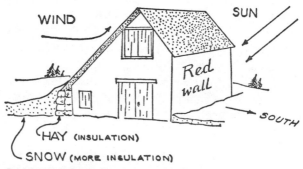

Red Barn: Solar Collector From Wilson Clark, *Energy for Survival*

"Before the advent of oil heaters, electricity and the air conditioning machines that homogenized the structure and shape of construction and housing, all buildings and homes were designed to use the natural factors of climate," observes Wilson Clark, energy advisor to Governor Brown.[21] Buildings were consciously designed to take advantage of the cycles of nature. Where "air conditioning and heating devices have replaced mental skills and ingenuity," Clark writes, the level of building design is "behind" that of the native architects of centuries ago.

The economic factor is also important in judging whether solar is practical in the colder regions. The home heating bills are infinitely higher in Ohio than in California, making the solar-conservation alternative more and more competitive. In fact, a 1970 study, republished in 1973 by Dr. George Lof and Richard Tybout, concluded that solar heat was economically viable for most areas of the U.S.[22] In six out of eight cities surveyed—Miami, Albuquerque, Phoenix, Santa Maria (California), Charleston (South Carolina), Seattle, Omaha, Boston—solar would cost less than electric heat at the then-prevailing rates which, of course, were before the oil price shocks began. California Energy Commission studies now show that solar is cost-competitive not only with electricity but natural gas as well.[23]

Introducing solar energy for water and space heating in the colder regions will displace and save natural gas, thus reducing the danger of shortages during national emergencies, freeing that much more gas for allocation to the high priority areas. But beyond these solar heating applications, the Midwest and Northeast can benefit from other conservation and renewable resource programs. It has been estimated, for example, that 30 percent of American homes (25 million) are without *any* insulation and millions more lack sufficient protection.[24] As much as 25 percent of energy use in the residential sector could be saved by serious efforts at weatherization.[25] In addition, previous energy-producing processes can make a major comeback. For example, in New England, over 100 hydro-electric sites have been abandoned because of cheap fossil fuel prices in the past three decades (hydro-electric plants produced one-third of America's electrical energy in the 1920's).[26] The windmill, a traditional farmland symbol, is going to become resurgent as the cost of electricity from conventional power plants rises. The use of wood stoves in New England has escalated rapidly since 1974.

The Feasibility of a Solar America

The potential of the whole nation moving toward a solar emphasis has been viewed favorably in three recent studies by very cautious sources, two within the federal government and the other in the Harvard Business School. The first, by the President's Council on Environmental Quality in April 1978 contained the following predictions for solar over two time frames:

MAXIMUM SOLAR CONTRIBUTION UNDER CONDITIONS
OF ACCELERATED DEVELOPMENT
(In quads-per-year of displaced fuel. Total U.S. demand in 1977 was 76 quads. Projected U.S. demand in the year 2000 is from 80-120 quads; and for 2020 it is 70-140 quads.)

SOLAR SOURCE	1977	2000	2020
Heating & Cooling (active & passive)	small	2-4	5-10
Thermal Electric	none	0-2	5-10
Intermediate Temperature Systems	none	2-5	5-15
Photovoltaic	small	2-8	10-30
Biomass	1.3	3-5	5-10
Wind	small	4-8	8-12
Hydropower	3	4-6	4-6
Ocean Thermal	none	1-3	5-10
Conservation	small	2-4	5-10
		20-45	53-123

"It is now possible to speak realistically of the United States becoming a solar society," the CEQ concluded, "...a goal of providing significantly more than one-half our energy from solar sources by the year 2020 should be achievable if our commitment to that goal and to conservation is strong... (This is) the most exciting energy news of our generation."[27]

The CEQ analysis is especially interesting because of the role that political will plays in determining the outcome. The estimates of what solar can provide fluctuate enormously; e.g., 10-30 quads from photovoltaics, 5-10 quads from conservation by 2020, and a projected energy demand ranging from 80-140 quads in the first part of the 21st century. *This vast spread of possibilities reflects the essential fact that the acceleration of solar depends more on political and social decisions than the removal of technical barriers.*

A second study, the 1979 Domestic Policy Review (DPR), illustrates even more completely the potential of public opinion in solar policy projections. When solar activists organized national Sun Day in May 1978, President Carter responded by promising the DPR, a procedure by which government agencies under White House direction drew up recommendations to the President. The DPR involved hundreds of consultations with citizens groups around the U.S., a process that included severe criticism of Secretary Schlesinger, the Department of Energy and even the President.[28]

In the end, the DPR reported three options: 1) "Continue existing Federal programs but make them more effective"; 2) "Expand the current level of federal effort . . . to accomplish cost-effective objectives"; and 3) "dramatically increase Federal support with a variety of programs that give solar energy high priority as a national goal." The first, or Base Case, was rejected as only continuing the status quo. The third, or Technical Limit, was questioned as being too risky and expensive. The middle path, defined as the Maximum Practical option, was preferred, a policy which would result in solar providing 20 percent of the nation's energy by the year 2000.

Arriving at this conclusion—close to that proposed by the CEQ, higher than that favored by Schlesinger—was a largely political process. For example, the frank reason given for rejecting the lowest projection was that "the interested public may conclude it is too modest to demonstrate a national commitment . . . Certainly, the nation's leading solar advocates will probably view it as inadequate and would prefer no goal to one set this low."

Here, then, is clear evidence that the nation's solar advocates can (and do) have a direct effect on the pace and amount of solar development. The other obvious implication is that solar's readiness for use is far ahead of its present application.

Perhaps the most important endorsement of solar in established circles has been *Energy Future*, a 1979 report by an energy team at Harvard Business School under the direction of Robert Stobaugh and Daniel Yergin. Reported on page one of the *New York Times*, the Harvard project became the first of its kind to advocate that "the only viable program that would politically reduce U.S. dependence on imported oil would be for the government to give financial incentives to encourage conservation and solar energy."[29]

The Harvard Project's solar projections for the year 2000 fall somewhere between the Domestic Policy Review and the Council on Environmental Quality. They too favor a "gradual transition to an increasingly Solar America in the twenty-first century," and it is worth emphasizing their analysis of the key factor in the process: *"It's the political climate, not the weather, that will govern the future of solar energy."*[30]

Thus, we see that in a period of less than a decade, solar energy has emerged from its status as an object of esoteric curiosity to a serious competing alternative in the energy debate, with respected authorities speaking "unblushingly"—as the CEQ report says—of a Solar America.

It is now time to begin to implement the vision. It is time for a program to convert California and the nation to solar energy as rapidly as is feasible, with the urgency of past national mobilizations. If we could massively go to war in Vietnam for what were foisted as "national security" considerations, we can certainly make a greater commitment to a safe energy future. If we could reach the moon in a decade, we can reach the sun in the same period.

Program for a Solar Transition

I. To begin with, there should be a planned *conversion program to a non-nuclear future*. It can be launched in states or regions with a heavy nuclear dependency, or nationally in cooperation with the federal government. The concept would be to prevent energy shortages and job dislocations during the phase-out of nuclear plants. Activists are realizing it is not enough to be anti-nuke, but that one must also prepare an alternative that answers the legitimate questions of people concerning their jobs and energy sources in a non-nuclear future. With a few exceptions, neither the anti-nuclear movement nor any state or federal agency has begun this process. Yet in the wake of Three Mile Island, with a majority becoming skeptical about nuclear plants, the question of alternatives becomes crucial. If it is not answered, the result will be a large number of people held hostage to the political necessities of life under the nuclear industry. Anywhere there is a nuclear facility, citizen groups can and should begin researching the employment and energy alternatives in their region, and the retraining and relocation costs that might have to be borne by working people during a transition. A possible model for this conversion program lies in the pioneering research over two decades by Professor Seymour Melman of Columbia University into the problems of shifting from a wartime to peacetime economy.[31] Regional studies have been conducted along the same lines by a California Assembly research team in 1969 and the Center for New Priorities in Long Island.[32] The Pentagon itself has a little-known department which helps cushion the community impact of military base closings, a possible model for nuclear plant phase-outs.

In California, this would mean that the Governor and Legislature should *direct* the Energy Commission and PUC to determine the steps necessary to keep Diablo Canyon nuclear plant shut down, and phase out the Rancho Seco and San Onofre plants, while meeting energy and employment needs by other means. By not taking such a deliberate step towards conscious planning, the state is doomed to a future which will be "planned" by the market influence of oil and gas producers, foreign imports and the nuclear industry.

In other regions more dependent on nuclear power, the conversion process will be far more difficult than in California. For example, in New Hampshire, the center of the anti-Seabrook demonstrations, the public uses more oil per capita and pays more for it than in other regions of the U.S. Nuclear power has been advertised as the way out of depending on oil, and promises to provide more than half of the state's energy needs. The New Hampshire League of Women Voters, on the other hand, is promoting cautiously the concept that "Less May Be More," and calling for the "development of decentralized energy systems, consistent and efficient use of renewable resources, and the application in the private and industrial sector of the principles of energy efficiency."[33] They can point to a few encouraging examples of using solid waste, water, wind, and wood, as alternatives to nuclear power: a paper company in Groveton generating its steam and electricity from the wastes of the town, a Burlington plan to obtain all of its electricity from waste wood by 1982, a Springfield proposal for a municipally-operated hydro-electric plant, and so on. What is not clear, as implied in the careful phrasing that "less *may* be more," is whether these new sources can in fact eliminate the state's nuclear dependency or whether a non-nuclear choice means greater dependence on disappearing out-of-state oil. Until such questions are answered, the New Hampshire citizen is likely to face a quandary regardless of what becomes of the Seabrook plant itself.

The same dilemmas apply to all of New England, and no simple solution is in sight. An excellent article on the search for answers is that of Rory O'Connor in the Boston *Real Paper*, "Can We Live Without Nuclear Power?"[34] O'Connor's answer is in the affirmative, but it is based on assumptions that a majority of taxpayers may not yet find reassuring. O'Connor's argument, based on the data of Barry Commoner's Center for the Biology of National Systems in St. Louis, is that Northeastern utilities keep an electrical generating capacity about 44 percent higher than what is necessary at any given time. Therefore, if all *oil*-based plants in New England were "jacked up" to optimal capacity (from 45 to 65 percent), nuclear plants could be shut down while the region maintained a "comfortable" reserve margin of 22.7 percent.

The only problem in this scenario, as O'Connor acknowledges, is that such a transition would require an annual *increase of 80 million barrels of oil* and a 10 percent electricity rate increase for consumers. O'Connor seems to realize that this is an unattractive alternative, and therefore falls back on drastic energy-savings as a way to cushion or avoid the increase in oil imports. He proposes more fuel-efficient cars, mandatory residential conservation programs, rate restructuring, and greater reliance on coal (which would add new problems). But without a planned conversion program, with guarantees of jobs and energy, these measures would have no chance of sufficient popular support or coordinated implementation.

Other approaches to New England's problems have been taken by the New England Federal Regional Council, the Maine Wood Fuel Corporation, and a Vermont Governor's Task Force, all emphasizing a massive emphasis on forest resources for heating and power. Over 44 billion cubic feet of wood used in New England by the year 2000 could possibly generate the equivalent power of ten nuclear plants.[35]

Disparate studies such as these should be drawn together by region to plot a safe and practical course to a non-nuclear future. If the federal government is unwilling or unable to do this, there is no reason why a new "states' rights" challenge cannot be mounted in those areas which want to determine their own energy path.

II. The second major need during a transition is to *harness the oil-energy monopolies to serve the needs of the American people.* Those needs are, first, for affordable prices; second, for steady supplies; and third, for a "bridge" to a decentralized solar future. Rather than meeting those needs, the oil industry is profiteering from inflation in energy prices, creating fuel shortages either by design or mismanagement, and investing in controlling power over coal, uranium, and centralized solar technologies.

In California, there are limited but real initiatives which can be taken to cope with the crisis. There is little that can be done about prices. But the Energy Commission can be more generous towards conservers with the federal allocation of "emergency" fuel reserves it has previously turned over to the oil majors. And the legislature can pass the proposal for a state oil and gas corporation, pioneered by former Assembly Member Charles Warren (before becoming head of the CEQ), and later carried by Tom Bates and Mel Levine in the State Legislature. Such an entity could make a public and independent analysis of reserves (now done in secret by the majors), and compete on state-owned lands for resources not profitable enough for the private sector.

But it is at the national level that major change can be made. We are facing multinational corporations too powerful for any one state to check and transform. The most important energy issue before Congress in 1979 was that of deregulation of prices. It is becoming clear that as long as the oil industry thinks higher prices are in the wind, it will make the sensible business decision to withhold production and supply of the millions of barrels of proven reserves still in the ground. It is also clear after six years of rising energy prices and tapering domestic production that there is no cause and effect relationship between deregulation and new discoveries or greater supplies of oil. Despite a 1970s "drilling boom unprecedented in its intensity," *Business Week*'s editors wrote, "all this drilling has produced very little new oil, and for the first time in 200 years, the lure of higher prices has not brought greater amounts of oil on stream."[36] Therefore, *price controls* should be re-imposed, not only to spare consumers the bombardment of inflation, but to give the oil industry a firm signal that regulated prices and profits are here to stay.[37]

This choice is neither simple nor easy, requiring as it does a basic choice between the environmental and consumer perspectives in the movement for a safe energy future. In the environmentalist perspective, higher prices (and profits) are often seen as a necessary means to the goal of energy conservation. Environmentalists of this type "uncomfortably" decide that Americans must be forced into saving energy by paying a higher price. They therefore align themselves with their enemies in the oil industry by blaming popular gluttony for the energy crisis and adopting forced austerity as the solution.

There are several problems with this solution beyond the alliance of strange bedfellows. First, it is not practical. There is no clear evidence, for instance, that higher prices lead to substantial conservation when people must still pay for necessities such as gasoline for transportation or housing in the suburbs.* Nor is there evidence that higher prices and incentives lead to more production of energy rather than diversified investments in more profitable sectors. As a matter of fact, prices and profits have been rising since 1973, while production has declined and levelled, and oil company investment in non-energy alternatives has increased. So the well-intentioned environmentalist argument in favor of deregulation only leads back to the doctrines of the federal government and Big Oil: *pay more for less*. Inflation as the proposed solution to the energy crisis is also self-defeating because it obviously prohibits an alliance between middle-class

*France, despite a tripling of gasoline prices since 1973, has seen a 21 percent increse in gasoline consumption. (*Wall Street Journal,* May 12, 1980)

environmentalists and those who are hardest hit by higher energy prices: working people and minorities.

A typical "solution" along these lines that has been much-publicized and applauded is the so-called "50-50" proposal at the heart of Rep. John P. Anderson's independent presidential campaign. Anderson would impose a 50 cent gasoline tax to push down automobile use, and "finance" the plan by a 50 percent decrease in Social Security payments. But it ignores those outside the work-force—students, housewives and retirees, for example—while discriminating against low and moderate-income people. A janitor making $6,200 per year would get back about $200 from Social Security, while his $25,000 per year supervisor would receive about $800—although both drive the same distance to work each day. Anderson's solution would discriminate as well against regions and classes of people more dependent upon the automobile for transportation than others, not to mention possibly drawing down an already underfinanced Social Security system of the future. Anderson's solution to the energy crisis, in short, is inflationary and it soaks the poor.

Re-imposed price controls, combined with gas rationing, would be more equitable and effective. Instead of rationing indirectly through the price system, as Anderson suggests, a better solution is offered by Hazel Henderson, called "white rationing." Attempting to avoid price increases and a government bureauc-racy as well, Henderson proposes issuing a prescribed number of ration coupons to all citizens over 18, instead of simply to drivers (20 percent of American families do not own cars). This would remove a major inequity, while at the same time putting enough rationing coupons into circulation "to make counterfeiting and black marketeering marginally unprofitable." There would be a stick to reduce consumption plus a carrot rewarding conservation, "by permitting those who do not own vehicles to sell their coupons to those who do at free market prices." The relatively easy availability of extra coupons would lessen the need for rationing boards and costly administration. "Thus a socially equitable solution to gasoline conservation might be possible without adding to inflation pressures, and improving consumer freedom of choice."[38]

Price controls and rationing, however, will be insufficient if the oil industry is allowed to invest in more lucrative areas outside the field of energy.

Divestiture—the prohibiting of oil companies from buying up alternative energy sources or diversifying into condominiums or other profitable non-energy businesses—is needed, like price controls, to give the industry a clear message that they are to be in the business of producing gas and oil only. It has been a historic mistake to leave our precious energy resources and policy in the hands of businessmen whose main purpose is making money, not energy. An ARCO executive gave this revealing description of his firm's priorities in 1979: "Why did we buy Anaconda instead of investing in oil? Obviously, finding oil is not as profitable. We're rational businessmen. We have an obligation to our stockholders and the community to remain a viable business. We must invest prudently and wisely."[39] An AP report noted, "the nation's big oil companies, looking down the road at a time when the Earth stops giving up petroleum, are sinking money into other areas."[40] For example, Mobil has acquired Montgomery Ward's retail chain and Container Corporation of America; Chevron explores for silver in Colorado, mines uranium in Texas, holds 260,000 acres of agricultural land in the West, builds condominiums in Southern California, and markets home gardening products throughout the world; Atlantic Richfield makes plastics in Texas, the Netherlands, Spain and Japan, mines copper in ten states and nations, produces aluminum, mines bauxite and coal, owns the London *Observer* newspaper, a solar photovoltaic plant in Los Angeles and in 1979 picked up Anaconda Copper.[41] Of course, the oil business is profitable, but the lack of divestiture laws makes it inevitable that oil companies will use their petroleum profits to expand into even more lucrative areas. Only through divestiture can the energy corporations be "ordered" to stick to the essential tasks of producing and supplying energy.

If price controls and divestiture were certainties in the eyes of the industry executives, a fundamental drama would begin. Either the energy conglomerates would "shrink" back, become oil companies again, and do their essential job for the next two decades of transition, or, more likely, they would resist and drag their feet. At that point, it would be justified to bring them under government control as public utilities while perhaps also creating a public energy enterprise to compete with them. The high risk and public service character of producing oil and gas would justify the conferring of monopoly status and guaranteed profits on such firms in exchange for their delivering secure supplies of energy. At that point, oil industry dictation to the government would end and government control of our energy destiny would finally begin.

Public control in the public interest should be the key theme of any attempted transformation of the energy industry. There are legitimate concerns, from left as well as right, about the bureaucratic dangers of nationalization. These could be met either by making sure that a new government energy company had regional branches with citizen and employee input, perhaps even with the use of the referendum for key decisions that would affect certain areas of the country more than others. But however one feels about the merits of Big Business versus Big Government, the key point to remember is that it is the *failure of the private energy sector which requires public intervention.* That failure, if allowed to continue, would guarantee a future dependency on shrinking resources with all the dangers of inflation, unemployment, pollution, monopoly and war which have already been mentioned, as well as stifling the growth of the solar alternative—problems far greater and more hazardous than any government intervention could create.

A publicly-controlled energy corporation, and a regulated industry, could play a vital role in the transition to a solar society. Continued production of certain levels of oil, gas and coal are going to be necessary for the rest of the century while the solar transition is being made. The danger is that, left in the present hands, the commitments to these fossil fuels will be made without any concept of transition in mind, and the nation will stumble from crisis to crisis. A new leadership is needed which will manage the *downcurve* of fossil fuel production while new technologies are introduced, accelerated and become dominant. During this process some conventional sources will continue to meet the ongoing needs of the disappearing fossil fuel age (transportation, for example). Natural gas, as Barry Commoner argues, may become the major "bridging" fuel to the future, gradually being replaced with biogas from waste materials introduced into the existing distribution system. An example of the "bridging" process is in Chicago, where citizens using gas-burning stoves are already relying for a fraction of their gas on methane from Oklahoma manure that is carried daily through the conventional natural gas pipeline serving Chicago.[42]

A scenario for a step-by-step transition to a solar future was first devised by Amory Lovins. That sketch, however smooth in comparison to the rude shocks of reality, serves as a good illustration of the decline of fossil fuels creatively *meshed* with the emergence of renewables that is possible with commitment and planning.

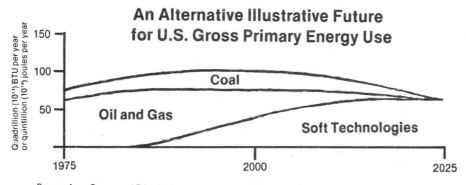

An Alternative Illustrative Future for U.S. Gross Primary Energy Use

Source: Anna Gyorgy and Friends, *No Nukes*

III. Besides planning for a non-nuclear future and bringing the oil industry into line, the parallel initiatives which must be taken are in the crash development of *conservation* and *renewable resources for the future*.

It is provable beyond a doubt that greater efficiency in residential and office building construction and use, in industrial processes, in transportation, is possible now. And it is equally provable that solar collectors and pumps, passive design techniques, windmills, methane digesters, and concentrating collectors are either economically feasible now or will be in the early 1980's everywhere in the U.S.

The fact is, however, that conservation and new solar technologies will never take their rightful place as long as the economic marketplace is rigged against them. It has been documented again and again that the oil and nuclear industries receive massive direct and indirect subsidies without which they could not survive. According to the CEQ report, government incentives to stimulate conventional energy production have totalled over $100 billion in the past generation.[43] And, the CEQ points out, usual economic comparisons between solar and conventional systems are unfair, incomplete and inadequate: "They do not, for example, cover an adequate range of costs and benefits—or subsidies and externalities—through the complete fuel cycle... in comparing solar energy to coal and nuclear, a full and fair analysis should include such frequently ignored cost items as occupationally-related deaths and injuries, environmental damage, the ecological and aesthetic effects of transmission lines, security and accident risks, government assistance, insurance and tax subsidies, and so forth." The conclusion one draws is that *there must either be equal subsidies given solar and conservation* (tax and investment credits, for example) or *existing subsidies should be stripped from the present energy industry.*

By changing the market so that solar makes sense, another transitional strategy becomes available: to *require solar and conservation where they are cost-competitive taking total long-term costs into account.* The city of Davis, California, did just this by tightening its building code in 1974 to require strict energy efficiency; energy consumption has dropped by between 10 and 20 percent without any serious effect on the quality of life. The County of San Diego in 1978 passed an ordinance requiring solar in new houses in all-electric areas by October, 1979, and solar in all new residential construction by one year thereafter. Many other cities and counties in California are looking at ordinances to ban the luxury use of natural gas (in swimming pools) and require solar in new buildings. The SolarCal Council's Action Plan, *Toward a Solar California*, encourages all such alternatives in the private and public sectors.[44]

The California Energy Commission staff recommends mandating of solar design in new residential construction, swimming pool heating, water heating in new homes, and conservation and solar in all residences at time of resale (the latter policy has been adopted by Santa Clara County). In addition, the Public Utilities Commission took steps in 1980 to end the wasteful utility practice

of offering free line or service extensions to builders using high-energy consuming appliances in their housing tracts. The PUC's new policy is to give credits for conservation or solar installations in new housing. Full implementation of these and other mandatory measures could lead to a major breakthrough of the energy stalemate in the 1980's. In "Decade of the Sun," a CEC staff plan for "maximum implementation of solar energy through 1990," the following phenomenal possibilities are projected:
—4.9 million passively heated and cooled residential buildings,
—5.5 million solar water heaters in residential buildings,
—400,000 swimming pool heaters.[45]
By 1990, this change would save annually *40 percent* of the natural gas used in the state's residential housing.[46]

In another far-reaching initiative, the California PUC decided in 1980 to order utilities to provide no-interest loans to consumers wishing to finance solar devices for their homes. This breakthrough, originally opposed by the utilities, may overcome the key barriers of initial cost and consumer confidence. Short-term loans for solar are considered far safer than long-term investments in nuclear plants for the state's utilities. For the consumer, the loans can be made essentially "free" since the utility would take into account the rising price of natural gas which the consumer would otherwise have to pay. At the same time, if consumer interests prevail, the utilities' involvement would be limited to finance and service, leaving small businesses to grow and compete for the new market. If carried out to the maximum, the PUC decision could result in the solarizing of 5 million California homes by 1990, nearly half the housing stock.[47]

As a result of these trends, environmental and alternative energy groups are quickly coming to a common recognition that only a strong, mandatory approach that rearranges market incentives profoundly has any chance of making a difference in the current energy stalemate before it is too late. The Natural Resources Defense Council, for example, in proposing a package of conservation measures (reducing end use in the industrial, commercial, residential, and transport sectors and different load management techniques such as off-peak pumping and power pooling) as well as alternative supply initiatives (wind, cogeneration, repowering, geothermal, hydro-electric, methane and active solar), comments that "a number of *mandatory* policies, directed at consumers, businesses, utilities and state agencies, will be required in order to achieve the type of energy system described in the alternative scenario." They propose that the California legislature direct state agencies to "ensure that the full cost effective level of conservation is implemented, and that the potential savings from conservation and supplies from renewable energy resources are exhausted before any conventional power plants and supply projects using traditional fuel sources are built."[48]

The term "mandating" may be upsetting to those who believe in the free market, oppose big government and yearn for personal choice. As with many aspects of the solar debate, the advocates of the new are attacked for fostering the very things that are acceptable within the status quo. We mandate, for example, the flush toilet in housing, with few people raising objections (except, interestingly, water-conscious environmentalists recently). We, in effect, have "mandated" a generation of waste in energy transportation and housing by allowing all-electric houses, cheap rates for large industrial users of electricity, office buildings with air conditioners and no windows, and Chevrolets which grew 500 pounds between 1968 and 1973.[49] All this waste was invisibly mandated by an economic system of rewards which made these choices inevitable. The "invisible hand" of the market economy can be just as dictatorial as any government bureaucracy.

To call for mandating is essentially to call for a new set of rules in the way we use energy. Instead of new rules being imposed in the market by private forces, they should be established by the decisions of duly-elected officials after public debate and participation. From the initial decision onward, solar power can be essentially democratic power because of its many decentralized and community-level applications.

IV. It still may not be enough to plan the non-nuclear future, control the private oil giants, and write new rules ushering in an age of energy frugality. A final part of the programmatic strategy will have to consist of *major government investments in the alternative energy future.*

If one goes to the Jet Propulsion Laboratory in Pasadena, California, one sees a beautiful slide show displaying the extra-

ordinary technology which—through government investment—
has taken Americans into the universe in less than a generation.
Yet if one looks closely at the very first jet propulsion engines
lifting small planes into the air in the 1940's, one is struck by how
awkwardly amateurish they appear. They almost seem to be
strapped onto the fusillage of the plane, threatening to come off at
the first unexpected winds. Yet from these early contraptions came
the sleek, futuristic, miraculous vehicles of today's space program.
The lesson of this is that when Americans wanted a jet propulsion
engine, they committed the government, the laboratories and
money to make it happen as rapidly as possible.

No such urgency surrounds the solar program of today. At
JPL, which created the solar electric (photovoltaic) cell as a
byproduct of the space program in the 1950's, there is a dedicated
crew of scientists working on its domestic application to the energy
crisis. They are good and intelligent people, perhaps the best in
their field in the U.S., yet one feels less than a sense of crisis about
their work. If one asks the head of their solar division whether
there is an energy crisis comparable to a wartime emergency, the
answer is no. "There is an energy *dilemma*, with many possible
solutions," he says, "not an energy crisis that demands a mobilization like in wartime."

This attitude is quite common in both government and corporate sectors, and reflects itself throughout the U.S. energy
program. In the field of photovoltaic cells, for example, there is a
continuous debate over various technological breakthroughs that
may be necessary before the cells are "competitive." In its own
terms, this debate may be entirely valid. One would not want to
introduce cells in the market before they are ready; that would be
an "inefficient" expenditure of funds. So the scientists will
continue their research, and solar cells will be introduced only in
remote applications (offshore buoys, mountaintop communication systems, etc.) where they are already competitive.

There is a completely opposite way of viewing this, however.
First, one begins with a concept of "crisis" rather than
"dilemma": a need to find immediate alternatives to nuclear
power and fossil fuel sources of electricity, as well as a need for
electricity among millions of villages beyond the power grid in the
developing world. Seen this way, the temporarily higher cost and

inefficiency of photovoltaics are good insurance against greater costs and dangers in the future. Therefore one might invest in creating a market by purchasing the cells so that, through mass production, their price would come down. In fact, a Federal Energy Administration task force made just such a proposal in 1974, for a $440 million Pentagon purchase of photovoltaic cells which they calculated would bring the peak watt price down to competitive levels by the 1983-85 period.[50] Their proposal was never taken seriously. In 1979, the Carter Administration proposed cutting photovoltaic procurement to *zero*, a move that was only slightly offset by Congressional action.

If one looks at the cells being studied at JPL today, one finds most research and development in the hands of Exxon, ARCO, Mobil and Motorola, companies with no special interest in finding a rapid alternative to nuclear-generated electricity. Among competing nations, France and West Germany are making major investments in photovoltaics. Thus, a product of the U.S. space program, created by taxpayer funds, is being turned over to the multinationals and foreign competitors when, with an urgent U.S. government commitment, it could make a major contribution to the energy transition we need.

Virtually the same analysis could be made, category by category, of the whole federal energy program. A panel of biomass specialists has found that the existing federal R & D program would lead to no more than the equivalent of 1.4 percent of today's oil demand by the year 2000.[51] The same criticism is levelled at the wind program.[52] Every possible alternative to conventional energy sources is being short-changed, stifled and put on the shelf until the next century.

The Politics of Solar Energy

Taken as a whole, the 1979 solar proposal of President Carter would lead to a 20 percent dependence on solar in the year 2000. While this figure is more than double the Department of Energy projections of three years before, it is still inadequate and deceptive. By defining "solar" to include hydropower, the President begins with a current estimate of 6 percent from solar to the energy mix. Accepting this as a fact, it means that solar is expected to grow at an average of less than 1 percent per year—14 percent in 20 years, to be exact—until 2000. Such snail's pace progress guarantees that solar will be a second-class energy solution rather than the ascendant technology, until the 21st century.

Up to now, we have discussed the energy crisis and a transitional program to meet it. We are at an impasse which is fast becoming a catastrophe. The impasse is between the proponents of conventional technologies and nuclear, who have vast organizational and financial power at their disposal, and who control our vital energy institutions today, on the one hand, and the proponents of solar and conservation who so far have only objective economic conditions and rising popular support on their side. While it is inevitable that fossil fuel will continue to become scarcer, more expensive and more concentrated in monopoly hands, nothing is inevitable about how the impasse is to be broken. It is indeed possible that those who command our major institutions will, like lemmings, carry all of us over a cliff of destruction—unless we stop them.

The logic of the choice we face might be made more graphic by an analogy that decreases the scale of the issues for simpler comprehension. Consider an island community which subsists primarily on a particular sort of fruit grown in one region of the island. Imagine the fruit has been plentiful for decades and the islanders have become accustomed to using it in many ways, some of which are highly wasteful of its nutrient value. Imagine too that a climactic change, a soil alteration—whatever—has begun to deplete the crop. The supply is becoming less each year even as the population continues to grow. There is still enough available—bacchanalias can continue in the short run—but such misuse brings the day of extreme shortages, hunger, and finally starvation ever closer. More, some islanders have begun harvesting another crop in another part of the island, and this shows tremendous promise as an on-going source sufficient for a desirable, though less wasteful lifestyle. Can you imagine a sector of the islanders fighting all attempts to conserve the old crop so it might suffice till the replacement is ready, and even hindering development of the replacement?

To make the analogy still more apt, assume that the work associated with the "old fruit" is very dangerous and boring, that its processing is difficult and pollutes the island. The new crop, on the other hand, requires more rewarding work with few risks and its processing has no detrimental side effects. Can you still imagine a sector fighting to limit efforts at enlarging the new crop or conserving use of the old?

No. It is impossible to conceive such irrationality unless we make the analogy still closer. We must assume there is a small sector of the island's population who have monopolized control of the current crop and who have made it available only at a very high cost which allows them, in turn, great power, prestige, wealth and comfort—freedom from the ills of pollution and the fear of hunger as well. We'd have to also assume that this "elite" was at least as yet unable to exert the same control over the new crop. Then, if the elite's sense of humanity had been totally corrupted by their greed and monopolization of the island's resources to date, the idea that they would oppose the new crop and use their power and prestige to bribe and manipulate others into doing so as well is imaginable, however socially irrational and immoral. For the islanders there is obviously a political choice to be made with conflicting interests at stake. Do the past rights of the elite justify their dragging down the whole economy? Or must those past rights be challenged in the name of the whole island's well being? Is it so far fetched to see ourselves living on such an island with solar as the innovative crop and oil as an old one and with nuclear power as a temporary replacement which the elite can easily monopolize and profit from till they find some way to "own the sun" as well?

In describing solar as a "political" issue, to get back to our more complex society, a narrow definition of electoral contests is not intended. Rather, politics means the process by which competing forces, in different forms of struggle, determine who gets what share of society's resources. In this sense, solar energy is at the center of a very powerful conflict that can determine the survival and direction of humanity, the struggle between many nations over the declining fossil fuel resources of the earth.

Many people, even solar advocates, do not think of their cause as a key political issue. Some think solar will come to reinforce the present system, making it simply more efficient and adaptable. They do not recognize that powerful interest groups with stakes in the status quo see solar as a threat. Those groups with investments in nuclear, oil, gas, and coal depend on the expansion of their energy sources at even higher rates of return, and view solar as a serious threat to their future. In the short run, they may often accept solar as a helpful supplement during national gas shortages. Some of them may even be enlightened enough to realize that their institutional base built upon cheap global energy is becoming obsolete, and may want to help usher in a new energy age. But for the most part, powerful institutional forces are at work keeping solar in a secondary, subordinate role.

There has been a tendency to minimize this underlying conflict on the part of many solar exponents. In Amory Lovins' brilliant *Soft Energy Paths*, for example, there is a magnetic passage in which solar is said to appeal to all classes of people: "a soft path simultaneously offers jobs for the unemployed, capital for businesspeople, environmental protection for conservationists, enhanced national security for the military, opportunities for small business to innovate and for big business to recycle itself, exciting technologies for the secular, a rebirth of spiritual values for the religious, traditional virtues for the old, radical reforms for the young, world order and equity for the globalists, energy independence for isolationists, civil rights for liberals, states' rights for conservatives."[54]

To be fair to Lovins, he realizes that there are formidable conflicts in society; in fact, he is really trying to point out that while "present policy is consistent with the perceived short-term interests of a few powerful institutions, a soft path is consistent with far more strands of convergent social change at the grass roots."[55] Yet his writings generally assume a compatibility of solar with "enlightened" corporate society. All that is needed is to "free some log jams of outmoded perceptions."[56]

Other studies make this assumption automatically, like the Livermore study applying Lovins' concepts to California. In one chapter, the authors recognize that "the energy industry in California is one of extreme concentration of power and supply in the hands of several very large companies," but draw no conclusion save that "in order to understand the nature of the problems involved in a transition to a decentralized energy future, it is imperative that more be learned about these firms and their operations."[57]

At another point in laying out the premises of the study, the authors state that "the structure of the economy is assumed to have remained generally unchanged" from 1975 to 2025![58] All that is needed therefore is to take out the present fuel tank of resources that makes the national economic engine go, and insert another marked "renewable resources." This is a most mechanical and unrealistic method of analysis. America has gone through its "petroleum age" in 100 years alone, and the next 50 promise to be fundamentally different as America's relationship to the rest of the world changes again. A compatibility between the interest of global oil companies and American consumers in this new age, or between centralized economic power and political democracy, cannot be assumed.

But the Harvard report goes farthest in asserting that the corporate establishment has nothing to fear from a solar future. Stobaugh and Yergin are contradictory to the point of schizophrenia in their analysis. They sketch the most terrifying picture of policies which lead to the danger of world depression or war. But then, almost to reassure the reader, they write that "Some might think that we are proposing a transformation of the market. On the contrary . . . the pursuit of profit has, after all, served American society well in the past."[59]

If that does not make them respectable, they go out of their way to dissociate themselves from more "radical" solar advocates: "the 'revolutionary' impact of solar has been exaggerated . . . a shift of this sort hardly means the disappearance of the utilities or a revolutionary transformation of society as some 'small is beautiful' advocates have argued."[60]

However, the real debate is not between moderate and militant solar advocates. The question is whether the corporate system can undertake and survive a rapid transition from depletable energy sources to renewable ones: the real test is whether the present corporate arrangements can "get the job done." The goal has to be the energy transition, not the preservation of current market structures.

What is one to conclude so far about the ability of the economic system to adapt? First of all, there is a tremendous vitality in the sector of "free enterprise capitalism," that is, in the growth of small, innovative businesses pioneering in solar energy.

Some are in the business purely "for a buck," but most are eager businessmen with a genuine interest in the social usefulness of the new products they are introducing—and they are beginning to make money as well. They are the innovators in the field, rather than the oil companies and utilities who may at most seek to acquire them. For the survival of these enterprises, there must be strong anti-trust laws (as passed in California in 1978) and government-backed loans made available to businesses and consumers for front-end costs.

That leaves the "corporate capitalist" sector where the picture is far different. There are a few enlightened large companies, like Grumman, who chose to enter the solar field early and aggressively. Their role is significant, and only needs to be balanced enough by government policies to prevent the smothering of small competitors by the larger firm's superior capital assets gained from their military and other sales.

But beyond them are the energy conglomerates who have no particular interest in solar except as a secondary source trailing behind conventional technologies. And largely aiding and abetting the giants with contracts and alluring policies has been the Department of Energy which, under James Schlesinger in 1978, had 20 top officials with a combined employment experience of 209 years in the Department of Defense, Atomic Energy Commission, Central Intelligence Agency, National Aeronautics and Space Administration, and multinational oil firms.[61] Trusting men like these with solar energy is akin to putting Dracula in charge of the community blood bank.

Barry Commoner, first in *The Poverty of Power,* and more recently in *The Politics of Energy*, has recognized the reality that "the decision to embark at once on a solar transition would mean an unavoidable clash between the national interest and the special interests of the major oil companies and the electric utilities [between the islanders and the island's monopoly elite]. In the solar transition, the major oil companies, among the richest and most powerful corporations in the U.S. or the world, would lose their dominant position in the economy."[62]

Painful as it may be to some, this has to be the point of departure for anyone who is *serious* about solar energy. There are many ways that many different kinds of people can play helpful roles in preparing the way for solar. But it has to be realized that a clash of interests is basic to the energy crisis. The largest corporations with specific stakes in the status quo will dominate the market with their preferences for oil, coal and nuclear. Small business will establish a beachhead in the market but go no farther. Only government initiative will both restructure the market arrangements and, where necessary, invest the capital necessary to follow the path to a truly new society based on renewable resources.

Only a powerful citizens movement will be able to liberate the instrument of government and turn it towards these more positive uses. If the vision is renewable resources, the mechanism has to be the government in combination with innovative entrepreneurs, and the means a movement of people desirous of democratic control over our energy future.

As Commoner concludes in his most recent essay, *The Politics of Energy,* "If we firmly embrace economic democracy as a national goal, as a new standard for political policy, as a vision of the nation's future, it can guide us through the historic passage that is mandated by the energy crisis, and restore to the nation the vitality that is inherent in the richness of its resources and the wisdom of its people."[63]

Beginning in the Community

For the transition to begin, as it already has, there is no need to wait for the federal government to respond, and no reason to be intimidated by the national power of the oil and nuclear industries. The transition to a conserving, solar society can and will occur through a renewed spirit of *community self-sufficiency.*

There are signs of this change everywhere. Citizens in Franklin County, Massachusetts, are burning wood in their stoves and saving money on their utility bills. A couple in upstate New York has started their own local "electric utility" by wheeling power out of the Hudson River. A Puerto Rican group in Jersey City contributes its "sweat equity" to insulating and solarizing neighborhood housing abandoned by absentee landlords. A professor in Massachusetts hooks up a windmill and cogenerator system to a school building. A Navaho group in Arizona, calling themselves the "solar savages," builds, sells and installs its inexpensive flat plate collectors. A community development corporation in San

Bernardino, California, builds a solar hot water system for a block of ghetto housing. A farmer in Iowa makes his own hydrogen and gasohol to power his tractor and truck. A couple in Davis, California build and share a neighborhood solar tract called "Village Homes." The society based on renewable resources rises into vision through the efforts of its pioneers. The basic change comes on a personal and community level, and can neither be controlled nor taken away from above.

The community-based movement is being organized and expanding rapidly. The SolarCal Council brought together over 50 local elected officials in California in 1979 to work together on conservation and solar ordinances; in less than six months, new ordinances had passed in more than a dozen cities.*

There was talk of "municipal solar utilities" as a mechanism for promoting, financing and servicing solar systems on the community level; the Energy Commission had funded pilot projects in Bakersfield, Palo Alto, Oceanside, San Dimas, Santa Monica and Ukiah. The SolarCal "hotline," with no publicity and only three staff, was receiving 500 calls a week from interested citizens across the state.

A solution is coming into sight: in cities large and small, a goal of maximum energy self-sufficiency. That means homes well insulated and shaded, commercial buildings retrofitted with energy-saving devices, factories using solar for process heat and cogenerators for power; farms using solar for drying and wind for electricity; recycling programs harvesting paper, glass and metal; food production happening in backyards, greenhouses and community gardens; schools, stores, hospitals and services being located within reach of bus lines and bicycles. Capital will be recycled like any other scarce resource, to those businesses and jobs within the community providing the energy services needed. The democracy of town meetings will become more meaningful in people's lives. And as Americans change from passive energy consumers to active energy producers, they will daily marvel at the possibilities concealed from them during the age of profitable

*For information on these ordinances, see *Capturing the Sun's Energy: Opportunities for Local Governments*, a publication of Western SUN, 1111 Howe Avenue, Sacramento, California 95825.

waste. They will learn, for instance, that a city's steaming temperature can drop by ten or more degrees in summer if more trees and fewer parking lots are planted, or that windows are merely passive solar collectors which, if properly shaded, can save up to half the energy used for air conditioning. And then they will learn it was Socrates who first explained to the West that "in houses that look toward the South, the sun penetrates the portico in winter, while in summer the path of the sun is right over our heads and above the roof so that there is shade," and that his countryman, the playwright Aeschylus, condemned those who were ignorant of solar energy as uncivilized people, who "though they had eyes to see, they saw to no avail; they had ears, but understood not. But like shapes in dreams, throughout their time, without purpose they wrought all things in confusion. They lacked knowledge of houses... turned to face the sun, dwelling beneath the ground like swarming ants in sunless caves."[64]

Through this relearning of ancient truths, Americans will discover that they have been separated from reality, from the very way in which things work by a system which mysteriously prefabricates nearly everything. They will come to lessen their need for "experts," and value instead the power of self-suffiency in a real community. The road to solar energy is also a road of self-reliance.

FOUR
HEALTH: PREVENTING
CORPORATE CANCER

In the area of public health, science, and medicine, the government has in the past traditionally stepped forward to tell the people to look out for something, to put them on guard, to prohibit dangerous substances. Way back in the days of Typhoid Mary, the government led that battle. The government maintained this leadership role until about the end of World War II, when it more or less threw up its hands. The government refused to face the complex health problems which have come to light in the last 20 years as a result of thousands of new chemicals and industrial processes...

It wasn't always that easy. We weren't always exposed to the extent that we are now. The interesting part of it is now we have a new Magna Carta of human rights, a declaration that makes it possible for us to hold our heads high throughout the world. It sounds good, and I think we ought to start applying it to our own people—defending their right to life, their right not to be killed in the name of profit, not to be sacrificed on the altar of technology.

> Hon. Miles W. Lord, Judge, U.S. District
> Court for Minnesota.

The final legacy of the petrochemical age may be a humanity and an earth in terminal states of illness. Both cancer and environmental poisoning are escalating at nearly epidemic rates. The key to a recovery of health, like a recovery from chronic energy crises and inflation, will only emerge from a new awareness of the limits of our natural selves and our natural environments.

The false assumption that the frontier environment was both a source of unlimited resources and a sink for unlimited disposal of toxic waste has given us a landscape pockmarked with poison. In

---

*I am indebted to Paul Blanc, M.S. Public Health, for the original research in this chapter, and for assistance in the writing.

addition to nine million cubic feet of high-level radioactive waste stored since World War II, the nuclear industry produces on the average 30 tons of radioactive waste per reactor every year—with the long-promised technology for safe disposal still not in sight.[1] Chemical waste is nearly as harrowing a problem for future generations: 70 billion pounds of hazardous waste is deposited annually in 30,000 dumps, many of which are already overflowing, leaching, flammable time bombs.[2]

A high-technology economy based on the faulty premise that it could expand forever in a world of finite boundaries and resources has given us, along with combined inflation and recession, death and disease that are caused by the system itself, and whose "treatments" ironically are one of the most profitable, high-growth industries in America. The petrochemical industry seeking to avoid any social controls on its ecologically destructive behavior works to convince us that disease is but a necessary by-product of progress. Its agents lobby to shift the financial cost of suffering to the victims and taxpayers. A society with an exaggerated faith in science and a mystified notion of illness is thus manipulated into massively subsidizing the search for physical or biological explanations of disease while mostly ignoring the possibility that health is a social, economic and political issue which citizens can do something about.

The issue of chemical contamination is also a moral issue, once again the "sins of the fathers" visited upon future generations who will suffer unprecedented health and environmental crises that could have been prevented by a simple concern for the future.

Cancer as the Modern Plague

Cancer may be seen by future historians as the paradigm disease of the petrochemical age. Current American Cancer Society statistics estimate that one out of four people in this country will be diagnosed in their lifetimes as having cancer, compared to approximately one of 25 Americans at the turn of the century.[3] The death rate from cancer has continued to rise in spite of statistical adjustments for an aging population and in contrast to the death rate for heart disease, which has begun to decline. The death rate from certain cancers which are known or suspected of being chemically related, for instance of the lung and pancreas, have risen dramatically. The World Health Organization and our own government have estimated that 80 percent of cancers are "environmentally-related"—due to workplace exposures, environmental contamination, diet or lifestyle.[4] The National Cancer Institute has estimated that 20-40 percent of cancer incidence in America is related to occupational exposures, for example, to asbestos.[5]

Nor is cancer the only disease which is an outcome of modern contamination. There are genetic impacts, like those discovered at Love Canal;[6] birth defects, like those from "Agent Orange";[7] "brown lung" like that created in North Carolina's textile industry;[8] and male sterility, from exposures to dibromochloropropane (DPCP) in Lathrop, California.[9] As long ago as 1970, the U.S. Department of Health, Education and Welfare estimated there are 100,000 occupationally-related deaths per year, many thousands from toxic exposure.[10] There are no estimates on disease and death in the general population beyond the factory door, exposed through their food, air and water. But the Environmental Protection Agency warns that only 10 percent of hazardous waste is disposed of in an environmentally-sound way. Every hour in 1975 Inland Steel's Indian Harbor plant poured 14,000 lbs. of sulphur dioxide and 6,000 lbs. of solid and liquid waste into the atmosphere. Across the country there are 108 waste dumps officially considered to be "highly serious" and over 100 classified as "medium serious."[12] Carcinogens have been detected in drinking water from Los Angeles to Long Island,[13] and studies in Louisiana have linked increasing cancer rates for those taking their waste water from the contaminated Mississippi.[14] Unusually high rates of birth defects have been detected in such disparate groups as nurses exposed to operating room anesthetic gas,[15] residents near forests exposed to herbicides, and communities adjacent to waste dumps.[16] Cigarette smoke, thought to be hazardous in itself, has now been shown to multiply the effects of such ubiquitous environmental toxins as asbestos.

In the era of American expansion, the notion of plague was often associated with foreigners, the uncivilized, the immigrants. Sometimes it could be imposed on others, as the U.S. Army did to the Native Indians by spreading smallpox on blankets, killing buffalo herds, destroying crops, thus weakening the "enemy's" health and sources of sustenance. But in the new era of limits and inter-relatedness, the same approaches to warfare have brought a modern plague home. The constant spraying of the jungles and croplands of Vietnam with "Agent Orange" and "Agent Blue" to weaken still another "enemy" has resulted in a rising incidence of cancer among not only the Vietnamese, but also the very American soldiers who flew the missions. In a horrible irony, thousands of GIs escaped being cannon-fodder only to find themselves cancer-fodder a decade later.

It is difficult to believe that American officials during the Vietnam War were either unaware of, or unwilling to admit, the hideous effects of the chemical spraying upon their own soldiers. They knew that the defoliant Agent Orange (2, 4, 5-T) contained dioxin, the most potent non-protein poison created by human science. They knew that even small amounts would kill people. They knew its effects on trees, crops, soil. (And those of us, journalists and anti-war activists who travelled to North Vietnam during the war, brought back detailed reports of birth defects among the peasants gassed by the U.S. helicopters). As they were callous toward the entire population of Vietnam so were they callous toward their own soldiers as well.

Now that cancer has begun to surface among U.S. servicemen exposed to defoliants in Vietnam, the official attitude is almost too cruel to believe. Like the most selfish of businessmen trying to avoid a suit from their maimed or injured workers, the U.S. Veterans Administration has resisted classifying the G.I. cancer cases as "service-related," thus far avoiding the need for compentesting on soldiers and civilians in the 1950's.[17]

It should not be surprising that a government which treats its own soldiers this way will have the same negligent attitude towards the rest of its citizens. And so, with little publicity, 2, 4, 5-T and related phenoxy herbicides such as 2, 4, D have been introduced in managing forest lands, in agriculture, and often even are in weed control around roads and city streets. The federal agency responsible for regulation of this herbicide, the EPA, did little to investigate the long term effects of such use. In places like southern Oregon, where spraying was particularly intense, citizens began to notice cleft lips and other deformities in their communities.[18] Some were so outraged that they threatened to shoot down the Forest Service helicopters, a final coming home of what began in Vietnam. Their protest ultimately led EPA to severely restrict the use of 2, 4, 5-T in 1979. But other phenoxy herbicides which have unknown and equally dangerous potential long-term effects, have not been federally banned.

The use of dioxin and other chemicals in warfare abroad also has come full circle with the assault on the lives of those Americans living near Love Canal in upstate New York. A legislative task force in New York found that the federal government, particularly the military, dumped their wastes from World War II in the Love Canal area near Niagara Falls. The site eventually came under ownership of the Hooker Chemical Company, a subsidiary of Occidental Petroleum.[19] Because of the Vietnam War, the Love Canal dump became the largest single disposal ground for 2, 4, 5-T in the world. When Jane Fonda and I visited Love Canal in 1979, the first persons we met were a family of Vietnamese "boat people" coming to live, with other Indochina refugees, in a new public housing project built at Love Canal. The chemical exposures they had apparently escaped in their homeland would be an immediate part of their new life in America. Perhaps more ironic, our "guide" for a tour of the Love Canal neighborhood was an American Vietnam veteran who had served two tours of duty, who described his war wounds as "an indirect hit" while he angrily charged that the Love Canal was a "direct hit" on himself, his family and community. One wonders who the "real enemy" is? We met mothers, fathers and children who knew intuitively what would be revealed months later by a federal report: that they were suffering genetic assault, chromosome damage, exposures to fearful and unknown diseases that would be passed on for generations. They were hard-working patriotic Americans who suddenly thought of themselves as mutants, as refugees, as expendables, as "motel people" because they were crowded like boat people into local motels while Hooker denied responsibility and legislators debated what their relocation was worth.

Love Canal is a stark signal of how far astray Americans have been led in our efforts to control, and therefore maintain, the "earthly paradise" that lured generations of immigrants here. In a nightmare of self-destruction, we have begun to inflict cancer on ourselves through a chemical assault on our basic environment. We have created a social and physical threat for which there *seems* to be no cure but more of the same: an expensive, uncertain search for chemical cures to chemically-caused diseases, for new chemicals to neutralize the toxic ones, a chemical arms race without end. How could scientific thought, we might ask, have been so short-sighted?

Production of Synthetic Organic Chemicals
in the United States from 1918 to 1976

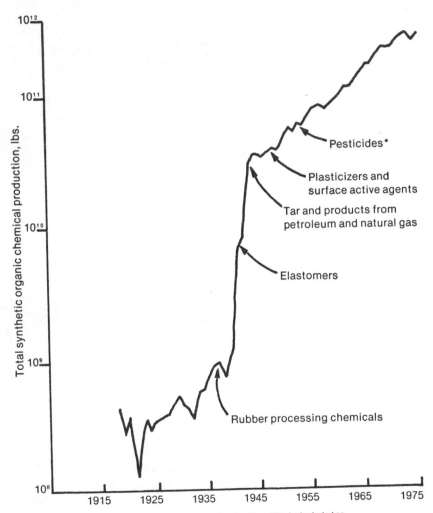

*Arrows indicate year when usage became sufficiently "significant" to be included as specific categories in Commission reports.

Source: U.S. International Trade Commission, 1978.

Origins of the Petrochemical Threat

The failure does not lie with "pure scientific thinking." There is nothing destructive about the quest for a deeper understanding of our place in the universe, nor of the universe itself, nor of the processes that enhance life or bring death. It is ill-conceived experiments or especially the subversion of pure science to the power of commerce and the priorities of states that breed our self-perpetuating cancer crisis. The petrochemical industry as we know it today is the institutional outcome of a 150-year history of "applied science" prostituted to the service of profit and growth. The petrochemical industry more than any other was able to exploit the scientific revolution of the last century because of its unique relationship to the crucial subject matter being researched —hydrocarbons themselves. If a naturalist like Thoreau might have held to the heights of objectivity in exploring the Merrimac River or the Walden woods, it was the mentality of Custer that marched with applied science in the valley below.

The petrochemical industry first arose from the 19th century discoveries that became the field of organic chemistry.[20] The new science was named "organic" because it was believed, until the mid-19th century, that these chemical compounds derived only from living or "organic" matter, which followed different laws than "inorganic" chemicals. It was generally believed that organic chemicals contained a vital "life force," since they were purified from living things. Therefore they could not be created synthetically. But then in the 1830s the organic chemical *urea* was synthesized in the laboratory solely from chemicals which were not themselves "organic." It quickly became apparent that what differentiated organic from inorganic chemistry was that organic compounds were those based on a structure of atoms of the element *carbon*. Carbon has certain relatively unique properties that make it particularly well suited to be the chemical kingpin of life. Above all, it is carbon's ability to enter into relatively stable chemical bonds where electrons are shared between and among atoms that is the hallmark of organic molecules.

The 19th century organic chemists concentrated on compounds derived from coal or coal tar distillates, knowing that synthetic creations were possible but not yet having a use for them. Then in 1856, William Henry Perkin, an 18-year old student, inadvertently dissolved his black sludge into a purple dye.[21]

Called "mauve," Perkin's dye could be used for coloring textiles, and so began the synthetic organic chemical industry. A whole generation of inventors discovered that synthetic chemicals could be produced for a variety of quite profitable uses. The color magenta was soon created, then other analine dyes, and then in 1869 one John Wesley Hyatt won a $10,000 prize offered by a billiard ball manufacturer for a synthetic alternative to ivory, calling the invention celluloid.[22] What had begun with the innocuous discovery of urea, and the accidental discovery of dyes, was now spreading from industry to industry. Within a few years, bakelite, the first synthetic resin was created, and research was leading rapidly to the development of modern explosives. The idea had been firmly established that chemistry research could be applied industrially with great financial profit.

Even then the first evidence of the human effects of this new applied chemistry was becoming available, but was ignored. By the 1890s a German study reported a high incidence of bladder cancer among workers in the dye industry. However, the industry was still small and limited. It was not until two subsequent developments—the production of petroleum and the advent of modern, mass warfare—that the petrochemical industry as we know it today was born.

When the first oil well was drilled in 1859 (three years after Perkins' discovery of mauve), the oil was chiefly processed for lighting fuel, and the new product's main competition came from sperm whales. The electric lightbulb changed all that, so the petroleum industry shifted to heating oil in the 1880s, and left the industry searching for a market for their heavy fractions from distillates (the light fractions were going to paraffin stoves). This need was resolved by the development of marine oils to fuel ships. The use which was to later predominate—automobile fuel—was now not far off. But oil refining, with "cracking" to produce octane rich fractions for automobile gasoline, presented another set of problems—a huge surplus of petroleum byproducts such as benzene and short-chain hydrocarbons, with no market big enough to consume them. The lesson of the dye industry was not lost on the petroleum industry. In *The Oxford History of Technology*, the writer R. J. Forbes states it: "Close cooperation between the universities and the refineries existed only in Europe, and there mainly in Russia, where Count Witte...had ordered the universities to *direct their research in organic chemistry to the promotion of the Caucasian oil industry....* However it took them (the American refineries) a long time to realize that progress was ultimately related to scientific research, which in the United States did not start in earnest *until the period of the first world war.*"[23]

In the first two decades of the century, the petroleum industry had the raw materials in the form of cheap hydrocarbon byproducts as well as a technological approach learned from applied organic chemistry. The search for the chemical solution to the problem of a synthetic replacement for natural rubber led directly to the creation of the modern plastics industry. This development came about because natural rubber and plastics share a common chemical characteristic. They are both *polymers.* Polymers are long chain chemicals made up of similar repeating subunits. As the physico-chemical properties of rubber became unraveled, these discoveries laid the foundation for the industrial creation of synthetic polymers: not just neoprene ("synthetic rubber") but also polyvinyl chloride, polystyrene, polyethelene, and so on. For polyvinyl chloride for instance, the basic starting unit for the polymer, vinyl chloride, had been first created in the laboratory in the 1830's soon after the synthetic creation of urea. However it was not until after 1910 that polymer research stimulated interest in the subject enough to show the vinyl chloride could be "polymerized" into PVC (polyvinylchloride). World War II led to the commercial development of PVC, initially as eletrical insulation material for fighter aircraft. By 1973, the first cases of liver cancer were reported in workers who had entered the booming polyvinyl chloride industry in the 1940's.

With these technical advances came a chemical explosion of almost incomprehensible magnitude. According to one history, plastics production grew from 500 million pounds in 1942 to 7.8 billion pounds in 1962, the U.S. came to supply 40 percent of the world's chemicals, production of synthetic organic chemicals increased at a yearly rate of over 10 percent, and in recent years it has been common for as many as 1000 new chemical substances to be created, adding to the approximately 70,000 now in existence.[24]

During precisely the same period, nuclear-generated power came into existence as well. Like the history of petrochemicals, the growth of nuclear power reveals a history of science subverted to the economic and political needs of profit-based industry. From the first discoveries of radium, the possible financial advantage of radioactivity has been consistently exploited to the detriment of the public good. Radium itself was early used as a luminous paint on the dials of watches. The women who worked in the factories painting these watch dials made fine tips in their brushes by painting them with their mouths; the radium they ingested led to bone cancer, facial disfigurement and death.[25] Radioactivity became more than a commercial curiousity (although large profits were also made in various medical applications which later proved to be successful only at causing future cancer) with the scientific discoveries showing that uranium could be "split" such that a resultant net loss in mass was released as energy, according to Einstein's famous equation $E = MC^2$. The Manhattan Project was the seed project for a huge industry: uranium milling, and mining, enrichment, and production. But only a few years after Hiroshima and Nagasaki, the uranium industry faced a potentially dangerous sibling rival in the more powerful hydrogen bomb. Fusion meant a terrible threat to the infant fission/uranium industry at least as far as weapons production was concerned, even though uranium processing for weapons would continue to be a relatively large budget item. The "Atoms for Peace" program was the solution. We would use the same mines, mills and processing facilities to produce uranium fuel rods instead of bombs. The history of government misinformation on the adverse effects of radiation extends from Eisenhower's suppression of the effects of atmospheric atomic testing to current mystifications about the possibility of technical solution to the problems of radioactive waste disposal. It demonstrates an economic commitment to nuclear technology regardless of its human costs. It is a paradigm example of the prostitution of pure science to inhuman ends. The interlocking connections between the oil, nuclear, and uranium industries, and their overlaps with the Department of Defense and former Atomic Energy Commission, make clear that we have created much of our energy economy for purposes of warfare and profit. No society can escape the fallout from such policies on its own health.

Can Cancer Be Cured?

There still are powerful voices denying that cancer is the plague inherent in a petrochemical society, not all of them industry public relations personnel. One of the most eloquent, for example, is Susan Sontag, the widely-respected essayist who wrote *Illness as Metaphor* in 1978.[26] Sontag's thesis is that illnesses such as tuberculosis in the 19th century, or cancer in the 20th, become metaphors of culture, economics and politics, when in fact they are real diseases that can be cured without any simultaneous cures of society's larger problems. Cancer, she believes, is "a good metaphor for paranoids, for those who need to turn campaigns into crusades...,"[27] ranging from the John Birch Society to Wilhelm Reich (who believed that cancer was a "stagnation of the flow of the life energy of the organism").[28] The view of cancer as "a disease of industrial civilization," she believes, is scientifically unsound. Her frontal attack on environmental-health advocates comes to the following climax:

> For the more sophisticated, cancer signifies the rebellion of the injured ecosphere: Nature taking revenge on a wicked technocratic world. False hopes and simplified terrors are raised by crude statistics brandished for the general public, such as that 90 percent of all cancers are 'environmentally caused'...[29]

While Sontag is surely right in criticising the Birch view that cancer and chemotherapy are somehow only a Rockefeller conspiracy, and that there can be a "world without cancer," there is something excessively negative about her rejection of the arguments in favor of *preventing* such cancer as can be prevented by changing the economic and energy environment. The case for prevention, of course, has a hollow ring to the one in four who already have the disease. Her's is an almost exclusive advocacy of an emphasis on chemotherapy and immunotherapy as opposed to prevention. Her hope is almost fanciful:

> ...all the diseases for which the issue of causation has been settled, and which can be prevented and cured, have turned out to have a simple physical cause—like the pneumococcus for pneumonia, the tubercle bacillus for tuberculosis, a single vitamin deficiency for pellagra— and it is far from unlikely that something comparable will eventually be isolated for cancer.[30]

And yet in another passage of the essay Sontag briefly notes that the National Cancer Act of 1971 failed to envisage the "near-to-hand decisions that could bring under control the industrial economy that pollutes,"[31] instead concentrating on only finding a cure.[32] But Sontag's essay makes the same mistake by emphasizing the hope for a cure over the practical possibilities which lie in prevention. A careful reading shows that she misunderstands the history of tuberculosis in exactly the same way. Only once does she mention the widely accepted observation that improved living conditions and sanitation did far more to eliminate TB as a major public health menace than the development of anti-tubercular drugs. The death rate for tuberculosis declined from 350 per 100,000 Americans in 1860 to slightly over 300 when the causal agent (tubercle bacillus) was identified in the 1880s, to only about 33 per 100,000 by the time the first effective chemotherapy (streptomycin) was introduced in the 1940s, and then with the drug technology mastered, to only a negligible 10-15 in the 1950s. It is true that the use of chemotherapy usefully sped up the rate of decline but, according to one history, "even without this therapy, it seems likely that the death rate would have continued its decline."[33]

Although unique in eloquence, Sontag is far from alone in her fundamentalist return to the traditional model of cancer as a disease which cannot be prevented but can and will be cured. Dr. Lucien Israel, a cancer treatment specialist whose influential book, *Conquering Cancer*,[34] is called by Sontag "the most intelligent, informative and useful book ever written on cancer," heavily emphasizes cancer treatments over preventive environmental change. He writes:

> The pollution that accompanies industrial development, which we have not yet learned to master, arouses vehement indignation in some people. But for all that, people do not stop administering carcinogens to themselves—tobacco and alcohol, for example... It seems that, instead, people have decided to go on poisoning themselves while they wait for doctors to find the magic pill that will enable them to do so without risk. This attitude reflects a touching confidence in science that is *diametrically opposed to the views of the advocates of zero growth. I share this confidence, at least*

*from a certain point of view. Otherwise, I would not have
written this book. . . . Cancer will be curable.*[35] (Emphasis
mine)

The acceptance of a deteriorating environment, and with it
the rise of cancer, as the "given" of the present human condition,
as an inevitable byproduct of industrial progress, and as a problem
which can only be solved by further progress of the same kind, is an
imperialism turned back upon the human self, as if cancer were
somehow part of the American manifest destiny. This outlook
reaches its most extreme form in the writings of Dr. Lewis
Thomas, particularly in his popular and award-winning *The Lives
of a Cell*.[36] Thomas is also president of the Memorial Sloan
Kettering Cancer Center in New York, making him an arch-villain
in the conspiracy theories of the Birch Society and others. And
these Rightist views, however paranoid, are not without a base of
evidence, it might be noted. For example, for a detailed description of Sloan Kettering's role in the official "cancer
establishment," and for an account of the number of representatives of large, polluting industries that sit on its governing board,
including the chairmen of Exxon, General Motors and American
Cyanamid, and of the ways in which they profit from cancer
research and chemotherapy, one can read Ralph W. Moss' book,
The Cancer Syndrome.[37]

Let us assume, however, that Dr. Thomas has no such conflicts of interest, and is permitted a mild paranoia himself when he
writes that "in so much of our thinking about cancer these days,
we keep looking for outside causes for the things that go wrong.
We imagine a kind of demonology."[38] Lewis' philosophy is a
subtle rejection of the whole idea of prevention in behalf of a scientific, chemotherapy fix. First, there is his rejection of the notion of
a fragile environment: ". . . it is illusion to think that there is anything fragile about the life of the earth; surely this is the toughest
membrane imaginable in the universe. . .".[39] Then there is un-
shaken scientific faith: "If we have learned anything at all in this
century it is that all new technologies will be put to use, sooner or
later, for better or worse, as it is our nature to do."[40] As applied to
the question of cancer his outlook is predictable: "we are systems
of mechanisms," the underlying mechanisms are "mysterious,"
cancer results when "host mechanisms" get out of control, and
"there is something wrong with the popular view that (such di-

The Cancer-Petrochemical-Bank Interlock

Of 50 Overseers, or directors, of the Memorial Sloan-Kettering Cancer Center, 18 are related to major polluting industries and 14 to major financial investment firms. They are:

Peter O. Crisp	Rockefeller Family & Assoc., Associate
Harold W. Fisher	Exxon, Chairman of the Board
James B. Fisk, Ph.D.	American Cyanamid, Director
Richard M. Furland	Olin, Director
Clifton C. Garvin, Jr.	Exxon, President
James D. Landauer	Consolidated Oil and Gas, Director
Thomas A. Murphy	General Motors, Chairman of the Board
Ellmore C. Patterson	Atlan ic-Richfield, Director
John S. Reed	Philip Morris, Director
Laurance S. Rockefeller	Exxon, Mobil, Standard Oil of Indiana, Standard Oil of California, etc., major shareholder
Robert V. Roosa	Texaco, Director
Benno C. Schmidt	San Jacinto Petroleum, Transcontinental Gas Pipe Line Corporation, Freeport Minerals, Director
Arnold Schwartz*	Texaco, Vice President
Frederick Seitz	Organon, Director
H. Virgil Sherrill	Commercial Solvents, Director
William S. Sneath	Union Carbide, President
T.F. Walkowicz	Rockefeller Family & Assoc., Associate
Harper Woodward	Rockefeller Family & Assoc., Associate
Peter O. Crisp	Rockefeller Family & Assoc., Manager of Investments
Albert H. Gordon	Kidder Peabody, Chairman of the Board (Investment Bank)
Richard D. Lombard	Lombard, Nelson & McKenna, Chairman, Ret. (Invest. Bk.)
Elinor W. Montgomery	Wife of George Montgomery, Jr., Vice President, White, Weld (Investment Bank)
Ellmore C. Patterson	Morgan Guaranty Trust Co., Chairman of the Executive Committee
John S. Reed	Citibank, Executive Vice President
James D. Robinson	American Express, Chairman; former investment banker with Morgan Guaranty and with White, Weld
Laurance S. Rockefeller	Rockefeller Brothers Fund, Chairman
William Rockefeller	Shearman and Sterling, Partner (Firm closely tied to Citibank)
Robert V. Roosa	Brown Brothers, Harriman, Partner (Investment Bank)
Benno C. Schmidt	J.C. Whitney & Co., Managing Partner (Investment Bank)
H. Vergil Sherrill	Bache Halsey Stuart Shields, President (Investment Bank, Stock Brokerage)
James H. Wickersham, Jr	Morgan Guaranty Trust Co., Vice President
Harper Woodward	Rockefeller Family & Assoc., Associate

*Died Sept. 10, 1979

The Top Chemotherapy Corporations

Company	1979-80 Profit Increase	Fortune 500 Rank	Interlocking Directors (partial)	Medical Interlocks (partial)
Pfizer	13%	123	Mobil, ITT, IBM	• Vice President for Health Sciences, Columbia University • National Cancer Institute Review Committee, Large Bowel and Pancreatic Cancer
Merck	24%	147	J.P. Morgan Co., IBM, Ford Motor Co.	• Institutional Policy Committee, Memorial Sloan-Kettering Cancer Center • President, Mehany Medical College
Eli Lilly	19%	163	Standard Oil (Indiana), Chase Manhattan, Mobil, Citibank, General Motors	• General Director, Massachusetts General Hospital • National Cancer Institute Committee on Developmental Therapeutics
Squibb	12%	188	Chase Manhattan, Olin Corp.	• President, Memorial Sloan-Kettering Cancer Center • Institutional Policy Committee, Memorial Sloan-Kettering Cancer Center

By Ralph Brave, CPPC, 1980

eases) are all the results of environmental influences— things we eat, or breathe, or touch."[41]

Sontag, Lucien Israel, and Lewis Thomas are by far the best defenders of the existing chemotherapy approaches. Indeed, their essays and articles intertwine and depend on each other. Not only does Sontag salute Israel for having written the best book on cancer,[42] she also cites Thomas' faith that cancer's cause will be isolated and destroyed.[43] Thomas, in turn, applauds Dr. Israel's book as a "solid, reliable, highly useful" work by an "able, compassionate and skilled clinical scientist."[44]

However expert, eloquent or authoritative these authors are, there remains something chilling about their common and superficial rejection of prevention. They are in effect denying the responsibility of the petrochemical and nuclear industries for cancer and, even worse, recommending that the laboratories of the same industries can be entrusted to come up with an effective cure.

The industry itself no longer denies that certain of its products and processes are linked with cancer. What they currently imply in defense of themselves is that *everything causes cancer.* The world is so inherently carcinogenic, they admit, that one can be struck by cancer from an innumerable, unknowable combination of sources outside and inside the self. Thus it cannot be prevented, but potentially can be cured once its invasion of the body begins.

What is frightening is the political implication of the worldview that "everything causes cancer." For if this is the case, why regulate anything which industry does? If the disease is inevitable, optimists can hope for a cure but not for control of cancer at the source, for that would be striking at the source of everything else. "Without chemicals, life itself would be impossible," goes the famous Monsanto commercial. In another one, workers come to the American home to remove all objects produced by the synthetic chemical industry; nothing remains but the frame to a brass bed when they leave.

But it would be more accurate to say that without a cancer epidemic, the profits and power of the petrochemical industry itself would be impossible. We are faced with a growing burden of cancer and genetic risk because we have allowed the sole factor which determines the introduction of novel substances and processes to our environment to be short-term profit by impersonal corporations whose only measure of health is the bottom line, and who will never foot the bill for the long-term damage they cause. Beginning with the dye manufacturers of the 19th century who experienced no liability for the bladder cancer of their employees, down to Hooker Chemical which sold the Love Canal site to a local school for one dollar, the citizens and especially the workers of this country have subsidized the cost of doing business with their own health.

The industry which puts itself forward as the only source of a solution, let us remember, is the same industry that once denied there was a problem at all. It is the same industry that promised to curb world hunger by the introduction of quick fix chemical solutions to the problems of pest control in agriculture, resulting in strains of resistant predators requiring ever increasing tonnages of expensive, energy-intensive, largely ineffective, poisonous and often carcinogenic pesticides with all the destructive effects described almost 20 years ago in Rachel Carson's *Silent Spring*.[45] And it is the same industry which for a generation promised that nuclear power was safe, cheap and plentiful.

Industry has long promoted the myth that deep in the research laboratories, where "disinterested" scientists labor round the clock, a scientific breakthrough will be fashioned. However, an interesting study, titled *Sources of Invention*,[46] calls this faith in the corporate laboratories into serious question. Choosing a number of "major inventions" of the 20th century, the authors examined the origins of each. The overwhelming majority came not from the research and development facilities of large corporations, but from independent inventors or scientists working in a relatively free investigative setting. Those independent discoveries included such diverse items as the helicopter, cyclotron, the electron microscope, the jet engine, the safety razor, insulin, penicillin, streptomycin, zippers, and Polaroid-Land cameras. Corporate R & D, on the other hand, has given the century such products as chlordane, aldrin, dieldrin, television, freon coolants, acrylic fibers, DDT, neoprene, tetraethyl lead, semisynthetic penicillins, and crease-resistant fabrics. A major failure of corporate R & D, according to the study, was the necessity of quick returns on investment, which tended to prevent the exploration of riskier, more novel technologies. "To sum up," the authors write, "a significant proportion of twentieth century inventions have not come from institutions where research will tend to be guided towards definite ends."[47] Even more significant is the difference in *quality* between the two groups of inventions, where the corporate inventions read like a passenger list on an environmental Titanic.

The petrochemical solution to cancer, not surprisingly, is to create more cancer as a cure. Cancer chemotherapy is remarkable in the wide gap between its original promise and its proven performance. As Dr. Samuel Epstein documents, the National Cancer Institute budget has risen steadily for several decades, reaching $5.7 billion for the decade of the 1970s.[48] Nearly all of those dollars have gone into the search for a cure rather than prevention. But over four decades, there has been "little overall improvement in our ability to treat and cure most cancers."[49] Except for important results with types of childhood leukemias and a handful of other tumors, cancer chemotherapy has been ineffective. The leading types of adult cancer—lung, breast, colon and prostate—have all been extremely resistant to such treatment. There has been an improvement in the numbers of victims surviving five years or longer, from 20 percent in the mid-1930s to 33 percent by the 1950s, but Epstein attributes these changes to "advances in surgery, blood transfusion, and antibiotic treatment, rather than specific advances of cancer treatment."[50]

The bulk of cancer chemotherapeutic agents act by selectively attacking cells which are proliferating, whether they are cancerous or non-cancerous; in general, they do this by interfering in various ways with the replication of DNA. This of course is also how chemical carcinogens seem to cause cancer. Anti-cancer drugs are themselves carcinogens. Aside from the implication that whoever is involved in producing them may get cancer on the job, the patient being treated is also at risk. We are to believe that the solution to cancer is a series of treatments which, if successful, will in themselves cause the same disease. This is not simply a "weaker" form of the disease being applied, nor is it a treatment which is worse than the disease: *it is the disease.* Furthermore, in the finest tradition of expanding end-use markets, cancer chemotherapy agents are being increasingly applied medically in conditions other than cancer, specifically where immunosuppression is a desired goal.

Where Sontag is correct is in the plain insight that prevention does the cancer victim no good at all, and that therefore the attempt at treatment and cure must remain an absolutely paramount concern. Any person should have the right to choose, through informed consent, the most aggressive "therapies" available, whether chemotherapy, radiotherapy, immunotherapy or surgery. They should also have the legal right to explore such alternatives as lactrile if they wish.

The alternatives of laetrile, diet modification, vitamin treatments, and certain immunotherapies have been the subject of immense controversy without yet bringing any proven reduction in the cancer burden. But so little is known about cancer, and so little has been accomplished by chemotherapy, that it seems mistakenly rigid to prohibit personal choice of the controversial alternatives. There is an instructive historical parallel to the laetrile controversy in the yellow fever crisis which hit Philabelphia in 1793. In the face of the epidemic, the Philadelphia Medical Society (which was the most advanced in America) became bitterly divided along partisan, political and ideological lines.[51] Although the cause of the disease was not understood, one group of physicians aligned with the philosophy of Thomas Jefferson favored a new cure consisting of bleeding the patient and giving him mercury compounds, while another group aligned with Alexander Hamilton favored the traditional regimen of quinine bark and wine. Dr. Benjamin Rush, a signer of the Declaration of Independence and ally of Jefferson, was viciously attacked for his support of bleeding. He, in turn, denounced bark and wine as a "Federalist cure." The city population became divided along Republican versus Federalist lines, their political tastes coloring their medical choices. In fact, neither side's treatment was particularly effective, and even 200 years later yellow fever, once contracted, is still a life threatening illness even with medical care. Yellow fever has disappeared in this country because of adequate mosquito control, and was further controlled because of vaccination against the infectious agent which the mosquito carries.

The laetrile controversy is similarly colored by a bitter philosophical and political dispute, in which all sides have one problem in common: their distance from understanding a cure for cancer.

Therefore, the alternative cancer therapies deserve the same research support, the same objective tests in the laboratory, and the same clinical controlled trials that traditional chemotherapy approaches receive, but this should not deflect from a course that will strike more directly at the known causes of cancer in our economic and energy environment. That course is prevention.

Towards a Movement for Prevention

The fact is that we are faced with a technology that has gone out of control, fueled by an illusion of plentiful hydrocarbons and vast profits to be made from their exploitation. Bringing that juggernaut under the restraint of a public policy with health as its priority rather than profit requires that this technology be examined, dissected and controlled the way the biologist hopes to control the cancer cell gone wild with a destructive growth that disregards the welfare of the whole organism. Major public health advancements, and the control of most of our illnesses, have come from exactly such public controls whether in basic health standards in building codes, requirements for the sanitary production of milk, restrictions on the adulteration of food, or the introduction of the basic engineering of water and sewage treatment. In short, the large-scale victories in the conquest of disease have all come through developments in public health standards leading to prevention rather than treatment of illness.

It should not be so difficult for health-hungry Americans to understand the concept of prevention. Childhood vaccination is an example of this approach which is well fixed in the public mind, perhaps because it fits neatly into the larger health care delivery system. To take another example, Americans are usually the first to apply public health/prevention criticisms to reports of Third World disease problems. Why don't they have better sanitation?, is a question Americans often ask of lesser-developed nations, but which could be applied as well to the health problems of this country. It has been pointed out, for example, that the major decline of tuberculosis in America came from changes in the environment.

This is only half the lesson that public health prevention has to teach us. The history of these improvements has not been an automatic and unimpeded march forward towards a distant goal of better health for all. Time and again these improvements, many of which we take for granted at this point, were bitterly opposed by those with a financial stake in the matter at the time. When Friedrich Accum wrote his "Treatise on the Adulteration of Food and Culinary Poisons" in 1820, which criticised practices such as the use of lead chromate as a food coloring, he made such powerful enemies that he was forced to leave England on fabricated legal charges. It took 40 years in that country until the passage of the Adulteration of Food and Drug Act of 1860.[52]

The history of similar legislation which came later in America is not much different. When Upton Sinclair wrote *The Jungle* in 1905, he provoked a vicious and deceptive counter-attack from the meat packing industry.[53] The publishers of Sinclair's book became hesitant about releasing it after sending page proofs to the managing editor of the Chicago Tribune. The editor sent back a lengthy response refuting Sinclair's charges about filthy and scandalous conditions in the industry; later the publishers discovered that the rebuttal to Sinclair was actually written by a publicity agent of the meatpackers and forwarded by the Tribune as the work of its own reporters. The first U.S. legislation in the area of food and drug quality, the Pure Food and Drug Act of 1906, came only because of the public concern created by *The Jungle* and the work of other journalistic muckrakers.

The history of water quality treatment is another case of overcoming greed as an obstacle to health. The linkage of contaminated water to cholera and typhoid in the 1850s created a public consciousness which resulted in the passage of laws such as the London Metropolitan Water Act of 1852. The treatment technology which the law required had been available for 20 years, but had not been introduced by the private water suppliers for economic reasons.[54]

The battle for sanitary milk in this country went on for one hundred years, illustrating many of the forces which have tried to block public health advancement. In the first half of the 19th century, the unlucky discovery was made that if cows were brought to near starvation they could be induced to eat the slop, or waste, products from distilleries. Their milk was of such poor quality that between 1814 and 1841 infant mortality substantially increased in New York City, where distillery milk was commonly sold, as well as in other cities where the practise was introduced. One historian has noted that infant mortality decreased in European cities during the same period where this milk poisoning did not exist. "The practise of feeding cows distillery slop persisted," he writes, "because it was financially profitable (to the extent of one million dollars per year) to the parties concerned in this diabolic agreement."[55]

The 19th century pasteurization of milk, which has been a major factor in the reduction of summertime infant mortality from intestinal infection as well as control of other infectious diseases, was bitterly opposed by the dairy industry which saw nothing wrong with having the consumers take their chances with every dairy purchase. During the pasteurization battle in Minnesota, the state's sanitation director "met with determined opposition from dairies, co-operative groups and even consumers... Opposition to pasteurization could be forceful, particularly on the part of legislators. Among the strongest supporters of sanitary milk were women's clubs... the mere fact that the Minnesota Board of Health had initiated a new public health approach did not mean that the state, in some magical fashion, automatically and quickly put into operation pasteurization plants."[56]

These examples are of more than historical interest. They also provide a political model for understanding our current environmental health crisis. As with past public health victories, cancer prevention will have to be won through the joint efforts of an organized constituency demanding specific reforms that radically reduce the contamination of the human environment. This is exactly what we have begun to see across the country. As in the struggle for pasteurization, it is often groups of women who have become alarmed as those around them, especially their own children, are exposed to the risks of chemical waste. We Who Care, a group of mothers from Rutherford, New Jersey, concerned with unexplainably high leukemia incidence in their community; the Love Canal Homeowners Association led by several women who have suffered miscarriages or birth defects in their children; Concerned Neighbors in Action, a neighborhood group violated by toxic waste leaking into their soil and water in Riverside, California—all these groups understand better than the National Cancer Institute the need for prevention as the highest priority. These are only a few of the groups, mostly unknown to the other, that have sprung up in anger nationwide in response to this public health threat. They are aligned with the many thousands of Americans struggling against the health hazards of nuclear power production. This disconnected but ever-expanding protest promises to write the next chapter in the long history of public health in America, this time focussing on the aggressions of the petrochemical industry against life itself. This new movement will have to develop cancer prevention strategies that are the modern equivalents of pasteurization, water sanitation and the original food and drug laws.

Immediate Reforms

In the short-run, stricter regulatory controls will certainly be crucial. Although popular political wisdom suggests that the public is hostile to government "interference," this is not the case when it comes to environmental health. For example, Union Carbide in 1979 published the results of their own poll showing that a majority of people favored fewer controls and taxes on business. What the corporation did not reveal, however, were the details of the poll which showed that with respect to environmental, health and safety regulations, the public wanted them strengthened even if they increased the final cost of the product to the consumer.[57]

Stricter regulation may take many forms but a common theme will be to force corporate accountability for the health effects of their operations. Federal legislation has recently been introduced which would extend criminal liability to management, including boards of directors, where they knowingly withhold information about the possible adverse health impacts of their industry on employees or the public. In California, a 1979 study by the center for Law in the Public Interest showed that on the state level criminal prosecutions were never sought for even extremely hazardous violations of occupational health standards. The average fines imposed on offenders were only $10 for a non-serious violation and $239 for a serious one.[58] Changes in both laws and their enforcement are necessary on federal and state levels to make corporate managers aware that "crime in the suites" will no longer go unpunished.

Financial liability must also be extended so that the true costs of doing business are internalized. Industry has with increasing frequency called for the application of "risk/benefit" analysis in the setting of environmental health standards. In this "Heads I Win, Tails You Lose" formulation, the benefits largely accrue to one group, those who profit, and the risks fall to another, those exposed to carcinogens in the workplace and the community. As long as criminal penalties are negligible, it will remain cost-effective to poison and pollute, and a competitive disadvantage to be a conscientious businessman.

The concept of *strict* liability is already applied in the marketing of pharmaceuticals and should be extended to chemical contamination of the environment and nuclear accidents. In environmental health however, state and federal laws require proof of deliberate or willful negligence in order to prosecute those whose actions ultimately lead to contamination. Strict liability in environmental health would mean that, in the case of ground water poisoning from a chemical waste dump, it would be beside the point whether or not the dump's operator knew that an underground stream flowed on his property. He would be held *responsible* for knowing, as part of his personal stewardship and business charter.

Another important change would be to modernize Workers Compensation laws to include protection against cancer. Some laws are so weak that a victim of occupational cancer is excluded from benefits because statutes of limitations protect the former employer from any liability. Others award benefits but based on a fee scale tied to the time when the cancer was caused (for example, 25 years earlier) without any allowance for cost-of-living increases. Workers compensation awards in general are so inadequate, as well as difficult to collect for occupational disease damage, that those affected by workplace poisons are forced to find compensation elsewhere. A December 1979 Department of Labor study entitled "An Interim Report to Congress on Occupational Diseases" found that the major source of income support for those disabled by occupational disease was Social Security disability (53 percent), with pensions supplying 21 percent, veterans benefits 17 percent, and welfare 21 percent. Workers compensation was the major source of funding for only 5 percent. The report estimated that occupational disease, including cancer, costs the Social Security disability and welfare systems about $2.2 billion annually.[59] This all comes from general revenues, a direct subsidy to industry that is double the projected bailout of Chrysler. With reform of workers compensation laws along with realistic fines for health violations, industry can be made to bear a truer cost for the diseases they cause. Then corporations might find it cheaper to make products that are safe for worker and consumer alike.

However, no fine, criminal penalty, or financial compensation can restore someone's lost health or that of one's children. Nor can increased penalties and fairer compensation sufficiently check the underlying tendency of the petrochemical society to produce and feast on poisons. Starting now, a transition has to begin to a world less dependent on chemicals and nuclear power for growth and profitability.

The workplace is a useful arena for beginning. Workers should have a "right to know" about the materials they are handling and be protected from the exposures which now make guinea pigs of them. The first seeds of a new policy approach towards the fundamental sources of contamination were sown in such reforms as the 1976 Toxic Substances Control Act and the 1980 generic chemical carcinogens standards of the Occupational Safety and Health Administration. The first law, in theory, requires pre-market testing of certain chemicals before they can be introduced into the environment, with the Environmental Protection Agency being empowered to prevent environmentally damaging substances from ever seeing the light of day. The OSHA standard would allow that agency to require implementation of alternative processes and products for those found to be cancer-causing and "replacable." In both cases, only a few chemicals will in fact be affected because of limitations, jurisdictional problems and overall regulatory weakness. However, the precedent they set is important: that the public interest should prohibit certain products from ever being created. To rephrase Monsanto's motto, life itself is possible only *without* certain chemicals.

A good model for a transition to a less chemical environment is being developed by those interested in reducing the use of pesticides in agriculture. While most Americans know that we could live without astro-turf, cool-whip and plastic swizzle-sticks, they are far less sure whether pesticides are a profitable extravagance of the petrochemical age or a necessity in food production. The development of Integrated Pest Management (IPM), however, has shown that high-yield quality agricultural production need not depend on the heavy use of poisons.

The California Department of Food and Agriculture's 1978 *Report on the Environmental Assessment of Pesticide Regulatory Programs* showed that IPM can largely replace conventional pesticide use patterns without major loss of production.[60] The key to IPM is greatly reduced use of pesticides, applying them only after careful monitoring of pest populations combined with alternative natural or biological controls. Overnight, the report indicated, pesticide use in California might be cut in half. With more sophisticated biological controls in the long run, their use might even be cut further.

A second element of the transition is to protect America against chemical dumping while reducing production of and reliance on superfluous chemicals. Michael Brown, author of an excellent book on Love Canal, proposes three categories of short-term and partial steps towards immediate and temporary clean-up: keeping chemical landfills away from major aquifers and populated areas, use of solid clay bases and improved construction and protective trenching, better training of maintenance personnel, increased research into more sophisticated disposal systems, and the like. But even this multi-billion dollar clean-up would be inadequate, since no landfill or technology is possibly safe forever.[61]

Therefore Brown proposes a second step, to actually ban the discharge of any chemicals into the ground except for unique and unusual reasons. "If such a policy, however startling or unacceptable it may now seem, is not effected before the beginning of the next century," Brown warns, "an intolerable number of acres will be rendered both useless and dangerous. In a nation that depends so heavily on the productive utilization of its soil, the dwindling of such a resource is intolerable."[62]

Most important, Brown concludes, is that "rather than

developing increasingly elaborate procedures for the destruction of toxic wastes, we can minimize production of such substances in the first place.'' This has to be the heart of any prevention strategy, ''an outright ban on the manufacture of highly dangerous substances until industry, so slow to protect our needs, has demonstrated ways of destroying their wastes, or of making them innocuous to all segments of the ecology.''[63]

Finally, the same transitional approach must be urgently applied to nuclear power. There can be no guarantee of human health as long as there is a growing stockpile of nuclear weapons and a proliferation of nuclear power plants. Even in a world without nuclear war, the destructive impact on human life due to radioactive waste would be measurable, growing and irreversible. As with chemical dumping, there is still no technical solution to the problems of radioactive waste disposal. Whole regions of the country are being considered, in Department of Energy terminology, as possible ''national sacrifice areas'' for dumping. We may soon see major areas of our country turned into wastelands where no human activity is supported or allowed. While research into waste disposal must continue to be a priority, several decades of failure should be evidence enough that only a phase out of nuclear energy and an international disarmament agreement can protect humanity from even greater damage than that already sowed in the 35 years since Hiroshima and Nagasaki.

Above all, it must be realized that what is healthy for the petrochemical industry means sickness and tragedy for the American people. As we come to the end of the open frontier of exhaustible resources, the system itself turns into a senseless and self-destructive creature, somehow living on, though pieced together from parts which are individually dying or dead. High executives and officials make decisions which doom their own children to cancer and hideous malformities, and which pollute and degrade the very environment upon which their wealth depends. Appeals to their reason and conscience should be tried for the sake of averting tragedy, but it is more likely that a solution depends on new generation with new consciousness emerging from the chemical deluge in which we are drowning.

Health as always is a political and economic problem as much as a biological one, perhaps more so today than ever before. The solutions to health problems must be found in linkage with solutions to the other crises of society: economics, energy, foreign policy, values. Those solutions together can create a transformation to a society that is inherently healthier: where technology must enhance rather that subvert wellness, where deliberate pollution is unthinkable, where fossil fuels and uranium are energy sources of last resort, where harming human beings is never profitable, and where prevention of disease as part of conservation takes precedence over the promotion of illness as part of progress. One component of any strategy able to attain these aims will likely be a program for economic democracy, the focus of our next chapter.

FIVE
POWER: ECONOMIC DEMOCRACY
OR A CORPORATE STATE

The corporation will either transform itself, or be transformed by the agents of the American public, into a unit
that formally and continuously considers the desires,
needs and concerns of the individual (be he or she
worker, customer, neighbor or shareholder) and forms
and executes its policies accordingly.
—conclusion, American Management Association
survey of 644 chief executives, 1975

In the last three chapters we have discussed economic trends,
energy options, and our country's physical and mental health. In
each case beyond specific legal and social reforms, the effort to
find lasting solutions to underlying causes pointed in the same
direction. If our economy is to provide us with sustenance and
social well-being, decision-making must be guided by more than
just the narrow material interests of corporate elites. The interests
of workers, consumers, and the public at large must be reflected in
our country's economic development. If there is a major economic
reform ahead in this country, on the scale of the New Deal, it will
be the achievement of economic democracy, an alternative to the
intertwined bureaucracies of Big Business and Big Government.
Giant corporations will no longer be considered "private" as the
American public feels the effects of boardroom decisions on
income, prices, human and environmental health, political freedom and world stability. In the wake of recognizing the "public"
nature of the giant corporation, rising pressures will be felt to open
up economic decision-making to those whose lives are affected as
employees, consumers and neighbors. One of two scenarios will
occur in response: in defense of their private privilege,
corporations will attempt to extend their power over government

153

and the public through a planned corporate state, or the crisis will be resolved by an enlightened new consensus which incorporates the public interest and democratic values into the goals and makeup of American corporations.

From Free Enterprise to the Era of Trusts

The leaders of the American Revolution and framers of the Constitution believed in the basic compatibility of capitalism and democracy, even though the first notion rested on private rights and the other on public control. The Revolution, limited as it was by slavery and male superiority, nonetheless represented the greatest simultaneous expansion of political enfranchisement and property ownership in Western history. In the new Constitution the rights to vote and own property seemed equally sacred and complementary. The boundless frontier seemed to guarantee a free path to expanded economic and political freedom, and the period of "Jeffersonian democracy" came close to realizing the promise. Business enterprises were chartered on state levels as vehicles for specific economic development that could not be achieved by artisans, craftsmen or yeomen alone, in a kind of state capitalism. These corporations served defined public purposes and owed their existence, ultimately, to the popular franchise.[1]

But within a few decades corporations grew larger and permanent, finally becoming legally "immortal." American law followed the path enunciated in the Old World by Blackstone's *Commentaries*, where it was claimed that "so great is the regard of the law for private property, that it will not authorize the least violation of it; no, not even for the common good of the whole community."[2]

The historian Howard Zinn has explained the irony of how the 14th Amendment came to mean more for corporations than for the ex-slaves it was designed to protect. Weakened after the Civil War as a legal protection for blacks, the Amendment's forbidding of the abridgement of individual rights began to be tested in corporate law. Were corporations, legally speaking, "individuals" with rights to "life, liberty or property" that were beyond abridgement by the government? In an early case, *Munn vs. Illinois* (1877), the Supreme Court ruled that states could regulate prices charged to farmers for use of grain elevators, on grounds that the elevators had a "public interest" to serve. The lawyers for the grain company argued without success that the corporation was deprived of 14th Amendment rights.[3]

But by 1886, the basic interpretation was reversed in favor of corporate power. In that year, Zinn notes, the Supreme Court overturned 230 state laws regulating corporations. Corporations became full-fledged, fully-protected "persons." Though they had to obtain their "birth certificates" from the state, they were from thence forward immortal. Between 1890-1910, of the 14th Amendment cases brought to the Supreme Court, only 19 dealt with blacks compared to 288 with corporations. The era of great trusts and combinations—permanent, large-scale corporate concentrations—was solidly underway.[4]

Capitalism thus had evolved from agrarian free enterprise to high levels of oligopoly, a condition of economic concentration where today four or fewer firms control more than half the market in sectors ranging from breakfast foods to oil. Oligopolies control 99 percent of the auto industry, 96 percent of aluminum, 92 percent of light bulbs, 93 percent of steam engines, 90 percent of breakfast foods.[5] While there are two million private firms in America, real power rests in relatively few. The existing competitive sector of genuine entrepreneurs and farmers has little weight alongside the major corporate and financial entities. The early capitalism, in which large numbers of people owned property, in which consumers directly faced sellers, in which there was a kind of economic democracy, was replaced by an impersonal corporatism beyond the structural control of the consumer or voter.

The Rise of Reform

From the 1880s to the New Deal, several remedies arose to check this growth of corporate power: 1) shareholders power, 2) anti-trust laws, 3) regulatory bodies, and 4) labor and collective bargaining laws. Though not without significant effects, these tools achieved far less than the "countervailing power" to big business sometimes attributed to them.

"People's capitalism" has become an empty phrase. The shareholder constituency is itself narrow and unrepresentative.

While there are 25 million Americans who hold some shares in the corporate world, studies in the 1960s concluded that only 1 percent of all shareholders held 72 percent of all corporate stock. Shareholders have not served as an effective check on the private powers of management. One 1973 study showed that 99.7 percent of corporate elections were uncontested.[6]

Nor has the anti-trust remedy been particularly effective. This tool is invoked only *after* a suspected "combination in restraint of trade" has been formed. The solar energy industry, for example, would have to be largely absorbed by a conspiracy of oil companies before the Justice Department could investigate what happened to it. These after-the-fact cases are time-consuming, often requiring as much as a decade to complete. Penalties are usually not significant enough to deter the conspiracy. Moreover, court interpretations have watered down anti-trust law to require that the restraint of trade be "unreasonable." Beyond these deficiencies, a root cause of the failure of anti-trust laws is that they only react to and attempt to contain a powerful, inevitable, and legally-blessed dynamic of competition which defines success as winning control of a market. Anti-trust can be only a weak prophylactic in this context, for as Adam Smith himself commented about businessmen, they "seldom meet together, whether for merriment and diversion, but the conversation ends up in a conspiracy against the public, or in some contrivance to raise prices."[7]

Neither has regulatory law served to significantly check business power. A 1970s study showed a revolving-door intimacy between regulators and regulated, with 350 officials of agencies having roots in the industry they are charged with regulating in the public interest. One hundred officials from chemical or drug companies, for instance, were deciding what drugs to sell and what chemicals to put in food.[8] The deeper problem with regulatory approaches, like anti-trust law, is that they serve as a defensive, reactive containing mechanism while leaving the basic thrust of corporate power intact. The close connection between regulators and regulated grows from the fact that few from outside industry have the "expertise" needed to regulate and stabilize behavior while keeping the underlying profit-hunger fed and investor confidence stroked.

The power of labor unions to offset corporate power is much

exaggerated. Unions can be contributors to monopoly and inflation in the private sector, particularly in concentrated industries,
but there is no "Big Labor" compared with the reality of Big
Business. In the first place, only 20 percent of the work force
belongs to unions, and the percentage has been declining for 30
years. In the second place, chronic unemployment lines have
served to make labor cautious at the bargaining table. But in a
more fundamental sense, union power is nowhere in America
legitimized as co-equal with management. Union power is not over
production and investment decisions, but principally over wages
and benefits. In the political sphere, only a few unionists have ever
been elected to the Congress and none to the White House,
echelons of political power frequently and consistently filled by
the rich.

In short, the traditional mechanisms thought to "balance"
corporate power have largely failed. In fact, these regulatory and
labor law "remedies" have helped influence the large corporations
to become *global* institutions, a development that quite literally
gives them powers beyond the law, beyond democratic review and
control, beyond the authority of the nation-state itself.

The Power of the Multinationals

In 1978, in a meeting with President Carter about economic
development issues, I voiced the opinion that the elected President
was not as powerful as the executives of global corporations whose
names we do not know and whom we do not elect. To my surprise,
President Carter interrupted to comment, "I agree with you, I
learned that my first year in office."

The extent of multinational power has been well documented
in such works as *Global Reach*, by Richard Barnet and Ronald
Mueller. The profit motive lies behind their departure from this
country with its minimum wage laws, environmental requirements
and the like; they find areas like South Korea charming because,
in the words of Motorola's president, the young women "will
work harder for less."[9] The reasons this "cheap labor" doesn't
organize and fight for better conditions and higher wages go un-
stated though they are clear to see and we'll discuss them further
later. First, our foreign policy provides the military equipment and
training to keep foreign regimes who deny the rights of labor in

power. In a crisis we'll even send in the Marines to defend these governments, and thus to indirectly defend corporate interests in cheap labor and resources (as for example in 1965 when the Marines went to the Dominican Republic). Second, international inequalities of wealth are so great that in many Third World countries, horribly underpaid and dangerous work is still better than the only immediate alternative, no work or income at all. As a result of these factors, jobs tend to be lost to cheap labor markets abroad; capital is exported as well, with U.S. banks increasing their overseas assets 16 times between 1967-75; technology also is exported, then used to make foreign branches of U.S. companies competitive with domestic firms; several billion in U.S. corporate taxes find their way into foreign treasuries because of tax and tariff arrangements. But more important, from the viewpoint of a democratic society, *power itself is exported to a global level.* As a result of these factors, "By 1990 more than 60 percent of the free world's output will be produced by just 300 firms, about 150 of them American multinationals."[10]

"The viability of life itself," in the phrase of New York Times reporter Leonard Silk, may depend on these private, profit-oriented decisions made without the knowledge of the American people or government representatives.[11] This trend to internationalized private power, it should be stressed, has not been caused by any inevitable economic trends, but has been a *conscious* decision by American bankers and corporate executives wanting ever greater private latitude in making decisions that affect the whole world. As a *Business Week* article points out, "the Eurocurrency markets were the result of an end-run by the private markets around government controls."[11]

The rise of the multinationals also raises profound questions about the nation-state and the meaning of patriotism. There are numerous cases where global firms have evidenced a higher interest in currency than country. An early, shocking and little-known example is that of International Telephone and Telegraph (ITT) during the second World War. In their German plants, ITT produced Focke-Wolf bombers to attack American convoys at sea. In their American plants at the same time, ITT produced frequency direction finders to protect those very same convoys. Then after the war, ITT collected $27 million in compensation from the U.S. government for war damage to its German factories. A similar behavior pattern was true of General Motors, Ford and Exxon, who produced fuel and military vehicles for the Nazi war machine.[13]

The Middle East energy and petrodollar crises combine to create a potential breeding ground for the conflict between America's corporate and national interests. The revelation on "60 Minutes" in May 1980 that Henry Kissinger had encouraged the Shah of Iran to raise OPEC oil prices massively in 1974 to obtain dollars to buy U.S weapons; the willingness of Exxon to provide Saudi Arabia with the information necessary for an Arab boycott of the U.S. military during the 1973 Yom Kippur war; the promotion of the Arab cause against Israel by Standard Oil of California for its narrow oil interests; the cooperation by many American companies in the anti-Israel boycott required of them for doing business with Arab states; the 1980 Mobil ads urging censorship of a film criticizing corruption in Saudi Arabia; and finally, the scandalous registration of Billy Carter as an agent of Libya: all of these are only specific examples of the way corporate economic needs can effect Mideast policies that affect the interests of a majority of Americans.

Unlike the era when America was the world's banker—roughly 1945 to 1971—the interests of international finance are most often quite different than the interests of American workers and consumers. In late 1979, for example, President Carter directed Paul Volcker, the head of the Federal Reserve System, to take steps leading to increased interest rates, which in turn would intentionally bring about a recession or worse. The devastating consequences for Americans in terms of inflation and unemployment are obvious, and it can be seriously questioned whether such economic ruin is a moral or practical answer to runaway inflation. But the point worth pursuing here is the *international*, rather than domestic, reasons for the Carter-Volcker move. America's allies, particularly West Germany, were plainly becoming impatient at holding large amounts of U.S. dollars which were losing value steadily because of American inflation and energy crises. The allies were not going to accept this burden unless America took drastic steps to slow down its inflation and thus stabilize the value of the dollar. An analysis of this dispute by the

English economist Andrew Shonfield appeared in the January 1980 issue of *Foreign Affairs,* widely perceived as the journal of the traditional American foreign policy establishment. Shonfield's article subtly indicates that the Carter-Volcker interest rate policies were carried out against the immediate interests of the American people in order to reassure the Europeans. U.S. economic expansion (and inflation) "had to be *publicly and unmistakeably decapitated.*" It is worth understanding Shonfield's complicated analysis at length.

> The dollar's recovery in foreign exchange markets thus became dependent on the belief that the series of measures taken by the U.S. authorities, culminating in the Volcker package, could be relied upon to push the United States into a recession... The form of the final deflationary squeeze and the degree of its severity were imposed by external forces...
>
> The monetary relationship between the United States and "foreigners" was, predictably, a great deal more complex than this simplified version of events suggests...
>
> It should be noted that although there is a tendency to talk of "foreigners" and "international speculation," those concerned frequently included quite a lot of Americans, taking what they regarded as rational precautionary measures in converting a part of their portfolios of assets into foreign currencies.[14]

America: Imperialist or Colonized?

Volcker's "decapitation" of the American economy was only the most damaging of a series of events that question whether the American people still possess sovereign control of their destiny. Throughout the 1970s, to take another example, Americans read of a rising tide of "foreign investment" in their basic resources and institutions. Tens of thousands of acres of California's agricultural land were sold to foreign interests; similar speculative deals elsewhere led to several state laws banning foreign ownership of farm land. The downtown skyscrapers of many cities, including those of Los Angeles, passed into foreign hands. A banking consortium that would allow Saudi Arabia's former intelligence chief a direct look into the inner world of American banking was created. Shopping centers, malls and residential housing became targets of foreign speculators. The community of Beverly Hills, it was said with sarcasm, had become a suburb of Teheran.

Foreign Direct Investment in the United States
1954-1977

Source: *Financial Invasion.*

What was less apparent was that the "foreign intrusion" was carried out with the direct involvement of *American* banks, developers and real estate agents, and with support from certain U.S. tax preferences not even accessible to American citizens. U.S. Senate Foreign Relation Committee hearings in 1976 documented the long-term ties of American banks to oil-producing Middle Eastern nations. The hearings showed that far from being secondary clients of the banks, the OPEC countries had come to have serious influence on certain of their decisions. Of $14.5 billion that came from the Middle Eastern OPEC nations in 1976, nearly 80 percent of it was concentrated in only six banks: Bank of America, Citibank, Chase Manhattan, Manufacturers Hanover, Morgan Guaranty, and Chemical Bank (there are, incidentally, 14,000 banks in the U.S. altogether). According to journalist Kenneth Crowe, "half of the funds in the six superbanks were in highly volatile short-term deposits payable in less than thirty days."[15] Billions of dollars, not simply from the Middle East, were being reinvested in the U.S. because of the lucrative advantages created by the U.S. Congress: tax shelters in the Nederland Antilles, for instance, not only insured absolute privacy to the investors but an exemption on capital gains taxes, a privilege not available to *domestic* American speculators. The result of all this was an economy dangerously dependent on international economic decisions, made either by the multinations, OPEC or the European banks, an economy absorbing the inflationary impact of foreign mega-dollars little concerned with supply-and-demand, an economy being sold out from under the feet of the American people. Imperial economic maneuvering on the *global* level by American banks and corporations was beginning to create a more dependent, increasingly "colonized" *domestic* economic order in America.

Political Democracy Vs. Private Economic Power

"We have reached a point in the country where in a standdown between a giant multinational corporation and the government, the government would have to withdraw," the late Senator Philip Hart told a Senate hearing several years ago.[16]

While the idea of private property has developed into a reality of global monopoly, at the same time the idea of democracy has continued to expand in a broader, more inclusive direction, further and further into spheres which once were considered private and sacrosanct. The American people have very nearly achieved a *political* democracy. Discrimination against women and most minorities at the polls has been abolished. Property ownership as a qualification for voting no longer exists. Younger voters have been enfranchised. In many policy areas, citizen participation is required by law. The progression has been reflected in new laws, but also in a growing consciousness of the "right" of people to be ever more involved in decisions affecting their lives. "A new idea has begun to rule America," says one authority, "the idea that no group or authority has a special claim to understanding, power, or influence."[17]

Therefore, from an early conception of compatibility based on both widespread property ownership and suffrage, capitalism —in its fully-developed corporate form—and democracy have now developed to a point where they begin to represent diametric opposites of private and public power. Many leading businessmen recognize the tension in exactly these terms, and are prepared to diminish or forego democracy in order to retain their private prerogatives. They "have begun to fear that capitalism and democracy may be incompatible in the long-run," according to N.Y. *Times* business writer Leonard Silk.[18] Reporting on a private 1974 seminar of the exclusive Business Roundtable, Silk found considerable sympathy for the executive who asked, "Can we still afford one man, one vote?" Many businessmen present, Silk wrote, remain unreconstructed Hamiltonians, believers "in government by an establishment of the informed, the propertied and the responsible."[19] (No less a corporate representative than Texas' John Connally echoed this view of businessmen as elitists in 1979 when he called 90 percent of them "mediocre, pompous, narrow, stupid neanderthals"—he later changed the figure from 90 percent to "most").[20]

Energy and the Corporate Crisis

An age of energy shortages and lessened U.S. power in the world means America is facing its first distribution crisis without an abundant frontier to turn to for the magic solution of new wealth. Under these conditions there is certain to be an intensified pressure for a business authoritarianism to replace democracy in America.

The threat is even totalitarian. The evidence is the oil industry. The finest student of the oil monopoly, John Blair, has documented how the original oil families, like the Rockefellers and Mellons, obtained nearly 25 percent of the privately-owned land in the country, created the oil industry, and diversified their power and income through the "greater petroleum economy" as a whole.[21] The successors to the old Standard Oil Trust, broken up in 1911—Exxon, Mobil, Standard of Indiana and SoCal—today control 32 percent of domestic reserves, 31 percent of domestic refining capacity, and make 26 percent of all retail gasoline sales, according to Blair's study in the mid-1970s. Nearly two-thirds of U.S. reserves are held by the eight largest firms, and over one-third by the four largest. "In a period of diminishing supplies," Blair says, this hold on reserves will be the "critical determinant" in bringing about even greater concentration of power. Moreover, six of the eight largest oil companies were interlocked in 1972 "through large commercial banks with at least one other member of the top group," so "when the Bank of America holds its board meetings, for example, directors of the three leading oil producers in the Far West (SoCal, Union, and Getty) sit down together." And if that is not enough, "further cohesiveness is provided by Western Bancorporation, whose board meetings provide a handy occasion for directors of SoCal and Union to meet together."[22]

The petroleum industry now accounts for a fifth of the entire capital investment of the country.[23] It is also the most capital-intensive of all manufacturing industries.[24] Oil companies today absorb one out of every six dollars in profits earned by all manufacturing concerns, up from one out of $13.67 just 14 years ago.[25]

On the day it was announced that consumer prices had risen faster in 1979 than in 33 previous years, Exxon was reporting a 55 percent profit increase to a record $4.2 billion. The giant's gross revenues increased 30 percent to $84 billion, "more than the gross national product of Sweden, for example, and much more than any other business had ever reported for a single year."[26] With profits such as these, Sen. Edward Kennedy has said, Exxon "could tomorrow buy J. C. Penney, DuPont, Goodyear, and Anheuser-Busch using only its accumulated cash and liquid assets."[27] With their capital, Exxon and other oil companies chose to invade their potential competitors, taking over 44 percent of the leased coal reserves and 51 percent of the nation's uranium reserves.[28] Controlling the conventional sources of energy more or less securely, they have conducted what Blair calls a "vigorous invasion" of the chemical industry, with 11 of the top 30 sellers of chemicals in the sixties being taken over by oil companies, including Standard of New Jersey, Occidental, Shell, Phillips and

Mobil.[29] "Exxon's Next Prey," according to a *Business Week* cover will be IBM and Xerox, the key to the information technology of the future.[30]

What is crucial about seizing the chemical industry is the universal role that petrochemicals play in American life after only 35 years of rapid development. Barry Commoner explains the reason for this lies in petrochemicals being a process industry, backed by enormous capital, thus able to devour other sectors of the economy by inventing cheap substitutes for everything. Petrochemicals have been the fastest growing sector of manufacturing since the second World War, growing at an annual rate of about 8 percent, twice that of manufacturing as a whole. In a classic passage of ecological analysis, Commoner cites the results:

> Detergents have driven soap out of a market that it monopolized for perhaps a thousand years; in textiles, synthetic fibers have massively displaced cotton and wool; plastics have replaced long-established uses of metals, wood and glass; food production has become heavily dependent on fertilizers, pesticides and other agricultural chemicals; synthetic drugs and toiletries have become a major enterprise in an area of commerce once represented by concoctions of herbs."[31]

Thus, the power of oil families has branched out to take over industry which has in turn devoured its competitors, consumed the greatest portion of American capital, made this country dependent on capital-intensive, high-technology sources of energy which it controls, and spread from there to dominate the basic processes by which food is grown, clothes produced, homes are built, health care is given, and—in the near future, communications are handled—bringing about the absorption of American society as a whole, for in Monsanto's advertising message, "Without chemicals, life itself would be impossible."

The ultimate in this totalitarian process appears to be the growing field of bioengineering, the artificial production of altered or new forms of life itself. Industry enthusiasts have declared that "biology will replace chemistry in importance in this country" by the year 2000.[32] As fossil fuels decline, industry is gearing up to genetically-engineer new compounds to supply the economy "with alternatives to oil-derived chemicals for making fertilizers, plastics, wash-and-wear clothes, pesticides, dyes, paints, and tens of thousands of other products." [33] Six of nine corporate sponsors of the National Academy of Science's initial conference on recombinant DNA and genetic engineering were pharmaceutical firms [34] and behind their enthusiasm was Standard Oil, which had declared bioengineering to be "the growth industry of the future." [35]

As with other technical advances of history, the re-assembly of our genetic structure is being heralded as a scientific solution to problems which have eluded human solutions—the elimination of hereditary disease, creation of new agricultural productivity, new ways of increasing the energy yield from biomass, in short, a possibility of overcoming the spectre of material scarcity via a technical fix. Major corporations now have received a patent right on the "creation of new life forms," an ironic next chapter in the history of a social contract that began with the public conferring "immortal" status on the corporation. The point is not to question "scientific progress" but to assert the public interest over private opportunities in this vital new field. Although the danger now seems remote, it will not be long before the oil-petrochemical-pharmaceutical "complex" has begun to profit from this new frontier of behavior modification, "solving" the energy crisis by biological substitutes for chemical products, and coming to control the evolution of the environment and life itself, all for narrow material gain.

All this means a grim threat to a democratic society and culture. An October 1974 *Business Week* editorial hinted at the "challenge" an era of energy limits would pose to democracy. Recognizing that "it is inevitable that the US economy will grow more slowly than is has," *Business Week* pondered on the consequences for a growth-oriented capitalism. Where would the necessary capital come from in a period of stagnation and decline? "Some people will obviously have to do with less," they concluded. Would the sacrifices come from the rich? No, "cities and states, the home mortgage market, small business and the consumer will all get less than they want... it will be a hard pill for many Americans to swallow, the idea of doing with less so that big business can have more." [36]

The political implications of a reduction of the majority's standard of living were not spelled out in detail, but the editors speculated on "totalitarianism" replacing democracy since "nothing that this nation, or any nation, has done in modern history compares with the selling job that must now be done to make people really accept the new reality." Since no people in history have *voluntarily* reduced their living standard, the new austerity will have to be imposed from above by a government committed to protecting the privileges of a few.

The Permanent Corporation

The energy crisis and "era of limits" are fueling this trend, but the seeds of a Corporate State are already inherent in the workings of the political economy. Since the free enterprise world of thousands of competing companies has been replaced by oligopoly, the government can hardly allow large corporations to fail. When Lockheed or Chrysler or Franklin National Bank face collapse, the economic well-being of thousands of workers, pensioners and depositors, and that of many regions of America, are so threatened that bail-outs and subsidies—"welfare for the rich"—are virtually guaranteed. The government "is compelled," according to one corporate analysis, "to shape national policy in terms of protecting the great corporations instead of letting the economy make deflationary adjustments."[37]

If government cannot let large business fail, however inefficient it is, neither does it exert much influence over investment decisions. This permits the corporations the key initiative in determining plant and job location, and plunges local and state governments into a supplicant role of making the fewest possible regulatory demands in order to keep businesses from leaving their locale. In this competitive game, the "winners" are often the regions most willing to sacrifice their workers' wages and community environments for the sake of corporate investment. The cities of the Northeast, for example, have been more receptive to New Deal liberalism, trade unionism and civil rights than the former states of the Confederacy. As a result, for several decades blacks (and Puerto Ricans) have migrated to cities like New York in search of economic opportunity, or at least a welfare income. At the same time, corporations have moved South in search of cheap (non-union) labor. Nothing illustrates how underlying economic "rationality" leads to negative public consequences: unemployment, declining tax bases, and reduced services go to liberal New York while jobs and investment go to the conservative Carolinas. Corporate investment decisions made primarily on the basis of profit are more powerful than government decisions made on the basis of social responsibility.

The government, being more directly responsive to the voting public than is the private sector, gradually comes to represent rights, justice, better living conditions, demands which in various ways impinge on corporate privilege and freedom. The resulting conflict between private capital and public demand must never preclude sufficient profit going to the private sector to guarantee the continued investment that makes the economic engine go. But in a time of limits, the rising public demands on the state create an increasing threat to the accumulation and investment potential of the private sector, forcing that sector to make economic war on the government for the maintenance of profits and continued growth. In such a time of limits on expansion as we now seem to be entering, *the corporations will tend to absorb and become the state.*

The trend towards greater corporate political power has been quite apparent in the 1970s. "The danger," say Silk and Vogel in *Ethics and Profits,* is that corporations "may seek to corrupt and capture the powers of government and transfigure national values and institutions to serve corporate interests."[38] Even the editorial writers of the New York *Times,* in a *pre*-Watergate 1972 opinion entitled "The Corporate State," argued that "the over-riding issue is how to prevent powerful special interests from frustrating the democratic process."[39] During the past decade there were 15,000 corporate lobbyists employed in Washington alone, and corporations made a *one thousand* percent increase in their total campaign budgets across the country.[40] An analysis of political contributions to the November 1976 general elections in California by the state's Fair Political Practices Commission, showed the following breakdown: corporate interests 68 percent, labor 17 percent, miscellaneous 15 percent. Business interests contributed between 75 and 80 percent of the money spent in political campaigns in California. In 1976 dollars, that worked out to *$250,000 per legislator* by business on the average.[41]

Not only do corporations today dominate the political process, corporate plans call for an *increase* of political efforts in the coming years. As the March 27, 1978 issue of *Fortune* trumpeted, "the business community has become the most effective special-interest lobby in the country... Suddenly, business seems to possess all the primary instruments of power—the leadership, the strategy, the supporting troops, the campaign money—and a new will to use them. Business has poured money and resources into Washington on an unprecedented scale." *Fortune* noted that the Chamber of Commerce had formed 2,300 "Congressional Action Committees," each made up of about 30 businessmen who personally know and lobby their members of the Senate and House.[42]

An Inventory of Corporate Abuse

Let us pause to briefly catalog what further corporate power over our lives would mean. The following list of negatives is not meant to erase or deny the many achievements of corporations which are positive. Rather, the list is intended to show the comprehensive, systemic effects of corporate behavior guided only by profit imperatives. *It is not a mere "abuse of power" which has to be corrected; the abuse lies in the nature of the power itself.*

1. *Further centralization.* A 1978 U.S. Senate staff study of 130 large firms discovered that Exxon was linked through its board of directors with more than half—74—on the list. The ten largest American industrial firms now employ about 16 percent of the workforce and possess 23 percent of the profits.[43] David Ewing dramatizes the growth of corporate power with an analogy to our history: AT&T has 939,000 employees, twice the size of Virginia, which was the largest American colony; moreover, 125 corporations have larger "populations" than Delaware, the smallest colony, in 1776.[44] The trend toward concentration is increasing; between 1948 and 1968, the largest 200 industrial corporations increased their share of industrial assets by 25 percent, and between 1955 and 1970, the percentage of workers employed by the *Fortune* 500 rose from 44.5 percent to 72 percent.[45]

2. *Income Distribution.* "The real threat to capitalism,"

Father Theodore Hesburgh, president of Notre Dame has written, "is the maldistribution of wealth across the globe. We cannot hope for world peace when 20 percent of the people in the world have 80 percent of the goods."[46] At home, nearly fifty years after the New Deal began, there has been little change in the comparative positions of haves and have-nots. The top 5 percent of all Americans hold 55 percent of the net private wealth, while the "bottom majority" of 60 percent get only 7.5 percent. The poorest one-fifth of Americans earn 3.7 percent of the national income, while the top one-fifth make 47.9 percent. The top one percent earn 10.5 percent of total income, just 51 times the per capita income of the poorest fifth.[47]

Corporate After-Tax Profits

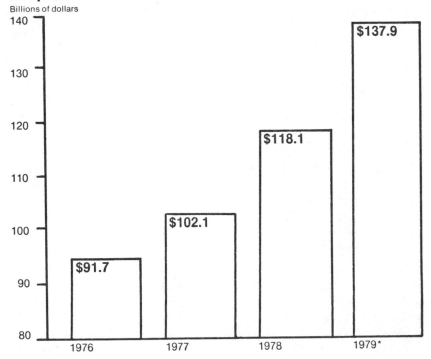

*First quarter annual rate.

Source: Commerce Department. Bureau of Economic Analysis.

3. *Loss of Jobs.* Since Henry Ford declared to his workers 50 years ago, "behave yourselves or we will go elsewhere,"[48] American capital has tended to move towards the cheapest labor markets available. The AFL-CIO estimates that over 1 million jobs were exported abroad between the years 1966-71 alone.[49] In California, a single corporate decision to invest $40 billion over 20 years in Indonesian and Alaskan Liquified Natural Gas (LNG) would produce only 42,000 California jobs; on the other hand, according to one study, a similar investment in residential solar energy would have created over three million California jobs.[50] Overseas profits are extremely attractive. More than two-thirds of the *Fortune* 500 companies derive 25 percent or more of their sales and profits from the operation of overseas subsidiaries and affiliates, with giants like Ford, IBM, and Citibank deriving half or more from foreign branches.[51]

4. *Inflation.* In May 1980, the U.S. Department of Agriculture announced that consumers were paying $16 billion a year more for food because of industry monopoly. The overcharging, they said, was due to profiteering and pass-ons of advertising costs to consumers. The Department's chief economist, Howard W. Hjort, reported that "pure competition is diminishing and oligopolies more prevalent," a situation which had been "increasing steadily for three decades."[52]

Prices have been rising in all the basic necessities—food, housing, medical care, energy—nearly twice as fast as the general inflation rate, according to the Exploratory Project of Economic Alternatives. This indicates that *inflation is profitable* for agribusiness, real estate groups, the medical lobby, and the energy conglomerates. Moreover, the existence of concentrated power can frustrate traditional Keynesian means of controlling inflation through higher interest rates and reduced government spending. Instead of reducing demand and "pulling" prices down, these inflation-fighting measures had little or no effect on monopoly prices in the 1970s. Instead, while monopoly prices remained high, unemployment also rose, creating a simultaneous inflation and recession given the name "stagflation."

5. *Declining technology and productivity.* American industry has become stagnant. One reason is that natural and human resources needed for technical breakthroughs and higher produc-

Price Increases for Oil, Gas and Coal
1965 to 1978

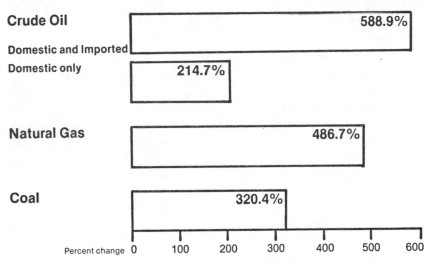

Crude Oil

Domestic and Imported — 588.9%

Domestic only — 214.7%

Natural Gas — 486.7%

Coal — 320.4%

Percent change: 0   100   200   300   400   500   600

Source: DOE Monthly Review, API Basic Petroleum Data Book, and EEI Statistical Yearbook of the Electrical Utility Industry.

tivity have been assigned to the military rather than civilian sectors of the economy. Another reason is that inefficient or backward industries like steel are powerful enough to harvest government subsidies that keep them in business while doing nothing to increase innovation. Shamefully, America now has to import the high-technology goods which are the key to innovations. Imports of chemicals rose 80 percent in the 1960s, non-electrical machinery 600 percent, electrical equipment 700 percent, transport equipment 680 percent. In the steel industry, nearly 20 percent is imported from abroad. In civilian electronics the percentages are even higher: 100 percent of our tape recorders, 35 percent of our TV sets. Key technological sectors face chronic problems of neglect. Telephone service is worsening. There are shortages of engineers for power plants. Our crumbling railroad system permits a top speed of 70 miles per hour from St. Louis to Chicago, while the Japanese and French are running trains at 250 miles per hour.[57]

New technologies, like solar photovoltaic cells created in the American space program, are being commercialized more rapidly in Europe and Japan than in the United States.

6. *Discrimination*. Inequality of opportunity and income has changed little in the past decade of affirmative action programs. Minority unemployment is nearly twice that of whites. Black males earn 69 percent of the wages of white males, while female workers earn less than 60 percent of the wage of their male counterparts.[54]

7. *Pollution*. Between 1946-71, the levels of industrial pollution rose by as much as 2000 percent, though volume of production grew only by 126 percent.[55] Industry creates one-third of all solid waste matter, one-half of air pollution and more than half of water pollution. The Environmental Protection Agency estimated that health and property damage from these sources in 1977 was $23 billion, the total budget of the State of California.

8. *Cancer and other health hazards*. The World Health Organization and National Cancer Institute estimate that 80-90 percent of human cancer is from the environment surrounding us. The percentage of Americans dying from cancer—one in 25 in 1900, one in five today—can only be explained by the emergence of the petrochemical age.[56] In addition, there are over 100,000 annual deaths from occupation-related disease.[57]

9. *Product safety*. DC-10's, Pintos and Firestone Radials are only the visible symptons of a system in which drug company over-prescriptions kill more than 60,000 people per year; cosmetics alone injure 60,000; and product-related accidents kill as many as 30,000, permanently injure 110,000, hospitalize 500,000 and force 20 million to seek medical treatment.[58]

10. *White collar crime*. Sixty percent of the 582 largest publicly-owned corporations have cases being pressed against them by federal agencies. Five hundred firms, including one-third of the *Fortune* 500, have acknowledged overseas bribery in the amount of $1 billion.[59] A record 100 grand juries are now looking into price-fixing conspiracies. Corporate cover-ups—for example, Johns-Manville's burying of reports on asbestos hazards, Hooker Chemical's concealment of dumping poison in the Love Canal, Occidental's secret poisoning of California wells—are apparently routine. The cost of all this corporate crime according to the Joint Economic Committee in 1976, was $44 billion to consumers.[60] The

health and environmental costs are more difficult to measure—
how much does it cost to take care of the victims of industrial
cancer? Can it be measured in dollars at all?

11. *Immorality.* "At Carthage, nothing which results in
profits is regarded as disgraceful," Polybius wrote centuries ago.
A more recent observation, by Professor Archie Carroll of the
University of Georgia, is that three-fifths of executives admit they
would commit unethical acts to prove loyalty to their seniors.[61]

12. *Manipulation.* The average person watches 40,000 commercials on television per year, each of which fabricates, distorts
or tantalizes rather than conveying information from a primarily
pro-consumer viewpoint. The 100 top national advertisers spent
$3.6 billion on commercials in 1974; if they had not, their sales in
all probability would have fallen. One study of fourteen industries
indicates that such lying is profitable: if advertisements were
limited to just 3 percent of sales revenue, their aggregate sales
would drop by 16.7 percent.[62]

13. *Decline in community and neighborhood quality.* Several
studies, including a comparison of the California towns of Arvin
and Dinuba in the 1940s, show that Big Business tends to depress
the level of civic welfare while small business tends to raise it, as
measured by unemployment, suburban sprawl, income distribution, home ownership, number of libraries, and per capita
spending for schools.[63]

These disquieting tendencies, some will say, are not the whole
story of corporate behavior. Of course thay are right. But the
defenders of corporate power are in danger of misunderstanding
the sum total of the "abuses," which taken together have a profoundly damaging effect on the whole society. And the defenders
fail to realize that the negatives will rapidly worsen in an era of
limits, at some point transforming the totality of abuses into a
general breakdown of society as we know it. Silk and Vogel
describe the coming danger this way: "Hard times, somewhat
paradoxically, *drive business to the right*—make it more hostile to
government social programs, more determined in the face of the
threat of economic breakdown and political hostility from the
rest of the population to preserve its own prerogatiaves and
autonomy."[64]

The Need for Alternatives

This bleak future cannot be avoided by anything less than a new vision at the center of our lives. We need a debate as historic, thoughtful and emotional as those which preceded the War of Independence and the Constitution, the Civil War and the end to slavery, the right of all people to vote, and the New Deal.

The choice is stark. The perpetuation of unbridled corporate power will destroy democracy. The long struggle for political democracy must now be broadened until the commanding heights of the corporations are scaled and entered by the citizens of this country. We must travel the road which led to political democracy even further, to economic democracy.

To clear away stereotypes, let us briefly define three common economic models—the New Deal (or corporate liberalism), socialism , and traditional free enterprise—to identify where they fail and where a new economic arrangement must begin.

The Death of the New Deal

The *New Deal* was based on government intervention in the economy to protect workers, small business and the elderly from chaos and suffering. While it broke the philosophical sanctity of the "free market," the New Deal did not re-arrange the *internal* structure of corporations. The crucial idea was the stimulation of demand which was thought to spark growth. The hidden, unquestioned assumption was that of perpetual abundance; from growth a surplus would be generated from which to redistribute revenue "downward" to the poor and helpless. The magic in the theory was that there were ultimately no losers.

But there was a major shortcoming in the New Deal that few noticed in the post-World War II economic euphoria. The New Deal did not end unemployment; World War II did. And victory in the war gave rise to an unparalleled set of new conditions that created a generation of prosperity: a burst of pent-up consumer demand after 1945, the emergence of American economic supremacy in the world, the availability of cheap energy, new industries (like aluminum) created by government investment, and so forth. These factors were in fact responsible for the achievements often credited to the theories of Keynes or programs of Roosevelt.

Now those underlying conditions have changed. No longer is it possible to spend for welfare, schools, freeways *and* tanks out of a rising national income. The crucial economic fact of the 1960's was that real buying power increased every year and, in 1969, average gross weekly earnings were 15 percent *higher* than in 1960 in constant dollars. By contrast, according to Michael Harrington, the real buying power of industrial workers in 1977 was $5 a week less than 1973—"and even a bit less than in 1969."[65] When real income levels off, harder choices between priorities become necessary. Where government fails to make those choices, citizens will take matters into their own hands. Proposition 13, the 1978 tax-reduction initiative in California, was very much a case of populist anger at expensive, bureaucratic government which was forcing the middle class to pay for welfare out of declining real income, and at the risk of losing their own homes due to rising property taxes. Proposition 13 represented the death knell of New Deal liberalism. Of course, certain liberals denied their ideological fate by criticising Californians for being "selfish." John Kenneth Galbraith called Proposition 13 "a revolt of the rich against the poor." On one level, he was right: the largest property-owning corporations were the greatest beneficiaries, receiving a $4 billion windfall out of the total $7 billion in tax relief. But the driving force behind 13, which brought support from virtually every constituency (public employees and renters voted for it by clear majorities, and 45 percent of blacks did as well), was the outcry against a tax burden which had become unbearable for working people and homeowners.

With the passage of Proposition 13, New Deal economics began to unravel. The first lesson to be drawn was that the tacit marriage between corporations and government was no longer working. Corporations, acting on their profit interests, were paying less in taxes to federal and state treasuries every year. Nationally, while welfare costs rose due to declining jobs in the private sector, the burden of paying was shifted from the corporations to the individual taxpayers; from 1960 to 1974 individual taxes rose from $41 billion to $119 billion, four times more than corporate taxes, which increased from $22 billion to $39 billion.[66] Hoping that a lowered burden would stimulate investment and jobs, the Federal government reduced its tax contribution from corporations from 23.2 percent to 13.8 percent of the US budget between the years 1960 and 1975.[67]

The tacit harmony underlying corporate liberalism was becoming a simmering conflict. When public interest groups and state officials called upon corporations to reinvest their Proposition 13 tax savings in California jobs, they were met by indifference and sometimes hostility. As much as $4 billion had just been removed from the state treasury by corporations under the spurious banner of "saving the American home." The effects were cushioned in the short-run by a bail-out from the state's accumulated surplus. However, by the early 1980s, California will be faced with three probable choices: a) to suffer the loss of $4 billion in services plus massive unemployment, b) increase other personal taxes by twofold to make up the difference, or c) recover the business windfall or raise corporate taxes, perhaps by repealing the application of Proposition 13 to sizeable corporate property holdings. A battle is shaping up over the question of starving the public sector or imposing more taxes and controls on the corporate sector. Whatever the outcome, a drastically-reduced state or a redirected corporation, the new "social contract" will go beyond the New Deal.

In addition to the strain imposed on New Deal *economics* by the era of limits, there is a further problem inherent in the New Deal *structure* as a model for the future of government. There is a legitimate public fear of more government bureaucracy controlling their lives. The modern state, as it has evolved for 40 years, has evidenced a bureaucratic, impersonal, expansionist character as serious in its own way as the problem of corporate monopoly is for "free enterprise" enthusiasts. The national government's budget has increased sevenfold since 1960, and shows little tendency to slow down. Granted, the reason for this cannot be entirely attributed to government; corporate domination, for example, leads to mounting payments for unemployment insurance, health care, and military defense, and the sheer complexity of modern society itself creates a mushrooming, overlapping jungle of communication and administration problems in political capitals. However, liberals and progressives cannot let themselves become ardent apologists for Big Government as if the 1980s were the early period of the New Deal.

There seems to be a problem inherent in the State itself. The existence of democratic elections does not guarantee that the office holders who are chosen will be accountable to either voters or platform. The primacy in democratic theory of office holders over the unelected permanent bureaucracy often works out the other way in practice: elected officials come and go, but Washington is forever. Furthermore, the incentives in the public sector for power and expansion, for careerism and conformity, seem as captivating as profit, status and production are in the corporate sector. Perhaps the tendency toward self-perpetuating power is built into any bureaucratic setting, public or private.

But our departure from New Deal liberalism does not imply agreement with the usual conservative critiques of government. The conservatives tend to promote big government in the form of the Pentagon, CIA and FBI while directing their anti-government rhetoric against programs for the poor, the elderly and the disabled. Ultimately and hypocritically, their concept of the state in practice becomes a giant armed fortress protecting the unfettered activities of the corporations.

Nor does our criticism of government bureaucracy imply that the basic problem is size, and that therefore "less government" is the answer to citizen frustration. There is nothing inherently better about less government: feudal states and petty dictatorships are reactionary despite their smallness.

The real questions emerging from the breakdown of the New Deal seem to be how to guarantee more *self-government* while eliminating remote bureaucracy, and how bureaucracies which are necessary can be kept accountable rather than insulated from the public.

Until these issues are faced and resolved by a more decentralized and accountable government structure, it will be difficult to justify expansion of the public sector. What is dangerously likely in the period ahead is a reduction of government services to the victims of corporate society, combined with "socialism for the rich" in the form of increased subsidies, bail-outs and tax breaks for ailing industries. This would be a "New Deal at the top," a bureaucratic and militarized capitalism dependent on the state.

The great achievement of the New Deal was the advancement of the dignity of labor and senior citizens. But in his last message to

Congress, in 1944, President Roosevelt acknowledged that our
"political rights proved inadequate to assure us equality in the pursuit of happiness." He therefore proposed a "second Bill of
Rights," including decent jobs, decent wages, freedom from
monopoly power, a decent home for all, adequate medical care,
good education, and "protection from the economic fears of old
age, sickness, accident and unemployment."

This *economic* Bill of Rights is more needed today than ever.
All Americans should be *entitled* to certain basic economic protections and opportunities. Yet after a generation of New Deal
efforts, there is a growing realization that the institutions and policies associated with Roosevelt are inadequate to achieve his vision.

Perhaps an *economic* Bill of Rights will only be achieved by
ordinary citizens beginning to think of themselves as being responsible for their own economic history, instead of leaving their needs
to be attended by public and private bureaucracies.

The Dilemma of Socialism

Here we come face to face with another possible economic
model, that of *socialism* or central economic planning and state
ownership of major economic assets. Is it desirable and adequate
as an advancement beyond the New Deal? Or is it too in need of
repair and amendment as an ideology and program? I would argue
the latter, without in the least underestimating its significance and
lessons. Certainly an America which freezes the socialist tradition
out of hearing is heading toward narrow-minded isolation in the
world.

One of socialism's historic strengths is its existence as the
only comprehensive critique and alternative to the *system* of capitalism. Socialism at least answers the old question, "what would
you do instead?" Its explanation of corporate capitalism demonstrates conclusively that piecemeal reform, or a little patchwork
here and there, is not enough to solve the problems of inflation,
unemployment or pollution.

In addition, the cooperative ethics of socialism are useful and
adaptable to an age of potentially fierce competition for scarce
resources. And its egalitarian notion of ordinary people being
qualified and capable of making history has been crucial to social

change in the past, and will be more so in the future.

The other lasting advantage of socialism over capitalism is its practical appeal to impoverished, exploited countries seeking some sovereign and collective path to economic development in a world of Western multinationals. It is no accident, given the history of colonialism, that the vast majority of lesser-developed countries in the United Nations incorporate the ideas and language of socialism in their vision rather than the model of Horatio Alger.

However, it is natural that all worthy ideals and programs develop new, often unforeseen problems or contradictions—as perhaps Karl Marx himself would argue. After a century of social-ism, and 60 years of various "socialisms" in power, those new contradictions have become manifestly apparent to all but the most dogmatic elements of the world left. Taken separately, these problems may be (or seem) soluble within the framework of social-ist theory. Taken together, they so strain that framework and its assumptions that one might conclude that socialism has been a meaningful ideology only for a certain historical age—and not for the age we are gradually entering. Seen in this way, socialism should be analyzed as an ideology and tradition by all serious students of social change, but only as a useful introduction to the continuing search for answers.

The first problem is with the "scientific method" of dialec-tical materialism. However reinterpreted, this view has always placed a determining emphasis on the growing material base of society—and its productive system—as opposed to the "super-structure" of consciousness, culture and institutional arrange-ments. For Marxists, class has been the defining factor of history. And yet, in the socialist and anti-colonial revolutions of the 20th century, successful upheavals did not occur in the capitalist nations which were theoretically most "ripe." Instead, the factors of nationalism, culture, and race seemed at least as determining as the economic factor, and where economics were crucial it was the peasantry's grievances against the feudal land barons that were far more decisive than the role of the small industrial working class.

Even today, material conditions alone do not seem to allow accurate predictions of where the next revolution, or next protest movement, will break out. In fact, none of the 20th century social-ist revolutions were predicted to happen before they did. Instead, there has been a zig-zag course from Russia to China to Indochina to Cuba, all "surprises" to most theorists of the time.

There is a further difficulty with class analysis as it applies particularly to the industrialized countries. To be sure, the United States is still more of a class society than most observers admit; the briefest look at income levels, occupational categories, and the economic ties of major office holders would show that. However, the predictive or explanatory power of Marxist class analysis is hampered by its inherent tendencies to dismiss *other* factors as merely "superstructure." Yet in the past generation, millions of Americans have been motivated by race, sex, age, by disability, by moral and religious desires, by consciousness. The superstructure itself, rather than the base, often seems to be the determining or at least operative factor in change. But because of a necessary adherence to materialist dialectics, Left groups have been left out, tending to view such movements as merely "progressive" but not "fundamental" because they did not arise from class factors. Some have tried to fit the new issues into a Marxist framework, trying for example to make the factor of sex as important as the factor of class and to give greater recognition to the importance of consciousness, but the Marxist concepts prove unyielding in the strategic analysis of most socialists.

A second problem with the material model has been a tendency to make the realm of economics a more fundamental focus of thought than politics, the latter again being merely "superstructure." In part, this tendency arises from the history of socialism being rooted in backward countries with minimal, militaristic and dictatorial governments. The key problem was to "overthrow" or "smash" the state. Detailed understanding of its operation was not crucial to success. The state was nothing but "the executive committee of the ruling class." After it was overthrown, a disciplined and victorious communist party would essentially build anew. The new state was then defined as a "worker's state," and therefore responsive because by definition its interests coincided with those of the population.

Later critics, from Trotsky to Milovan Djilas, and more recently Rudolf Bahro, noted with alarm a tendency for the state to mature a new "class," or bureaucracy of its own. Perhaps the most thorough and pertinent of these critics was Antonio Gramsci, the Italian communist of the early 20th century. Gramsci's views, at least as interpreted in modern "Euro-communism," were that the one-party state was too narrow and exclusive to represent the complexity, richness and need for participation of modern Western societies.[68] The method of "smashing" the existing order and building socialism anew could not be appropriate, Gramsci thought, to a society already well-developed and largely democratic. Instead there needed to be a multi-party system, the preservation of voluntary associations, independent trade unions and the like. The problem of the state under socialism was being taken seriously.

But there is more to this issue than can be solved by the existence of multiple parties. The problem of the state as a self-perpetuating bureaucracy remains. Having five parties would not change its character as a mechanism with a life and therefore interests of its own. A theoretical orientation that slights the importance of political dynamics per se won't pay sufficient attention to these facts. But the U.S. public does understand, at least intuitively, and so nationalization seems an unattractive alternative to corporate power, both in the theory and the everyday experience of most Americans. In fact, public ownership and control has often proven to be as bureaucratic as corporate ownership and control.

This by no means rules out public ownership or public enterprise as a legitimate alternative, and one which may make a major improvement in people's lives in comparison with the corporate sector. For example, the public education system, from neighborhood schools to public universities, is a kind of "socialism" which most Americans support. Similarly, the Tennessee Valley Authority brought electricity and growth to an impoverished South during the New Deal. Public power continues to be generally cheaper than private power today, and the nationalization of the oil industry has distinct advantages over continued private control—access to information, redistribution of profits, better national security and so on. Nevertheless, there is a tarnish on traditional socialist proposals that will remain as long as the modern State seems equally dangerous and no more productive than the giant Corporation.

There is a further problem with class analysis in a country as deeply wedded to individualism as America. It is the tendency, whether in theory or practice, of socialism to lessen the significance of the individual and his or her liberty. I do not here mean to celebrate the American individual's "freedom" to buy a color television and "choose" between packaged candidates, nor to minimize the individual protections of work, health care and security that socialism usually provides. Nor do I doubt that countries like Cuba today are better off than 25 years ago despite repression of certain freedoms. But there is something in socialist theory itself which tends towards the dangerous reduction of the individual to a class destiny. Even if one could justify this orientation in Third World revolutions—which I cannot entirely—and even if one could dismiss the Stalinism of most Western communist parties as an old-fashioned attitude to be simply outgrown, it is unimaginable that social change should come about in the United States at the expense of individual freedom. Certainly the unrestrained competitive individualism of the frontier needs to be stopped and balanced by a cooperative ecological ethic, but the individual's self-actualization still has to be a central purpose of life, and the key to political and economic health. This is not understood by those socialists who view individuals as expressors of class forces.

There is still another serious inadequacy even within the way socialists usually think about class definitions in modern capitalism. For after easily identifying the owners of corporations as "capitalists," the picture gets very murky. Is everyone who works for a wage or salary a worker: doctors, engineers, managers, teachers, factory operatives, and construction workers alike? Or are there differences? In popular usage we often hear the term "middle class" but who precisely does this refer to? Do the scientists and technocrats who chart the future course of institutions like Three Mile Island have the same interests and inclinations as the workers who mine uranium for that plant, just because an orthodox Marxist lumps them all in one class? And this confusion arises even before we ask about the impact of unemployment, state versus private employment, and welfare rolls on "class relations." No, even in the rare case when racial and sexual differences between people don't lead to a weakening of the predicative power of traditional Marxist class analyses, often the very intricacies of our economic terrain are still too complex for the old concepts to fathom.

Further, with reference to countries that follow the Soviet central planning model, the confusion over "class analysis" obscures an immense economic failing. In these societies it is central planners, elite technocrats, and managers who make economic decisions, not workers, consumers, and community residents. There is an on-going class division built into this approach which causes work in a Leningrad steel factory to be just as alienating as work at the River Rouge Ford plant in Detroit. The Soviet model is the opposite of what we are seeking, the extension of democracy into the economy itself.

And for one final reason, the socialist tradition faces major re-examination or declining relevence—and that is the central theme of this book, the meaning of the disappearance of the frontier. Since the time of Marx, socialists have been prophets of growth and technology, the "expansion of the forces of production." The revolutionary notion has depended on the increasing conquest of nature, the consequent creation of abundance, and the fair distribution of material goods so that humanity can move "from the realm of necessity to the realm of freedom." For this reason, Richard Barnet has argued that "the notion of systemic limits is threatening to capitalists and socialists alike," and "the fundamental philosophical choice—can human beings dominate nature or are they limited by nature—now divides both capitalism and socialism."[69] Socialists, like capitalists, often fail to understand or incorporate an ecological ethic in their visions and for the same reason: such an ethic challenges their underlying belief that humans are here to dominate nature in the name of virtually endless economic growth.*

*I don't mean to suggest that all socialists or Marxists make the errors catalogued here, nor that none work to overcome the shortcomings of old theory. Such scholars and activists as Michael Harrington, Barbara Ehrenreich, Sam Bowles and Herb Gintis, the editors of In These Times, Richard Flacks, the French activist Andre Gorz, Robert Heilbroner, J. Kenneth Galbraith, William Domhoff, and many others are all obviously making great contributions to our understanding of how modern societies work as well as how they might be improved. However, the socialist label no more conveys the content of their thought than my Democratic Party label indicates what an economic democrat stands for. All the same, the problems and weaknesses I have enumerated do afflict the programs of almost all socialist groups and certainly the economies of all societies which today go under the label "socialist."

Capitalism: No Looking Back

Having taken this long detour through the problem of the state under both New Deal and socialist systems, for our third example we return to the problems of corporate capitalism. One of the most popular reforms of capitalism proposed as an alternative to state-centered systems is the notion of a *return to competition*. But is this turning back of historic time somehow a path to a better future? It is most unlikely.

There are, let us acknowledge, certain satisfying and useful qualities to the entreprenurial reform of capitalism. These have been summarized in a recent staff report of the House Committee on Small Business. In terms of political philosophy, the preservation of small business is in keeping with what the chairman of the Federal Trade Commission, Michael Pertschuk, calls the "American belief that power should be fragmented and that decision centers should be multiple."[70] There are more concrete benefits in terms of prices, innovation, jobs, and productivity:

—estimates of the cost to consumers where competition is stifled run between $100 billion and $175 billion annually.[71]

—small companies produce four times as many innovations per research and development dollar as medium-sized ones, and 24 times as many as the largest firms, according to a National Science Foundation study of the years 1953-73.[72]

—small business is labor-intensive. The House report finds that while the top 1000 companies contributed less than 2 percent of the new jobs between 1969 and 1976, "small business accounted for what can be considered virtually all the new private sector employment in this country."[73]

Basic to the appeal of capitalism is the chance to personally *own* and *create*, however twisted these aspirations may become in our society of glib advertising and consumer frenzy. The ability to own and create seems to be necessary to freedom and dignity, and to a society that is both caring and forward looking. In agriculture, for instance, there is little doubt that the land would be better tended and more productive under the stewardship of family farmers than under high-tech, capital-intensive corporations exploiting their tax shelters. Beyond the farm, it has been the health food entrepreneurs who marketed nutritious, quality, life-supporting alternatives to the inferior packaged products of agribusiness. Most would agree as well that communities in general are better serviced and healthier for all where there are networks of locally-owned businesses rather than remotely-controlled chains. And it is a fact that the genuine pioneers in solar energy technology, whether in flat-plate collectors or windmills, have been small entrepreneurs, inventors and architects. Similarly in the world of media, it has been the entrepreneurs of the "alternative press" who took risks, exposed Vietnam and other forms of corruption, and introduced and popularized new ideas long before the larger corporate media discovered investigative journalism. And in music and film, it has been risk-taking individuals who have succeeded in introducing new ideas and themes.

For these and other reasons, there are some who advocate a new "entrepreneurial revolution." One of the most insightful of these is Alvin Toffler, author of *The Third Wave* and an astute observer of workplace developments.[74] Toffler anticipates "the breakup of huge corporations into small, self-managed units," a growth of "mini-companies" or "ensemble groups" that would contract with larger entities for specific tasks. One of the driving forces behind this devolution of enterprise, he believes, is the rapid growth of electronic terminals for communication, information processing, office work, and business management. As this technology becomes available to individuals, "they would become, in effect, independent entrepreneurs rather than classical employees—meaning, as it were, increased ownership of the 'means of production' by the worker."[75]

In addition to the factor of technology, Toffler sees in the "new entrepreneurialism" a response to over-centralized systems in general with their built-in tendencies to inflation, inefficiency and indifference. A value shift towards self-suffiency is everywhere noticeable. In the early 1970s, for example, 30 percent of all electric power tools were sold to individual do-it-yourselfers, and 70 percent to professional workers; by 1980, the ratio was exactly reversed. In addition, Toffler cites an industrial research report which concludes that between 1974 and 1976, "For the first time, more than half of all building materials...were purchased directly by homeowners rather than by contractors doing work for them"—which did not even include $350 million spent by consumers for home repair jobs costing under $25.[76]

The "do-it-yourself" movement in America has mushroomed across the board, registering a 200 percent increase from
1974 to 1977, and becoming a $16.5 billion-a-year business. Mean-
while, something like 32 million American households are involved in backyard and community gardens, again twice the number ever recorded before, producing goods worth over $13 billion
on the market.[77]

These are most positive and significant trends, and will
undoubtedly involve millions of people in tasks which inherently
decentralize American life. But do they represent a revival of free-
enterprise capitalism as a *system,* an emerging alternative to the
giant corporation and state? The answer must be no, for several
reasons.

The essential reason is that there is no possible turning back
of the clock to an earlier form of capitalism. The reasons capitalism evolved in stages towards oligopoly and globalism are *inherent*
in capitalism—the need to expand for profits, and to use those
profits for further expansion, is the very nature of the system. A
policy statement of Hooker Chemical Company, the poisoner of
Love Canal, New York, expresses the desire for infinite expansion
thusly: "Rather than manufacturing known products by a known
method for a known market... the research department is now
free to develop any product that looks promising. If there is not a
market for it, the sales development group seeks to create one."[78]

It was not a fascination with "bigness," nor a technological
imperative, nor a power thirst for world dominion that made
capitalism grow—though all of these factors have been significant.
Capitalism is a system which *competes* for scarce resources in
order to generate profits which are reinvested in the drive for
wealth. There is no inherent limit in competition, no "fair play,"
except where government imposes limits through regulations. But
even those rules and regulations, we have seen, are circumvented
by the dynamic of the economic system itself—or if the restraints
truly work, the system begins to lose its own incentive structure
and stagnate.

For this reason, the system works to transform today's Henry
Ford of solar energy into tomorrow's solar equivalent of the Ford
Motor Company. Or, more likely, it pressures the solar entrepre-
neur into becoming a bought-out subsidiary of a larger company.

"The role of small businessmen," said one oil company executive in 1977, "is to be absorbed."[79] Similar pressures have driven family farmers into the choice of large-scale corporate farming or migration to the cities, health foods into another expensive product line of the food conglomerates, alternative media into economic ruin or incorporation into the larger commercial system. A quote from the previously-mentioned House of Representatives study concludes with this description of the system:

> Starved of capital, deprived of incentives, submerged in bureaucratic red tape and surrounded by the burgeoning bigness of the corporate giants, the small business sector has become a victim of the upheavals and recessions of the 1970s. It is a matter of national urgency that the small entrepreneur, while not yet extinct, has become an endangered species.[80]

Therefore, while the "new entrepreneurialism" should be welcomed, encouraged and protected, it can neither gradually replace nor for long co-exist alongside "the burgeoning bigness of the corporate giants." The problem of the large corporation in a profit oriented market system must be taken on directly.

Changing the System from Within

We live in a crisis of both *means* and *ends*, during a historical epoch with at least three related characteristics: the decline of affordable fossil fuels, the transformation of competitive capitalism into bureacratic corporatism, and the emergence of a state socialism with its own problems of bureaucratic tyranny. Both "capitalist" and "socialist" systems have been based on the ability to control and exploit non-renewable resources. The path to a renewable resource economy—and the new security which that implies—will more than likely be retarded by bureaucracies, public and private, with vested interests in the fossil fuel age of growth. Therefore, economic democracy—a challenge by citizens to the centers of economic power—will be necessary in both advanced capitalist and socialist states. In capitalist countries, the corporation will have to be democratized and redirected; in socialist countries, the state.

Economic democracy, then is a provisional concept that draws upon the best lessons learned since the days of Adam Smith and Karl Marx, and tries to translate the notions of freedom and democracy into an era of limits. This outlook includes an affirmation of economic liberty and community level enterprise, a commitment to the equality of all people before the law, a belief in the public entitlement to the basic resources of the planet, and a strong preference for a direct and decentralized democratic process. As the centralized economic and political system suffers greater crisis, the themes of economic democracy will be translated, often a step at a time, into practical and positive alternatives.

In the immediate future, for example, we are likely to see the rise of cooperatives and bartering systems at points where the system has begun to fail people. Since the first Rochdale cooperative experiment in England in 1844, cooperatives have been slow to grow in America—but they have continued to show life, especially during the chronic inflation of the 1970s when millions enrolled in consumer co-ops of all kinds. Rural electricity is produced by nearly one thousand co-ops servicing 9 million farms at relatively cheap rates. As much as one-third of the oil supplied for farm use comes from 3000 oil co-ops.[81]

By one careful estimate, at least 71 million Americans belong to cooperatives "obtaining credit, health care, food, housing, car repairs, electric power... outside the profit-centered business system." Credit unions alone grew from 17 million members in 1965 to 32 million in 1977.[82] The co-op movement operates on certain principles of economic democracy: democratic decision-making among the members, return of profit to the contributing membership, support of community education and outreach programs, structuring the workplace along cooperative and democratic lines. While the co-ops have grown up in the "cracks of neglect" within the system, and are sure to expand with passage of the National Cooperative Bank bill, they still tend to exist alongside the larger corporate economy and bend significantly to its commercial pressures.

Barter systems are on the rise, too, and are likely to increase with stagflation as people trade labor and goods without the medium of currency. Marilyn Ferguson catalogs the rapid growth of labor pools and service collectives around the U.S. in *The*

Aquarian Conspiracy: "commercial barter companies... swap and credit goods and services to their members through sophisticated bookkeeping. One barter company does a yearly business of around one hundred million dollars in reciprocal trade agreements, recycling surpluses and mistakes, advertising space and hotel rooms. About seventy-five bartering groups in the United States are franchised under the International Trade Exchange."[83] According to *U.S. News and World Report*, 4.5 million Americans obtain all their income, and 15 million some of their income, from this invisible economy outside the reach of corporations and the Internal Revenue Service, doing their bargaining by cash or barter.[84] While these institutions operate on principles of economic democracy in many respects, they too represent more of a "survival" program than a structural alternative to the great corporations.

The Movement for Corporate Reform

How, then, is the problem of the giant corporation to be tackled? Essentially, by the development of a variety of citizens movements concerned with corporate abuse, the creation of a climate demanding basic reform, and the development of a blueprint for an alternative corporate structure. Let us examine the factors of building a movement and climate briefly before examining a detailed structural blueprint.

Specific movements for corporate reform have grown rapidly in the past 15 years, largely in response to glaring abuses. The movements have made some gains, but have failed to fundamentally change the process by which unfair, unrepresentative, unproductive and irresponsible decisions are made. As affirmative action efforts fail to break open the boardrooms, as union members see their pension funds invested against their own interests, as shareholders experience the futility of proxy fights, as religious activists encounter the lack of a corporate conscience, as communities find themselves helpless to prevent runaway shops and left-behind toxic dumps, as environmentalists tire of suing only after the damage is done, as laborers experience a downturn in real income, as taxpayers are asked for increasing bailouts, as these and a thousand other abuses mount, the call for an alternative will be heard, more loudly and incessantly everywhere.

A climate of discontent with the corporation, and a demand for greater accountability and access, already has grown enormously—though in fits and starts—during the 1970s. "Public anger at corporations is beginning to well up at a frightening rate," according to a Harvard Business Review editor. A 1976 Peter Hart Poll found that 66 percent of the public agreed "they aren't given enough to say in decisions which affect their jobs," 52 percent supported a system in which "employees determine broad company policy," 66 percent favored working for an employee-owned and controlled company, and 74 percent wanted to see consumers "represented on the boards of companies that operate in the local regions."[85]

Alvin Toffler, while endorsing the "new entreprenurialism," also sees the giant corporation becoming obsolete in the face of several historical trends. The corporation, he writes quite accurately, can no longer be considered a narrow "economic" institution vested with rights of privacy like ordinary individuals.[86] The very notion of "production" is rapidly being expanded to include the *side effects produced* as well as the goods and services generated. Responsibility for the environment, for social effects such as unemployment and community disruption, for providing vital information on everything from safety tests to investments in foreign countries, for respecting the law and the elected government, for promoting a decent ethical climate, for contributing to world peace rather than tension—these new responsibilities adhere to giant corporations simply because these entities affect the environment, communities, information flow, democracy and foreign affairs *directly*. Insofar as they have public effects, they will increasingly be held to the standard of the public interest. Inevitably, this pressure will reach inside the internal decision-making structure of the corporation itself.

The same point was made in a 1974 report of the prestigious Stanford Research Institute, *Changing Images of Man,* a volume which created more requests for reprints than any previous SRI publication.[87] "Giant corporations," the SRI study noted, "today are feeling the challenge put to the divine right of kings two centuries ago." They are "in an important sense public institutions" since "they are owned by a large fraction of the public" (through life insurance policies, annuities, mutual funds, etc), since "the public uses the goods and services they produce," and since the public "suffers the environmental degradation they produce." As they become more powerful than most nation-states, the report declares, "it becomes essential that their operative goals shift to resemble those of public institutions." In conclusion, the SRI authors propose that the priority of corporate goals be changed

> 1) to carry on activities that will contribute to the self-fulfillment of the persons involved,
> 2) to carry on activities that contribute directly to the satisfaction of social needs and accomplishment of societal goals, and
> 3) to earn a fair profit on investment, not so much as a goal in itself (as at present) but as a control signal which monitors effectiveness.[88]

The widely-respected *Reshaping the International Order* project of the Nobel laureate, Jan Tinbergen, came to similar conclusions from a global perspective. Multinational corporations, they concluded, can use their vast marketing, communications and technical skills in a "positive role in improving the living conditions of the poor masses in the Third World insofar as they comply with rules, formulated nationally and internationally, directed towards this end." Among the standards they suggested were a shift from economic to "social" profit, control of technology by human values, and conservation of resources; the structural changes included placing labor and consumer representatives on corporate boards, creating "public international enterprises" to manage the oceans' resources, and development of an enforceable code of "minimum standards of behavior."[89]

Real change has to begin with consideration of the very principles of legitimacy that entitle corporations to exist and guide their behavior. There needs to be a new birth, a new constitutional beginning, if the corporation is to be remade in a democratic and useful way. We must realize that corporations are not permanent and immortal, existing by some natural law or mysterious annointment beyond the reach of the citizen. The corporation is a creature of society, created by laws passed by generations of elected officials, functioning to serve a general interest. Since it no longer serves those interests, it is the right and duty of every American to extend the idea of citizenship to the economic world to make the corporation accountable again.

The bedrock principles for democratic reform of the corporation would be:

1. *That large corporations be guided by standards of total economic and social performance instead of profits alone.*

2. *That the public have a voice in corporate decisions in proportion to the effects on their lives.*

3. *That corporate management and boards be accountable to employees, customers, and communities affected by corporate decisions, not simply to investors in stock.*

1. The Need For a New Charter

Any blueprint for implementing these principles must begin with the *chartering* process by which corporations are created and have their responsibilities defined. This is the point at which the "social contract" between business and society is written. At present more than half the *Fortune 500* are chartered in Delaware, for the simple reason that Delaware provides the most "favorable"—that is, non-restrictive—climate to corporations. Thus, corporations are "born free," Delaware's treasury is enriched by fees, and the public suffers—because the national standards of corporate behavior are defined in effect by the state most willing to be servile to corporate power if the price is right.

This problem has been addressed by both legal scholars and the Securities and Exchange Commission, and by the U.S. Senate Subcommittee on Citizens and Shareholders Rights and Remedies chaired by Sen. Howard Metzenbaum. Under Section 14(a) of the 1934 Securities and Exchange Act, the SEC has the duty to establish corporate proxy rules "as necessary or appropriate in the public interest or for the protection of investors." [90] We shall explore what a duty to the "public interest" might mean in a moment. The official hearings have passed by this possibility to focus instead of what might be done for the "protection of the investors." A self-perpetuating managerial elite exists in most corporations, able to maintain itself through control of the proxy machinery which is scarcely available to ordinary shareholders. The minimal thrust of reform efforts has been to allow shareholders more information, greater access to the proxy machinery, easier ability to nominate candidates and "cumulative" voting which makes it easier for dissidents to be elected to boards of directors.

A somewhat stronger approach favored by Sen. Metzenbaum comes from William Cary, former head of the SEC, who advocates a Federal Corporate Minimum Standards Act. The basic notion is to stop the "downward" competition among states to lure businesses to incorporate. Cary's "minimum standards" would be national, and would include the abolition of non-voting shares, make frequency of transactions subject to shareholder approval, and create federal fiduciary standards for directors, officers and controlling shareholders.*

A related proposal by Harold Williams, present chair of the SEC, is that all corporate directors be "independent," i.e., neither employed by the corporation, doing business with it, or related to its officers. A variation is that the committees who nominate new directors consist entirely of "independent" directors, and the audit committees be composed of "independent" directors.

These reform efforts have value in that they make management more accountable, and may allow either the election of dissident, active directors or passage of certain shareholder resolutions such as requiring disclosure of ownership information, or disinvestment from South Africa. But they are severely limited in their potential to remake the giant corporation. The difficulty is that reform proposals are based on what Fred Branfman calls two myths of shareholder democracy.

The first myth is that shareholder democracy is possible at all. The key holdings in corporations today are by banks and institutional investors who generally defer to management. Beyond the possible issue of increasing shareholder dividends, there is hardly a conceivable situation where management can be beaten by a bloc of individual shareholders. Management has over 50 percent of the votes before balloting ever begins, through proxy solicitations mailed out and received back before the annual shareholders'

---

*Much of the research on this topic is by Fred Branfman, "Public Control of Corporate Managers" (Calif. Public Policy Center, 1979).

meeting. That is why the typical corporate election of directors is similar to the Soviet system of choosing government officials. In both cases management proposes a one-party slate, and the elections are little more than a ritual.

The second myth about shareholders is that their interest coincides with the public interest. It does not. The shareholders' basic interest is dividends, and if that goal is served by shutting down a plant, polluting a well, or keeping bribery a secret, the shareholder will almost always go along with management's plan. Equally important, today's modern corporation has measurably greater impact on workers, consumers and the surrounding community than on its own shareholders—yet those larger constituencies are left out of the corporate governing process altogether. The shareholders cannot act in their own interests.

A much stronger proposal for making the corporation more accountable "to the public interest," as the 1934 SEC law requires, through restructuring from within, has been made by Professor Christopher Stone of the University of Southern California, in *Where the Law Ends*. His key proposal is that the SEC, or a new federal agency, appoint "general public directors" to 10 percent of the seats on corporate boards. The "general public directors" would work substantial hours at being "superegos" assuring that laws were being observed, checking internal accountability and bookkeeping systems, preparing "corporate impact" studies, and serving as intermediaries both inside and outside the corporate world. They would have staffs, access to all internal reports, seats on management committees, a voice in promotions and dismissals, and the right to go to court for redress against corporate officers.

Stone proposes that "Special Public Directors" be appointed by the courts or government, almost as probation officers, to deal with corporate compliance when a company breaks laws or regulations involving environmental harm, worker health and safety, or consumer protection.

These proposals would go a long way towards creating a "checks and balances" system on runaway corporate behavior. However, they too are limited, in this case by the assumption that the government would appoint truly different kinds of directors. The current coziness of government and corporations creates a suspicion that the "public directors" would be little different than the former executives who now serve "public" functions with the Pentagon or Food and Drug Administration. There is no guarantee that the public—in the form of employees, consumers or community people—would move towards genuine control of corporate management.

2. From Secrecy to Free Information

Disclosure of corporate information is another goal often suggested by those seeking corporate reform. Management's control of vital information needs to be broken if "independent directors" of government regulators are going to perform competently. More important, the corporate monopoly on information must be broken for the sake of democracy. What the average citizen primarily sees today is only an *image* of corporate behavior, designed by public relations and advertising firms. Reporters, investigators, and even shareholders often have to fight fiercely to obtain pertinent information which corporations closely guard as "private." Greater disclosure is important because it is impossible to have a real democracy when major institutional centers are shrouded from public view.

A trend towards greater disclosure has developed during the past two decades, mostly over the objections of the corporations, environmental impact reports being the most controversial and obvious example. But other nations are far ahead of the U.S. in disclosure requirements. France, for example, has a far-reaching law requiring all companies with over 750 employees to publish reports containing 94 categories of information. Such a proposal, if offered here, would leave most businessmen aghast at the "invasion" of their privacy. When even a moderate version of requiring these "social indicators" was suggested by Commerce Secretary Juanita Kreps in 1977, it was immediately recalled and dropped from sight.

Ralph Nader and others propose to build upon the subjects disclosed already by corporations, thus requiring only the minimum amount of paperwork necessary. They suggest that current affirmative action information include the number of women and minorities in *top* job categories and *comparable* salary data, and that such information be made public. In addition, they ask for data concerning pollution control performance, a "right to know" requirement for workers encountering chemicals and toxic substances with complicated labels, information concerning accident and illness patterns among workers, and, perhaps most important, disclosure of the real identities of the largest institutional owners of stock and corporate creditors, as well as data on the overseas operations and tax policies of the multinationals.

The American people are entitled to know who owns and runs this country, and how well they do it. If corporations resist disclosure, it is because they have something to hide. They prefer private control of information necessary to make their competitive moves, thus denying the American people the information necessary to plan a safe economic future. The corporate refusal to provide crucial information further demonstrates the need for a fundamental design of the corporation to make it an *open* institution contributing to, and benefitting from, the free flow of information which is the lifeline of democracy.

3. A Public Voice in Investment Decisions

Other corporate reformers emphasize *influencing the flow of capital,* particularly the crises of plant closings and relocations which impose shock and hardship on countless workers and communities. Even the *Wall Street Journal* has recognized that "a company may have a responsibility not to leave its employees or its hometown in the lurch." [92] But the entire tax system encourages the runaway shop by allowing a firm to write off its old plant against other profits, deduct the cost of relocation as a business expense and obtain further credits for its new plant and equipment.

Ralph Nader's organization points out that in the Netherlands, the government can actually prohibit a corporate relocation unless management provides good reasons along with a plan for aiding the people thrown out of work. A more moderate proposal, originating with the Ohio Public Interest Campaign (OPIC), would require pre-notification of a plant closing, a public hearing to justify the move, and a payment to ease the hardship on the employees and affected community. Although OPIC and the steelworkers untimately lost the court fight to keep U.S. Steel from abandoning the Mahoning Valley, they did win a temporary court ruling that envisaged a new legal concept of corporate accountability to community. U.S. Circuit Court Judge Thomas Lambros said that since the people of the Mahoning Valley had "given and devoted their lives to this industry... U.S. Steel cannot leave that Mahoning Valley and the Youngstown area in a state of waste, that it cannot completely abandon its obligation to that community, because certain *vested rights* have arisen out of this long relationship."[3]

This is part of a much larger problem, that of the corporate compass pointing to the dollar sign over and above any other need. Not only are jobs and capital moving to the "sunbelt," but the same migration is taking place from America to other countries with cheaper labor and lower taxes. Economic democracy would require stringent controls, with public participation, over the flow of capital—from city to suburb, north to south, America to foreign countries. There are many avenues of control—anti-redlining laws, repeal of the incentive of "right to work" laws, revisions in the tariff system, export controls, etc. The key point is that decisions to move massive amounts of capital cannot be considered "private" when workers, communities and even national economic sovereignty are at stake.

4. Law and Order For the Corporation

Yet another approach to corporate accountability is the *strenghtening of civil and criminal penalties against "crime in the suites."* "Property is theft," wrote Proudhon.[4] If this proposition seems outrageously exaggerated, it is at least true that *inherent* in the process of doing business under capitalism is a market tendency to put profits above people, to lure the consumer into the highest price possible while conceding the lowest wage possible to the workers, magnifying the positive qualities of a product while minimizing its problems. It takes an extraordinary person to succeed in business while being honest and charitable. The line between doing well in business and breaking laws is thin, fine and easily crossed.

Therefore, penalties for business misconduct should be clear enough to follow and severe enough to deter. A business crime, which can affect a whole community or perhaps even the next generation, should be considered an even more serious offense in some respects than personal crimes. But it is not. There remains a double standard; between white collar and poor people's crime, the law is not "collar-blind." The jails are full of the poor and the minorities. The crooked businessmen are on probation or given negligible fines. For example, the average fine in recent years for firms found guilty of breaking California's Carcinogen Control Act has been only $240.[95] Despite an increased official interest in the subject since Watergate, federal and state law enforcement efforts against white-collar crime have been minimal. California's two-term Attorney General Evelle Younger, for example, virtually closed down the units charged with investigating crime. A House Judiciary Subcommittee on crime found in 1977 that only 5 percent of the Department of Justice resources went to combat white collar offenses.[96]

Therefore, the Nader group is extremely justified in calling for such measures as notification and restitution to victims, "double damages" as fines, disqualification of convicted executives from further corporate duty, on-site probation officers for recidivist firms, and stiffer penalties for health and safety violations.

It remains to be seen, however, how much real enforcement of tougher laws would accomplish in an economic system based on cut-throat competition in the race to profit. A change in the inner dynamics is needed as well.*

---

* It is not only the undemocratic nature of each firm, its lack of accountability to employees, consumers, and community citizens which breeds these ills. Market competition is also a serious factor promoting anti-social results. "Buy cheap and sell dear," "look out for number one," and "nice guys finish last," are all bits of common sense which apply in our society not due to some hypothetical greedy component of human nature, but due to the requisites of competing blindly for scarce resources.

As we seek ways to make corporate decisionmaking more socially conscious we will therefore also have to find ways to overcome the adverse influences market pressure can have. It will not do to improve matters within corporations individually only to have their clash in the marketplace undo all our accomplishments.

Certain of these notions—disclosure, criminal penalties, redirecting capital flows—have been advanced as part of an overall strategy of corporate reform first outlined in *Taming the Giant Corporation,* by Ralph Nader, Mark Green and Joel Seligman. Subsequently, these ideas were incorporated in a draft "Corporate Democracy Act" which awaits introduction and debate in the U.S. Senate. The virtue of these corporate restructuring proposals, the most important since the 1930s, is that they go beyond "shareholder democracy" to begin recognizing the broader constituencies of the corporation as possible participants in decision-making. Nader proposes a new *federal charter* designed to set national standards for corporate behavior. The heart of the proposal has to do with extending democracy to both the board-room and the workplace. Rather than nitpicking through the Nader group proposals, let us here focus on the basic theme.

5. Democratizing the Board Room

First and most important of these charter proposals is the need to *broaden the composition and powers of corporate boards of directors.* Professor Abraham Chayes of Harvard has noted the need for broadening the interests represented on corporate boards. Shareholder democracy is misconceived, he writes, "because the shareholders are not the governed of the corporations whose consent must be sought." The shareholders are protected "if financial information is made available, fraud and over-reaching are prevented, and a market is maintained in which their shares may be sold." Chayes insists there be a "more spacious concept of 'membership,' and one closer to the facts of corporate life," in which board members be drawn from "all those having a relation of sufficient intimacy with the corporation or subject to its powers in a sufficiently specialized way."[97]

Current corporate boards are narrow, ingrown and ineffective. A full disclosure of top corporate management in America by class, race, sex and age would give a picture more typical of an exclusive country club than a group of decision-makers reflecting the full spectrum of the society they affect.

Corporate executives show every sign of wanting to keep it that way, except for cosmetic changes, despite mounting pressures for change. Take, for example, a Business Roundtable report made to the SEC on this issue in 1978.[98] The Roundtable takes the issue quite seriously judging from the companies the Roundtable asked to help in drafting the report: Bank of America, Coca Cola, Crown Zellerbach, Dart Industries, H. J. Heinz, LTV, Standard Oil, Sun Company and Union Pacific Railroad, were all represented and the panel was chaired by J. Paul Austin of the Coca Cola company. We are entitled to think of this committee's observations as among the most enlightened of the corporate world. And yet the document reads like a public relations cover-up. For example, the Roundtable committee asserts that women are now included on 28 percent of manufacturing company boards, and that blacks are on 17 percent of manufacturing company boards and 32 percent of non-manufacturing company boards.

But these are deceptive claims, for we are not told how *many* women and blacks are represented. It is likely to be one per board in the one-third of companies which have "integrated." A *Business Week* survey in 1975 found there were only 15 women among 2,500 senior executives of large firms, and a 1977 Fortune report found ten women among 1500 key officers surveyed.[99] The same lamentable figures would be found for minorities, for labor, for consumers.

The real corporate agenda may be to meet the pressure for "new faces" in the boardroom by bringing in the chief executive officers of other companies. In a 1979 *New York Times* article by Thomas Hayes, we are told that "the most avidly sought candidates" are other CEOs, "not the women, the minority group members (or) the 'professional directors.'" Many corporate officers, the article goes on, "tend to look for their own kind as directors." This is because "in contrast to newcomers, they speak the businessman's language."[100] So it appears that the corporate response to appeals to open the boardroom is being met by the Custer attitude of pulling the wagon trains more tightly around the headquarters.

But even an increase of women and minorities on boards, while important in breaking down discrimination, would not in itself change the governance of the corporation. The first requirement for change is *a shift, approved by federal charter, in the goals of the corporation from profit to "overall performance," and then the structuring of boards and management to meet that broader objective.*

Alvin Toffler believes that corporations have to become "multi-purpose" rather than solely profit-oriented institutions. Some firms are experimenting with "social audits" and other mechanisms to measure overall performance according to broad social and environmental objectives. One multinational, Royal Dutch Shell, has gone so far as to require three equal standards in making decisions about investments in new projects: a) what is the potential profit, b) what is the technical feasibility, and 3) what are the potential adverse impacts socially. According to a Shell consultant, the firm has decided to study the social impact *first* and, if it is judged to be negative for any number of reasons, cancel projected plans even where they are profitable and feasible from a technical standpoint.[101] Now if it were local community representatives who conducted this priority first-step study, we would have an example of a principle of economic democracy at work.

Once the traditionally "external" factors of production are brought into consideration on an equal or superior basis to profit, the justification for narrow, profit-centered business and banking executives on corporate boards begins to disintegrate. To be specific, take the 1978 board of Pacific Lighting, the largest umbrella utility in Southern California, responsible for planning an energy future filled with dangerous choices and fateful effects on millions of lives. Their 14-member board in 1977 included three of their own officers, three corporate lawyers, two investment counselors, and executives from insurance, savings and loans, a bank, a department store, and an architect for developers. These men presumably are experienced at making money from traditional energy sources, and at investing utility funds in Hawaiian shipping centers and resorts, industrial parks, condominiums and pistachios in California, citrus in Texas, lemons in Arizona, apples and peaches in Maryland—all of which they were doing in the late 1970s, often at a loss.[102] But there is no reason to believe they can lead us into a solar age, or keep an intense concern for the environment, or assure that farmworkers receive decent wages and living conditions. Only a broader set of directors, with experience in solar and alternative energy, environmental management and workers' health and safety, could begin to meet these broader obligations.

What is needed is for the concept of shareholder to be broadened to that of "stakeholder." All those affected by corporate behavior, the general public, workers, consumers, and the surrounding community—ought to have some representation on corporate boards, chosen from their own constituency bases instead of by shareholders or management. The "public" representatives might be appointed by government officials or the SEC, as suggested by Stone. Consumer representatives might be chosen from the ranks of major customers, as defined by their charge accounts or receipts that prove a permanent stake. Or in the case of utilities, consumers could be chosen by changing the regular monthly billing mechanism periodically into a ballot with information and phone numbers for various "consumer candidates" for the board. Representatives of the community could be elected from the existing political jurisdictions around a plant. Workers could choose their representatives by a process similar to union elections, with the SEC, or perhaps the National Labor Relations Board, certifying the elections. All of these directors would be full-time, like government office-holders, with staff and access to information. All would have limited terms, and would tend to be responsible for board committees on health and safety, jobs and investment, product safety, accounting and budget, environmental protection, and community services. Obviously they would need to be directly accountable to and recallable by their constituencies. Indeed, it is not hard to foresee democratic councils of workers, consumers, and community residents—economic town meetings—evolving to provide direction for these representative decision-makers. Moreover, for these representatives to have the skills and knowledge essential to good decision-making, and for their constituencies to be likewise well informed and capable, a great expansion of our understanding of the importance and purpose of public education will be necessary.

In any case, certain immediate results of even a simple broadening of boards of directors could have dramatic impact on economic life. Corporations would be unlikely to poison the local water supply (as Occidental has done) with community representatives on the board, or arbitrarily shut down (as Firestone has done) with worker representatives on the board, or conduct secret DES experiments on women (as Eli Lilly did) with consumer advocates on the board, or bribe Italian politicians (as Exxon has done) with an independent audit committee present, or market unsafe, flammable cars (as Ford has done) with consumer representatives at the table, or plan second-class wages for women and Third World people (as Cleveland National Bank has done) with affirmative action directors voting, or cover-up illegal activity (as Johns-Manville has done) with public representatives checking up on them.

The Corporate Defense of Elitism

Two objections to this scenario are certain, one having to do with "efficiency" and the other with "qualifications." Put another way, wouldn't this new arrangement bog down corporations to a point of paralysis-through-democracy?, and are there enough people who have the experience and skills necessary to be independent and effective directors?

These are questions, one might note, that have been raised in objection to every forward step of democracy in history, in objection to the independence of every nation struggling against colonialism, in objection to every ethnic group trying to climb the ladder of advancement. That is not to say the questions are unfair, but that they are classical and long-standing, and have always been answered in American history—after much pain and deliberation—with an affirmation of human growth and democracy. When Toffler writes that "in corporation after corporation we can expect to see an internal battle" over these sorts of issues he is not discovering something historically new, but the extension of a very old debate into the boardroom where it at last belongs.

Corporations should be the last to defend their prerogatives on the issue of efficiency. They are *inherently* inefficient because they are now allowed to externalize their true costs—in shortened lives, broken arms, alcoholism, polluted lakes—while internalizing all the benefits for themselves. This creates the appearance of balanced books and a sense of button-down neatness that is essentially deceiving. Moreover, most large corporations are so unable to survive the rigors of the traditional marketplace that they have long since turned to government handouts for survival—and government has rewarded them, efficient or not. According to Mark Green, "the best research indicates that most large companies are far larger than required by minimum efficient scale."[103] The same conclusion has been drawn about family farms versus large-scale, absentee agribusiness in studies for the Department of Agriculture. Green cites the report, *Barriers to New Competition,* by Joe Blain, which concludes that "efficiency does increase and unit cost does decline as plants become larger—but only up to a point." Beyond that point, which many large firms have passed in their quest for power and profit, "there are either no further efficiencies to be gained or, in fact, actual inefficiencies incurred."[104]

A reformed, widened board of directors could hardly be less efficient than the present ones which are often filled with retired executives or persons seeking ornamental status without responsibility. Full-time board members, with staff, can create the kind of efficiency that comes when all viewpoints are fully considered, when all costs are factored in, when all problems are anticipated, an efficiency that is *synergistic* and humane. This kind of efficiency concentrates on *making things work* for the parties and constituencies involved instead of compulsively focussing on neatness, order and narrow material profits. It is more efficient, for example, to pay decent wages and involve employees in designing their work environment than it is to autocratically cut costs and corners only to create greater absenteeism, lower productivity, and higher turnovers on the job. It is more efficient to involve community organizations and senior citizens groups in planning for low- and moderate-income housing in a new development than to fight taxpayer and environmentalist lawsuits for 10 years. It is more efficient to provide thousands of no-interest consumer leans for solar energy installation than to lock billions of dollars into investments in a nuclear industry that is going belly-up. These kinds of efficiencies can only be achieved by the democratic participation of affected constituencies in long-term planning decisions.

Ultimately and ideally whole constituencies will become more familiar with political democracy. Where the current hierarchical workplace (or that of Soviet style economies) stunts the social instincts and skills of an alienated workforce, economic democracy promises to awaken new social concern and initiating powers in workers who will then be that much more effective participants in the body politic as well.

What the defenders of the corporate realm are really saying when they argue their version of "superior efficiency" is that they want to continue giving management unchecked and self-perpetuating control of internal corporate decisions. Pressed further, they would usually like to roll back *all external* restrictions on management as well, in the form of environmental, consumer protection and labor laws. A factory process produces cars, for example, but it also affects workers on the job, uses irreplaceable resources, affects consumers by built-in obsolescence, and local communities by the creation of pollution. Being "socially and democratically efficient" means taking all these factors into account to get the most socially desirable results for effort expended. Being "technically efficient" means getting as many cars as possible per effort expended regardless of environmental costs, boredom and danger on the assembly line, and unnecessary deaths on the highway. But for the corporate leader, efficiency is a still narrower concept—it is oriented neither to society, nor to levels of output, but only to profit. The factory is efficient if it accrues the most profit possible per effort expended, even if this means holding production back, and again no matter the debilitating impact on workers, consumers, and the community environment. So corporate efficiency is a very callous and undemocratic efficiency which some would simply call absolute power. And, in the final analysis, most Americans would choose accountability over tyranny, even if it meant taking more time deciding their future.

The elitism inherent in the corporate definition of efficiency comes to the surface when executives are asked who is "qualified" to make decisions. "Hell, I don't want anything from them except to go along and agree with me," is a typical way one executive described the qualities he preferred in board members, as quoted in *Directors—Myth and Reality*, a widely-read study by Myles Mace.[105]

There is a common belief among managers that board members are not qualified to make more than limited decisions. Mace's interviews of executives identified three functions they thought boards should perform: advice and counsel (on how to implement decisions already reached by managers), some sort of discipline (by asking questions), and act in crises (as bankruptcy, or choosing a new board president). Significantly, Mace found that most boards rarely if ever perform even these functions.

Many corporate theorists actually want to *narrow* the function of directors. Melvin Eisenberg, a corporate law scholar at the University of California, has written that policy-making "is usually beyond the competence of the board, since a corporate organ cannot be meaningfully involved in making business policy unless its members are highly active, and it is not realistic to expect a high degree of activity from the board." Eisenberg opposes the notion of "professional" directors because there are not enough persons with qualifications; sees "full-time" directors as unnecessary; and "fully-staffed" directors as too expensive and potentially disruptive. He believes that boards should be limited to selecting and monitoring the chief executive officer.[106]

Executives who think their present narrowly-constituted boards are unqualified are unlikely to welcome notions of citizen, worker and consumer participation. Nader, Green and Seligman have responded with a proper democratic faith:

It has been objected that there are not enough qualified directors to staff all major firms. This complaint springs from that corporate mentality which, accustomed to 60-year-old white male bankers and businessmen as directors, makes the norm a virtue.[107]

A new kind of director might not be qualified in the sciences of management, and perhaps there ought to be certain such qualifications required. But *administration,* after all, is what management is for. In any corporate reform, there would still need to be a management to *implement* board policy, as Branfman argues, by planning budgets, arranging loans, floating bonds, and performing other traditional management functions. "What is needed in board members controlling corporate management in the public interest is not a knowledge of the intricacies of accounting," Branfman concludes, "but a commitment to serving the public interest and the competence to assess a variety of economic and social factors to ensure that basic decisions are made in the overall interest of both the corporation and society at large."[108] Corporate managers trained in administrative techniques of maximizing profit are not qualified to judge an overall performance in the public interest. In fact their narrow economic orientation and management role frequently diminishes their ability to see problems in a broader context. Here, for example, is a sample of

the limited social thought of Howard Johnson, chairman of the
board of the firm of the same name, as given in a 1978 interview:

Q. Do you have an affirmative action plan?

A. No.

Q. How much success have you had, then, in moving
women and minorities up through the ranks?

A. Some of our best managers and staff heads are
women and . . . we already have women in some very sen-
sitive areas.

Q. Such as?

A. Well, menu planning and banquet planning. . . . You
know, gals have some attributes that men don't have.
They like to keep cleaner kitchens, generally speaking.
They're a little fussier in terms of orderliness and
cleanliness.

Q. Do you have any women corporate officers?

A. No . . .

Q. What about minorities? Are they moving up through
management?

A. . . . We have no Negro corporate officers. . . . You
know, it has a lot to do with ability. We've given chances
to some of these people, but I haven't really felt that one
is ready for a general manager's role in the field.[109]

Perhaps the head of Howard Johnson's is not a typical
business leader. But his thinking represents a direction, however
representative, that is an unwitting danger to American society.
No one could be elected President of the United States if they
claimed women and minorities lacked qualifications to serve in the
Cabinet. By the same standard, Howard Johnson should not be
qualified to run Howard Johnsons.

Democracy in the Workplace

The corporation can never be opened to democracy in the
boardroom unless it is also democratized in the offices and shops
where millions of Americans work.

Under current law, millions of employees—well over 50
million, perhaps as high as 80 percent—without unions in the
private sector can be dismissed without cause. This threat of

arbitrary firing automatically makes workers more conformist, cautious and accepting of their lot than they might otherwise be. The First Amendment does not enter the workplace.

In this regard, the U.S. is very backward among nations with a capitalist economic system. As long ago as 1928, for example France enacted a law making the employer liable for malicious, capricious or arbitrary dismissals. In Germany, England and Japan, dismissal without "just cause" is regarded legally as an abuse of power.

New laws are needed protecting workers against being fired, demoted or otherwise punished without just cause; protecting the rights of speech, assembly and press, and rights to privacy, conscientious objection and after-hours political activity. It is necessary to checkmate the kind of arrogance reflected in a California bus company memo to its workers: "The company requires its employees to be loyal. It will not tolerate words or acts of hostility to the company. . .or criticisms of the company to others than. . . superior officers." The Bill of Rights and the First Amendment should be extended to the office and shop floor.[110]

However, recognizing freedom of speech at work is a long way from full democracy in economic institutions. In *Democracy At Work*, Daniel Zwerdling identifies several *levels* of worker participation: 1) in which workers gain greater control over their jobs but "within a larger framework which has been dictated by corporate management," 2) joint labor-management committees on the quality of life, which involve workers directly in the *process* of workplace humanization, 3) worker-ownership models based on control of actual stock, ranging from Employee Stock Ownership Plans (ESOP's) as remuneration to actual producer cooperatives, 4) *worker self-management,* the most participatory form of worker involvement.[111] This latter arrangement rests on the principles of regular participation in decision-making, a frequent return to employees from what they produce, access to management and centralized information, guarantees of job rights, and an independent mechanism of peers for judging disputes.

There is nothing easy in moving beyond First Amendment rights to participatory democracy in the workplace. Even though millions of workers resent being "cogs" in a machine and desire respect on the job, there is also a broad and deep disinclination to participate in making decisions. Many workers doubt their own qualifications or those of their peers, a conditioned mentality which is generations old. Greater worker participation cannot be imposed or granted, or created as a social psychology experiment. It must be actively desired and legitimized by working people first. The *psychology* of economic democracy comes along with its workplace achievement.

Even then a more democratic arrangement will create a new set of issues. Democracy is never smooth, but it is a growing process. Group dynamics can become ridden with jealousy and internally-destructive; committee life can be wasteful and paralysing; authoritarian leaders can dominate formal democratic decision-making; "ultra-democratic" tendencies can damage respect for competence, leadership and seniority.

The alternative to democracy, however, is an alienating workplace and a society whose citizens are subordinated to arbitrary authority for most of their productive hours. Such a society cannot fail to suffer from its massive waste of human potential in countless ways.

At its best, greater workplace democracy can foster a self-respecting citizenry, make the office and factory safer places to be, enrich the quality of work itself, create a better product, overcome the suspicion between customers and corporations, and—most important in the long run—meet the economic challenge of the vanishing frontier.

That challenge is to improve the productivity and quality of work without being able to rely on the cheap resources and American technical superiority that made abundance and economic growth possible in the past. In the future, there will be only one economic resource with infinite potential: the human beings of the work force. As Hazel Henderson has remarked, "We must now conserve our natural resources by more fully using the talents of all of our people. We must therefore now run our economy with a leaner mix of capital, energy and materials and a richer mix of labor and human resources." [112] The most successful and competitive corporations of the 1980s may be those who can tap and mobilize the potential strengths of their employees. The most successful economic and environmental management efforts will rest on a popular sense of stewardship.

This "participatory management" will require a vast shift in consciousness and redefinition of work, stressing inner quality as the means to outer success. A return of belief in *craft* over "gamesmanship," an emphasis on *process* in addition to production quotas, an effort at finding *consensus* instead of giving orders, a leadership that is elected and *accountable* rather than imposed and unreachable, and a *democratic sharing* of sacrifices instead of automatic layoffs and shutdowns, are some of the possible directions to which the psychology and institutions of economic democracy will lead.

Here, when we discuss economic democracy in terms of real life, we reach the limits of blueprints and begin to return to the question of the pathway forward. Blueprints can be carried only so far because life and history are not like buildings. They are dynamic, they flow, they are unpredictable. The vision of an alternative like economic democracy only becomes clearer when people, of faith and necessity, commit themselves and act.

In 1979 a process began in Detroit which shows how economic democracy, haltingly but steadily, begins to grow where the system has failed. The Chrysler corporation, unable to free itself from the automotive fantasies of an earlier age, became a terminal case of mismanagement and runaway debt. Accordingly, the company turned to the federal government for a bail-out.

By the traditional laws of free enterprise, Chrysler simply would have been allowed to go belly-up. However, under the rules of the oligopoly system, where the fate of powerful corporations with thousands of workers is at stake, the pressure becomes enormous to save the firm with a subsidy.

It is at this point that the question of economic democracy sharpens. If public capital is to be used to save a corporation, aren't the taxpayers serving the traditional function of the private investor? And if so, shouldn't the taxpayer-turned-investor get a "return" for taking the investment risk? Why shouldn't the public, through the government, ask for a new management, more efficient cars, a commitment to mass transit, and a different approach to plant closings? Why shouldn't the workers too gain a new level of self-management over their now publicly subsidized workplace? This very notion was raised by the United Auto Workers themselves in response to the Chrysler affair. Instead of a bailout, the UAW suggested a *direct government equity invest-ment* in the firm, on the grounds that "the public should not assume financial risk for a private corporation in the absense of an equitable degree of control." The union also proposed *worker* participation "at all levels of the Chrysler Corporation, from the shop floor to the board room," with equal authority in reaching decisions on plant location, product planning, capital spending, pricing policies, production planning, quality control, health and safety and overtime.

UAW Vice President Marc Stepp explained the union's view this way: "There are real limitations in our economic and political system—a system that encourages plants to be closed and people's lives to be disrupted for the sake of profits. We believe that this shameful system can be changed so that workers and communities don't have to bear the total burden of such economic 'progress.' That's why we are demanding not only the right to workers' par-ticipation in the decision-making process, but also new provisions to deal with the plant-closing problem."[113]

By early 1980, a first step with major historical symbolism took place: UAW President Douglas Fraser was appointed a Chrysler director.

There are certain to be many more Chrysler-type failures in the years ahead. If the corporations have their way, there will be bail-outs with no strings attached, a total prostitution of the public interest before the private. But if the taxpayers realize that they are paying to correct the mismanagement of the corporations, they will begin to demand a seat at the decision-making tables. And it will not seem at all like a radical idea, but *the only path of common sense in a democracy*.

This is not to suggest that implementing economic democracy is going to be a straightforward easy affair in the years ahead. Even democratizing firms like Chrysler will be exceptionally difficult. Those who believe in corporate and not social efficiency, who would rather have profits than real progress, and who are philo-sophically fixed in frontier mentalities are going to rather fight than switch. Even when it comes to reforming one firm, they will realize the showcase power of any successes for economic democ-racy and try to slow such gains. But nonetheless a steady accrual of victories is surely possible to foresee. And when we speak of economic democracy penetrating all corporations and of the values of economic democracy and the inner frontier redefining our national politics we know we are talking about a hard and long fight on largely uncharted waters. But to deal with inflation and unemployment, energy needs, our health and the furtherance of our national culture and wisdom, nothing less will do. We must make immediate advances, begin now to elaborate structural and legal reforms, and progressively enlarge the new vision and practice of economic democracy.

Our vision of democracy, however, should not lead to the illusion that economic reforms alone will provide true equality for women and racial minorities. The victims of discrimination find themselves second-class economically, but also carry burdens of a social and cultural oppression as well. Economic democracy as a framework will have to remove the economic reasons for discrimination, but promote a kind of cultural pluralism too.

Economic Democracy and Women

Feminists have demonstrated that the power and privilege men monopolize in a patriarchal society will never be transformed by persuasion alone nor by mere economic restructuring. To equalize the opportunity for men and women, to eliminate the stereotypes and institutional bars which deny women intellectual and cultural advance as well as political power, to eliminate rape and other violence against women from our culture will require a long struggle by feminists not only in the economy, but in the spheres of socialization, education, culture, and politics as well. ts

To think of economic democracy without also thinking of ending male supremacy is to engage in self-deception. The whole concept of democracy in any form is hollow in a context where women are denied skills, confidence, and power to express themselves. What kind of democracy is it that operates without half a population. Further, there can be no true democratic consciousness and energy among men so long as the personality of Custer is our archtype. The struggle for economic democracy in the economy and the struggle of women against patriarchy in all its forms are thus connected and interdependent. For either movement to fulfill its profound promise, both will have to embody norms of behavior and develop programs respectful of the other's values.

The attainment of economic democracy, while it can't alone mean an end to patriarchy, will certainly be an advance for women. It would mean the implementation of the Equal Rights Amendment in the economy. No longer would women be subjected to inferior wages, earning only $.59 for every $1.00 earned by males in comparable situations as they do now. No longer would they be denied quality jobs or face discrimination in Social Security, insurance or credit programs.

The application of the ideas of economic democracy to women's role in the economy means that women's needs must be taken into account in the wage structure, the definition of work roles, and character of the products we produce, and the manner in which they are advertised. The principles of economic democracy mean that in workplaces women must be able to exert power over decisions affecting their lives, and likewise women as consumers and as community residents must also be in a position to exert power over the decisions of corporations which produce goods they need, or help create the cultural climate of their communities.

Therefore, when womens' power can manifest itself in our economic institutions, the changes will be profound for all. Women will escape from what is called "the secondary labor market" and attain not only equal pay for equal work, but also equal access to desirable jobs. In the short run affirmative action should be continued and elaborated still more broadly. But in the longer run the very character of workplace relations must alter— women will no longer permit men to relegate them to lesser work, to do only clean-up and be ornaments, and to hold fewer positions of leadership. More, women will not allow the maintenance of a primitive shop floor ethic causing them to endure not only psychological indignity but such barbaric practices as forced compliance with sexual demands to attain promotions. Women would not allow men to decide that pregnancy doesn't constitute a justifiable reason to be off work, and would certainly no longer accept losses in seniority or even unemployment because of pregnancy. As women consumers exert economic power over the structure of U.S. industry, equally profound changes can be expected. If medical treatment of women is no longer under the sole auspices of male administrators and doctors, it is less likely that prohibited or unsafe birth control will be forced upon an uninformed public. In a society practicing the principles of economic democracy where workers, consumers and community people—fifty percent women—control economic life and where women will have still greater power with regard to those issues most important to the quality of their own lives, obviously there will be great and important changes paralleling those brought about by feminist victories in other spheres of life. Can anyone conceive, for example, that with economic democracy we would allow a pornography industry so large that its yearly revenues exceed that of the combined yearly revenues of the movie and record industries? Would the quality of life be so grotesque, would the archaic Custer-like notions of masculinity and femininity that currently allow such a deplorable allocation of our human energies and resources continue to prevail? It is hardly likely. And so while the intricate relationship between the evolution of economic democracy on the one hand and of feminist struggles for advance on the other are still to be clarified, the obvious importance of the two trends to each other cannot be denied. Indeed, without overcoming the differences in economic opportunities afforded to men and women, the unequal wages they can earn, and the culturally backward character of the content of many economic roles and practices, how can any really lasting women's gains be made in the economy, or for that matter in the rest of social life?

Economic Democracy and Racial Minorities

The frontier was supposedly the avenue of advance for all racial and ethnic minorities, and for their projected integration into the mainstream of a homogenized America. In the brilliant analysis of James Ogilvy, the direction was to be an absorption into

> a universalist culture whose customs represent the unacknowledged imposition of Wasp values in the name of universalism. The price of Americanization is then the adoption of an individualist ethic of autonomy girded by strong internal restraints rather than external bonds of

brotherhood with one's group on whose customs, however parochial, one can depend for guidance.[114]

It is hardly an insight to note that the experiment failed. In California, the end of the frontier has not meant the end of ethnic identity and the emergence of a new Americanism, but a pervasive sense of *non*-identity among whites surrounded by tides of separatism among minorities. In the eastern, midwestern and southern U.S., even the whites have begun to redefine themselves in ethnic, tribal fashion instead of experiencing the fate of the melting pot. The issue of race is still, in W. E. B. DuBois' words, the issue of the twentieth century.

To date Native Americans, hispanics, blacks, and Asian-Americans have yet to get on the ladder of upward mobility or above the bottom rung. The pervasive racism in our society, with roots in the virtually genocidal European settler approach to Native Americans, slavery, and the expropriations and on-going "imperial" relations with Mexico and Puerto Rico have largely prevented the corporate largesse from ever reaching these most disenfranchised people in our country. Moreover, racism means hard work at low wages, a pool of unemployed, and a scapegoat group against which white workers may be played off to distract their attention from real problems. Racism has been profitable for corporations, creating an incentive to further the minorities' sad heritage. And now, when minority communities are faced with the dire necessity of improving their circumstance, the outer frontier closes. Further advances will have to be a function of a new kind of justice.

Once at a Christmas party of senior citizens in Watts, I gave a speech attacking "Scrooge in the White House" and promised to fight for poor and oppressed people. At my table afterwards, an older gentleman leaned over, politely, and said it wouldn't happen. He recalled growing up in Louisiana when Governor Huey Long called for "sharing the wealth." The white people this man worked for said Huey Long wouldn't live two weeks—"not with talk like that. And sure enough, he didn't live."

Since Huey Long, the list of dead or jailed populists, progressives, chicano activists, Native Americans and black leaders has grown. The number of petitions, rallies, demonstrations, riots; of books, educationals, studies, registration drives and militant confrontations has been enormous. Yet change has been slow. Our ambivalence is still not shared.

Admittedly however, there have been some gains, a testimony to the energy and determination of people like Cesar Chavez, Dennis Banks, Martin Luther King and Malcolm X, as well as to the vast movements they have inspired. Historic court decisions and legislation have been passed. Millions of southern blacks live in a safer desegregated environment, and have voted over a thousand blacks into regional offices. There are non-white mayors in some of our largest cities, even more in the professions, and the problems of rural America have begun to be recognized throughout society.

Yet these changes are not enough to keep hope and expectation growing, not enough compared to the sacrifices made. The underlying conditions are tending to worsen. Ten years after the Watts uprising of 1965, a Los Angeles County Grand Jury concluded that conditions "are worse than they were at the time of the Watts revolt." And as the 1980s come upon us, the situation is still worsening. The Miami uprising of 1980 is indicative of the pain and the irrationality simmering in our cities waiting to explode once again.

In this cruel context any talk of progress is bound to seem hollow or token. The right to vote has not included the right to decide the range of economic choice. Political power has not included economic power. Even the political takeover of city governments by minorities has been mainly a takeover of underdeveloped areas which white business neglects or leaves behind.

While it is true that the end of discrimination depends largely upon effective community organizations of blacks, latinos, Asians, Native Americans and other minorities, it is also true that broader economic changes are crucial. The growth of a labor-intensive, rather than capital-intensive economy, one in which investment priorities are directed to the nation's distressed areas rather than to lucrative cheap labor havens abroad, is the only way to create the *economic context* for an end to racial conflict over narrowing opportunities.

But the establishment of that new economic framework is not alone enough to solve the problems of racial exclusion. It simply means that blacks in a Detroit Ford Plant, or Native Americans mining uranium, or chicanos in California's vineyards, will be in an improved position to exert democratic power over their economic situations. Black autoworkers would be able to resist any racist mentalities that now pervade the climate of work on the assembly line. They would have recourse to oppose placement in the most dangerous jobs, arbitrary firings, and second-class wages. As consumers and voters they would be in better position to demand a reorienting of priorities to address the plight of the ghettos and the need for improved health care or schooling.

The broad impact of a move toward economic democracy will also work to the advantage of Third World communities. As inflation and unemployment, poor working conditions and unsafe communities due to corporate pollution are all problems that affect Third World people even more viciously than white workers and consumers, gains in these areas will help diminish racial inequalities while also improving everyone's living conditions.

But there can be no solution to racism merely and automatically by creating economic democracy. The movement for economic democracy will have to consciously realize that minorities will always have reason to suspect a democracy that works according to majority definitions. The concept of economic democracy must include some kind of guarantee of minority rights, including the right to remain culturally different. Instead of the drive towards homogenization of the old frontier, we will have to adopt what Ogilvy calls a "multi-dimensional" culture and society. Without this cultural pluralism, economic democracy either will not win support from a majority, or its "victory" would be rhetoric stripped of any moral content.

Summary: Pioneers on the Inner Frontier

As the frontier declines, Americans face a choice of scrambling for fewer and fewer jobs and possessions, or changing their focus to the quality of life, work and community. The first road goes only to social, economic and racial chaos, the undignified thrashing of a defeated people. The second way is the only means to find a positive national future beyond the declining empire of the corporations.

When the outer, physical frontier ends, the inner, endless frontier begins. Having stormed the continent, plundered the earth, erected our monuments to technology, reached the pinnacle of prosperity, we are now facing the questions that always return when the avenues of escape are closed. Why the rat race? Does a Gross National Product measure the quality of life? Does "life, liberty and the pursuit of happiness" mean the right to make as much money as possible? If money is a goal, why did all the religious prophets including Jesus Christ disclaim its importance?

These are not abstract, philosophical questions. They are as closely related to our practical choices as the Protestant Ethic was to the emergence of early capitalism. These questions underlie the problems of daily life, from runaway children to runaway shops, from alcoholism and drug abuse to violence against women, from absenteeism at work to competition over jobs.

We need a new generation of pioneers. This time the frontier will be harder to conquer, since it is not so much trees to be chopped down as it is the barriers we have built in the name of our own freedom. The role of rugged individualism today is not to oppose the King of England, but the monstrous Corporate State that has grown out of our free enterprise dream.

The original frontier was always unlimited, romantic, a dream. People did not come to America as stowaways, trek across Europe with nothing to their name, sacrifice everything for their children for the sake of material possession or subservience to the malefactors of great wealth. No matter how much the material incentive was a motivation, it is hard to believe that people would give up their homes, traditions, and if necessary their lives, for a dollar. Certainly the dollar was crucial, as it is today to the illegal Mexican immigrants who send their clandestine earnings home to their families. But the dollar was always a *means* to the pioneering soul, a step toward opportunities to a richer life in a less-material sense. The key to that richness was dignity, and the key to dignity was a sense of personally participating in the decisions affecting one's life.

Today the monarchies from which our ancestors fled are no more. But they have been re-created in new form, for we worship the Almighty Dollar in the Church of the Multinational Corporations.

The time has come to cease worshipping false gods, to bring down the great temples, and return to the religion and philosophy of the heart—that all of us are equal, deserving of love, obligated to contribute, and have a right to be represented and recognized for the work we do.

Economic democracy means that decisions about production and consumption must be made by the people most directly affected by means of a cooperative calculation taking into account not only material relations, but also human and social relations. Factories do not produce only material commodities, nor only commodities and material by-products like pollution. What goes on in production also affects workers' well-beings, skills, and consciousness, as well as the social relations of community life. Economic decisions, to be democratic, must take into account all these so-called "externalities," for these are at least as critical to the character of our lives as decisions about material efficiency alone. As we move toward economic democracy, increasing our understanding of its contours as we proceed, certain steps will prove path-breaking: opening corporate decision-making boards to equal participation from workers, consumers, and community residents; democratizing life within the workplace itself; and redefining methods of allocation so that people needn't compete but can instead decide cooperatively what is best for all. Only these broader aims of economic democracy promise the new vision and ethics necessary to offset our attachment to old frontier beliefs, and to sustain our efforts to create changes. Yet we needn't cross our arms and await an ultimate cataclysmic, all at once change— corporate power one day, economic democracy the next—at some distant time in the future. The principles of economic democracy can guide efforts to gain a long sequence of reforms, whose accomplishment will at each step make further gains more accessible while also enriching our consciousness for the tasks ahead. The change from outer to inner frontier, from Custer to Thoreau, is not accomplished in an instant with a magic incantation, but over a long period and by a continuous process of interrelated improvements.

Economic democracy is not merely a "structural" proposal which is morally and emotionally barren. It requires a self-confident and proud sense of citizenship from the average person in the face of the giant corporation, just as the original American Revolution required a similar sentiment against the monarch of England. Two centuries later, it is only logical and inevitable that a mature people would want to wrest control of their lives from a new economic royalism.

SIX
GLOBAL VIEW: THE
FRONTIER OF PEACE

There are three billion people out there. They want what we have.

President Lyndon Johnson

Concessions obtained by financiers must be safeguarded by ministers of state, even if the sovereignty of unwilling nations be outraged in the process...the doors of the nations which are closed must be battered down.

Woodrow Wilson

Simplicity and nonviolence are obviously closely related. As physical resources are everywhere limited, people satisfying their needs by means of a modest use of resources are obviously less likely to be at each other's throats than people depending upon a high rate of use.

E. F. Schumacher

In an age of limits U.S. foreign policy is dangerously likely to focus on restoring the old frontier of the "open door." Instead, America should begin to consider the new national security implications implicit in a world of closing frontiers and looming scarcities.

In a world of limits, a foreign policy based on expanding national ambitions can only lead to confrontation; in a world of energy shortages, a foreign policy based on unlimited access to oil only invites the tragedy of war; in a world of majority frustration with minority privilege, a foreign policy seeking "peace through strength" can only mean a peace of the starving or World War III.

Iran as a Mirror

The Iran crisis offers the latest example of the convulsions to be expected as America's role in the world changes. Since the early 1950s, the Shah's regime was a powerful outpost of the American frontier, serving the interests of the U.S. oil industry and in particular the Chase Manhattan bank. When a protege of David Rockefeller, Henry Kissinger, became U.S. Secretary of State, the linkages with Iran tightened even further. Under the Nixon-Kissinger Doctrine of "regional sub-powers" looking after U.S. interests, Iran was defined as the bulwark of the Middle East. The Shah received more military aid than any other American client, and there is even evidence that Kissinger supported Iranian and OPEC oil price increases as a means to increase the Shah's capacity to buy still more American weapons.[1] A powerful Iran was seen as a dependable regional "policeman" in the struggle with the Soviet Union over spheres of interest, and in the looming struggle with indigenous nationalism over control of oil in the Middle East as well.

The subsequent U.S. failure in Iran, beginning with the Khomeini-led Revolution in 1979, must be seen as part of a deeper collapse for a strategy of world dominance. The several specific lessons of Iran can be generalized to understand the choices facing American foreign policy in the 1980s.

Over-emphasizing the Cold War: One lesson is that the U.S. over-emphasized the global Cold War definition of reality, and under-estimated the internal crisis caused by the Shah's rule. Kissinger was the most vocal, but not the first, architect of foreign policy who saw the world as a chessboard of power politics in which the U.S. and Soviet Union confronted each other through proxy nations. The billions in aid and weapons sent the Shah were designed to show an American commitment to a powerful world role, particularly after defeat and withdrawal from Vietnam. The Soviet Union, Kissinger thought, must not get the impression after Vietnam that the U.S. would retrench, become isolationist, and withdraw from its Cold War priorities and alliances. The fatal error in Kissinger's emphasis on the "great powers," however, was in not realizing that the very U.S. aid that made the Shah formi-dable *externally* created the conditions *internally* that led to his downfall.

The Soviet Union and its allies in the small Iranian Tudeh party did not overthrow the Shah. Rather U.S. policy created conditions that infuriated and motivated sufficient numbers of Iranians to overthrow the Shah themselves. For example, by aiding in the creation of the SAVAK, or Iranian secret police, and by providing technical aid and training the U.S. was complicit in brutal torture and repression; for certainly the Shah via the SAVAK was one of the world's most vicious human rights violaters.*[2] Iranians, generally speaking, are hardly fond of the Soviet Union for nationalistic, religious and historical reasons. But their most extreme hatred and alienation has been towards the U.S. because of its embrace of the Shah. Is it any wonder, with many families having personal scars to show? In fact, U.S. policy may even drive the Iranians *closer* to the Soviet Union for reasons of trade and national defense, thus increasing the prestige of the Tudeh Party within Iran itself. Again and again, the U.S. policy of supporting dictators and antagonizing popular masses of people seems to lead directly to the very Soviet influence or communist "takeovers" that American policy professes to prevent.

For our policies aim firstly to insure that U.S. corporations and multinationals will be able to enjoy international economic advantages. From less than $5 billion in 1945, the direct investments of U.S. companies abroad multiplied more than twenty fold to over $150 billion in 1970. In the words of the editors of *Business Week* magazine, "Teheran under the Shah had become a virtual Mecca for multinational corporations."[3] Citibank, America's most rapidly growing bank, derived more than 80 percent of its 1978 profits from its operations in ninety three foreign countries.[4]

If this economic gain requires dictatorships to keep indigenous populations from their own resources as dominion of their own power rather than multinational power, so be it. But then the ensuing dictatorial oppression leaves those populations no options other than turning to the East. Perhaps the well being of these countries *and* U.S. security could be better served by subordinating corporate profit making to new norms of international

*The close relationship between SAVAK and the U.S. has been admitted by Kermit Roosevelt Jr., a former CIA assistant deputy director for overseas clandestine operations in the 50s: "SAVAK, the security service originally trained by the United States after 1953, had established a tight and discreet control over all U.S. Embassy contact with Iranians." (Los Angeles *Times*, July 30, 1980)

cooperation.

Exaggerating the value of military might. The second lesson is that the greater America's military might becomes, the more impotent it is to control events. Like the regime of South Vietnam only a few years before, the Shah was outfitted with one of the most impressive arsenals in world history. And yet the Shah was overthrown by the superior force of revolutionary nationalism, anti-imperialism, and a desire for religious identity. Like South Vietnam, Iran became a country where victorious revolutionaries inherited billions of dollars' worth of the most advanced U.S. military equipment and technology.

Rather than learn this lesson, the U.S. seems bound to repeat and intensify its mistaken military obsession. The tragic "rescue mission" of May 1980 seemed almost a metaphor for the fate of those who follow the tradition of Custer. In the wake of the catastrophe, a sense of respect for the Americans killed in Iran seemed to block any national discussion of what would have happened if the mission had not aborted in the Iranian desert. President Carter assured Americans that the actual rescue of the hostages would be the "easiest" phase of the operation, but a careful review of the known facts suggests that a "successful" rescue mission would have led to war.

One week after the helicopter failures, the New York *Times* reported that President Carter was prepared to use C-130s for strafing the U.S. embassy area in Teheran, as well as A-7 and F-4s for bombing runs launched from aircraft carriers in the Persian Gulf. However, we were reassured, the bombing and strafing would only occur "in the event the 90-member assault team ran into trouble."[3] In other words, if there was any foul-up as the rescue mission reached Iran, President Carter was planning to begin a war while the American people were literally asleep.*

In retrospect, the rescue attempt was defended by Zbigniew Brzezinski as somehow serving notice on Iran and others that the

___

*Later revelations about the tragic rescue mission expose the problems of high-tech military solutions. In the first place, the pilots were not briefed about haboobs, the rare dust storms that disoriented the mission. Second, a helicopter experienced the burn-out of its tactical navigation system, and its omni-directional radio receiver for reasons still not understood. Third, another helicopter lost a 13-pound hydraulic pump; no one brought a spare, even though the same pump had broken down in practice. Most shocking, however, was the Pentagon

U.S. would try anything, including force, to get the hostages back. Allowing for Brzezinski's need to put the best possible cover on an embarrassing catastrophe, his explanation is extremely disturbing in its psychological implication. It calls to mind the statement of Richard Nixon, revealed on the White House tapes, that behaving like a "madman" was an excellent tactic for bringing other nations into line. By implying that the U.S. would "do anything" to free the hostages, Brzezinski seemed to be justifying the suspicions of U.S. allies who had been lied to, substantiating the complaint of Iran that the U.S. was seeking a military solution, admitting the continuing deception of Congress and the American people, and giving credence to a rising apprehension across the world that the U.S. might start a war with catastrophic implications for those nations dependent on Iran's oil supply, and for the people of the Middle East, if not the whole world. In arguing that the threat of irrational military action by a great nation is a positive tool, Brzezinski was admitting a serious lack of reason and morality in American foreign policy, a military mindset gone wild.

Understanding the Importance of National Rivalries Over Resource Use: A third lesson of Iran is that American national security is increasingly threatened by the worldwide corporate scramble over resources rather than the superpower rivalries of the Cold War. Iran had come to be a virtual possession of several American oil companies and bankers pursuing a strategy of over-consumption for the sake of rising profits. Looking forward to a continuing flow of crude from Iran, the American oil industry was reducing its stocks in 1978, apparently tightening supplies in order to create a climate for achieving higher, decontrolled prices. During the Iran "shortfall" after the 1979 Revolution, the U.S. faced a loss of 500,000 barrels of oil per day, or about three percent of American consumption. This was a relatively minor shortfall by comparison with the 1973-74 OPEC embargo in which 2 million barrels daily, or 12-13 percent of supply, was denied the U.S. for five months. Yet the combination of the oil industry's priorities and the Iranian cutbacks caused sudden gas lines, massive price hikes, widespread social anxiety and even violence.

admission that a "successful" raid would have left 15 hostages and 30 American attackers killed or injured. "Thus, there was a chance that only 38 hostages would have been rescued safely—at a cost of 45 casualties." (*Newsweek*, June 30, 1980)

There can be no doubt that such crises are the shape of things to come. There is now an increasing amount of what Daniel Yergins describes as "hostile oil" in the world. Fully 30 percent of the world's oil in 1978 came from countries hostile to the U.S.— Iran, Iraq, Libya and Algeria. More ominous are the clear signs of turbulence in Saudi Arabia, a nation the U.S. depends on more than any other in our history. Saudi Arabia as a nation state has only existed for less than fifty years; its population is divided into conflicting religious groups with an imported workforce including (restless) Palestinians. Its repressive regime permits no freedom of the press or political parties, and the country is swept by the conflicts over "modernization" and "westernization" that preceeded the Shah's fall in Iran. In 1979 alone, there were revolts suppressed by military force in Saudi Arabia's oil fields, and the nation's stability was proved an illusion by the takeover of the Grand Mosque in Mecca by 700 religious militants.[7]

Misunderstanding the Relation Between Foreign Policy and Domestic Policy: The final lesson suggested by Iran is that the pursuit of the Cold War, of dominance over world resources, and of military superiority abroad leads to a National Security State at home which endangers democracy itself. This threat became most apparent in the Nixon White House when the pursuit of an unpopular war induced mounting levels of manipulation, deception, harassment and repression of domestic critics. It was apparent more generally in the growing realization of the mid-1970s that the U.S. could not afford both "guns and butter," that the imperial emphasis abroad would be more a burden than a benefit to working people and minorities at home.

Jimmy Carter was elected on a campaign pledge to reverse these American priorities, and create a foreign policy that reflected the social progress, democratic spirit and achievements of the American people. In response to the Iran crisis (and the Soviet invasion of Afghanistan), he quickly jettisoned his original conception in favor of a more secret, and unfortunately, familiar regressive one. The domestic fortunes of the "unreconstructed" Cold Warriors began to rise again. The author of the new Cold War doctrine, Vietnam hawk Samuel P. Huntington, re-emerged from several years of partial exile where he had been blaming an "excess of democracy" for the American failure in Vietnam.[8]

Carter's rescue attempt in Iran violated the War Powers Act, passed by an anti-Nixon Congress in 1973, which expressly requires the president to consult congressional leaders about any initiative which could lead to war. The CIA, held in the doghouse of public disrespect since the Nixon years, was suddenly reauthorized to go forward with covert operations without the new charter of accountability that had been widely proposed after Watergate. Domestic public opinion showed a major rise in support for military spending for the first time since the 1960s. Were these outcomes the very reason for inviting the Shah to the U.S. in the first place? The American Ambassador to Iran, William Sullivan, warned of military danger. Kissinger and Rockefeller prevailed on Carter to welcome the Shah anyway. Was this loyalty or a desire to provoke a further erosion of the foreign policy restraints that had emerged in the aftermath of Vietnam? The lament of one business executive provides a clue to possible motives. "It was easy in pre-Vietnam days to look at an area on the map and say, 'That's ours,' and feel pretty good about investing there. That is no longer the case. . ."[9] There is no way to determine motives for sure, but whether orchestrated or not, the results of the Iran events were ominous. The country's leadership began shifting to the right in ways that could have only harmful economic effects, damage democracy, stifle the calls for new priorities, and set the stage for increased polarization and bitterness in the 1980s.

In brief then, the crisis in Iran raised five foreign policy questions we must address in the eighties: a) what is the proper emphasis to accord Cold War superpower rivalry with the Soviet Union, b) what is the future of the "Western Alliance," c) what is the relation of increasing military might to foreign policy failures, d) is future national security more likely to be threatened by the scramble for resources or the invasion of foreign armies, and e) what effects will an expanded American military empire have on domestic democracy? These questions together reflect a single, larger issue: What should American foreign policy be in the era of limits? As with domestic policy, there may have to be certain tinkering and adjustments for the sake of short-term solutions, but the more dire need is for a comprehensive vision and policy based on the need to preserve America's most cherished values while adapting to new global realities.

Returning to the Cold War: The Question of Soviet Intentions

National jitters over Iran, compounded by Afghanistan, threaten to drive American society backwards into the Cold War instead of forward to an alternative vision of the world. Evaluating the nature and intent of Soviet behavior is limited to assessing this trend.

Until the Afghanistan invasion, Soviet behavior was widely regarded as cautious and conservative, placing more emphasis on material growth and East-West detente than on the active fomenting of revolutionary violence. The Soviets were perhaps not as conservative as American planners wished, supporting Vietnam as they did with military and economic aid throughout the long war with the U.S.; but neither were the Soviets the ardent champions of Third World revolution that the Cubans, Palestinians, or black Africans wanted. Increasingly, the Soviet Union was categorized by Third World nations as part of the white, westernized world of "haves." Fewer and fewer voices perceived them as the hub of an "international conspiracy" with plans to overrun Western Europe and rule the world, nor as humanitarian abettor of poor nations seeking to overcome neo-colonial regimes. Given this view, how does one explain the Afghan invasion? Was it a change in policy? Kabul prior to the invasion was a satellite within the Soviet Union's defined sphere of interest, the regime was facing internal rebellion as well as subversion from Pakistan, and therefore was effectively occupied militarily by Soviet troops for the same reasons that the U.S. sent troops to the Dominican Republic in the spring of 1965. In this analysis, the invasion was not so much an expansionary thrust by the Soviets as an awkward and brutal attempt to maintain a grip on its bloc, or empire. Moreover, one may interpret the Kremlin decision to risk detente for a military adventure as a *response* to an American foreign policy which was actively strengthening West Germany and China, the two nations most feared by the Soviets. Only months before the Soviet move into Afghanistan, the U.S. had pushed for hundreds of new nuclear missiles to be located in Western Europe, and declared a policy of "parallel interests" with China, providing Beijing with advanced computer technology that could modernize its military forces. These policies signalled a toughening American stance, and were certainly a provocation in Soviet eyes. These facts may have entered Moscow's calculations when choosing between a SALT II agreement or an Afghan invasion.

But there may be something a bit too convenient about this dovish view. Like certain economic ideas, it nourishes a long-term, bitter dispute betweeen dovish and hawkish assessments of Soviet behavior and American policy. The assertion that the Soviet Union is a status quo power is basic to the dovish agenda of lower military spending, efforts towards disarmament, controls on the CIA, and greater attention to social needs. The conservative depiction of the Red Menace likewise is a buttress to an agenda of greater military spending and aggressive intervention abroad at the expense of domestic needs.

In this debate, which began almost with the Russian Revolution, the dovish viewpoint has been more often right than wrong, particularly during the years of the Cold War. But history changes, and viewpoints based on historic conditions must constantly be reassessed. In the Cold War period after World War II the Soviet Union was cautious and conservative for a reason: it was infinitely weaker than the U.S. in its industrial base, Gross National Product, and arsenal of weapons. The U.S. absolutely dominated the arms race, controlled the Free World, and often carried out aggressive interventions abroad. The Soviet Union concentrated more on developing industry, science and technology, and a deterrent nuclear capability.

Since the mid-sixties, however, the American dominance has at least begun to decline, and the balance of forces in the world has changed. In the new correlation, the Soviet Union is relatively stronger than before. Its economy, while less productive than the U.S., is infinitely stronger than in the devastating 1940s, when the Soviets bore the brunt of the war against Hitler. Its military-industrial complex is formidable. Its weapons have helped certain Third World Countries like Vietnam become stronger. The policy of detente reflected this new balance as it emerged in the early 1970s. Bleeding from Vietnam and facing major economic problems for the first time in a generation, the U.S. needed a retreat from its Cold War emphasis. Having achieved rough equivalence in the arms race, the Soviet Union needed a way to improve its domestic economy and pursue its foreign policy objectives without risking nuclear war.

It is possible the 1980s could be a period *beyond detente,* in which American weaknesses become accentuated and Soviet strengths increase by comparison. If this is so, it would explain why the dovish view of Soviet behavior, correct in the old Cold War context, could become obsolete in the 1980s. Moscow began to display a new aggressiveness in the 1970s. They gave crucial support to Cubans fighting in Angola and the Horn of Africa, and to the revolutionary government in South Yemen. Whether for worthy aims (stopping South African troops) or dubious power politics (Ethiopia over Somalia), these military forays were a new step beyond traditional Soviet strategies, allowing as they did the "export of revolution" by direct Cuban entry. Then came Afghanistan, the first direct Soviet push beyond its borders since the Czechoslovakian intervention in 1968. It is not foolhardy to cautiously assume there will be more Angolas, South Yemens, and perhaps even Afghanistans in the next ten years.

There is no doubt that the Soviet invasion of Afghanistan planted or confirmed the Cold War view of the world in millions of American minds. The televised arrival of tanks and troops, the reported (but unsubstantiated) use of nerve gas, the destruction of villages, and the obvious hatred of the people of Afghanistan for the puppet regime, provided visible and overwhelming evidence for the views of America's hard-liners. The irony is that such Soviet behavior strengthened the hawks in America at precisely the moment that their views were becoming discredited. In fact, in most regions of the world, the U.S. is reaping what the first generation of Cold Warriors sowed, with extremely damaging results.

Under the banner of the "free world," the U.S. Cold Warriors propagated a doctrine that rendered even neutral countries, like India under Nehru, suspect of subversion. Even worse, the U.S. supported a brutal, and often preposterous, set of dictators on the grounds that they were allies in the struggle against communism. Their right-wing dictatorships, unlike those of the left, were defended as "necessary" or "temporary" measures of defense while the conditions of economic development, and therefore freedom, were being prepared with the assistance of American advisors and, occasionally, troops. Thus, America actively participated in overthrowing the "left" governments of Arbenz in Guatemala (1954) and Patrice Lumumba in the Congo (1961), while working to consolidate the dictatorships of Diem in South Vietnam, Batista in Cuba and the Shah in Iran, as well as such neo-Nazis as Stroessner in Peru. Obviously the real motive had little to do with promoting "political freedom." More important, it would seem, was the protection of economic and strategic interests no matter the effects on indigenous populations.

The results of these Cold War policies have not surprisingly been tragic and counter-productive. The Third World countries where the U.S. intervened—the Congo, Dominican Republic, Guatemala, Indonesia, etc.—showed no signs of economic or social improvement as a result. They continue to languish under corrupt and dictatorial governments, they remain among the impoverished nations of the earth, and they continue to be centers of revolutionary ferment despite repression and terror. Among the European countries, none have become "Soviet satellites," but the problems of Greece, Spain, Portugal and Italy remain very much the same as before the Marshall Plan of the 1940's—political corruption, economic stagnation and unemployment, violence and counter-violence, and polarization between left and right.

Perhaps the most tragic, and widely forgotten, of America's Cold War adventures was the Korean War. Many thousands of Americans died to create a "free" South Korea, only to leave a military dictatorship for 25 years. The people of South Korea showed their dissatisfaction with this result by overthrowing Singman Rhee's regime in 1960, only to have it replaced by a new strongman, General Park Chung Hee. General Park choked off liberties and foiled his political opponents for two decades until he met an embarassing end for a Free World leader, assassination by his own Chief of Intelligence. Within a few weeks of Park's death, the new military rulers in Seoul had placed over 100 top politicians and student leaders in secret detention centers, opened fire on people in the streets, and issued Martial Law Decree 10, which was summarized in this way by the *New York Times*: "no political activity, no assemblies, no free press, no strikes, no rumors, no criticism of the present President or his predecessors, and no college."[10] What, it should be asked in retrospect, did a generation of Americans fight for in Korea? A profitable haven for runaway electronics and petrochemical-firms who leave the sons of Korea veterans jobless here in America?

The dictatorial "dominoes" which still stand, like South Korea, South Africa, Zaire, Pakistan, Peru and Chile, will surely face growing revolutionary and economic pressures in the 1980s. An attempt to revive the Cold War on their behalf will only lead to new foreign policy failures for the United States and still greater suffering for millions of people. If we prop up the General Pinochets of the planet, we will only disgrace ourselves while provoking the very process of communist-led revolution we claim to be containing. On the other hand, if Cuban soldiers shed their blood in South Africa against apartheid, most of the world will justifiably respect them as heroes while Washington, with corporate billions invested in Johannesburg's diamonds and chrome, feebly points out how far Fidel has strayed from his borders.

Perhaps a comic example can prove the futility of following a path back to the Cold War. "A Tiny Exporter of Revolution?" is the way *Newsweek* defined the latest "ominous note of instability" in the Carribean in March, 1980.[11] They were referring to Grenada, a nation of 110,000, which was fast becoming "the world's first English-speaking socialist state." Grenada's president, "left-leaning lawyer" Maurice Bishop, is described as "exporter of revolution," an instrument of Cuban (and therefore) Soviet expansion. The U.S. is alarmed and stepping up aid to other countries in the region like Antigua, St. Kitts-Nevis and Trinidad.

Let us make the assumption that all this is true, that the eastern Caribbean is about to fall to communism, an assumption that certainly requires great imagination. The unexamined issue in the *Newsweek* editorial is what the U.S. has been supporting as a better alternative. The editors mention in passing that before the appearance of the left-leaning President Bishop, Grenada had been a "sleepy little island" with a 35 percent unemployment rate living under "the repressive eccentricity of the island's dictator, Sir Eric Gairy—a devotee of voodoo who liked to lecture the United Nations on UFOs." Little wonder that Sir Gairy was overthrown, but what does the United States see in voodoo doctors that makes them a viable alternative to communism? Certainly not an avenue to an advancing well-being for Grenada's population, yet only that could forestall increases in overtures toward the Soviets.

Breakup of the Western Alliance

The first Cold War cemented a "Free World Alliance" against the Soviet Union. The second Cold War revealed a basic weakening of that alliance. A last policy drawback of excessive fixation on the "Soviet threat" is that it detracts attention from a less suspected realm of potential new conflict. The token and grudging support from Western Europe and Japan for U.S. sanctions against Iran symbolized a basic global realignment. The "Free World Alliance" between America, Western Europe and Japan, at the heart of U.S. foreign policy during the Cold War, is fast disintegrating into economic rivalry and political tension. America's slippage from the role of world policeman and banker has been accompanied by a revival of German and Japanese power, the re-appearance of trade wars and protectionism and a weakening of Western military alliances. Reacting to American multinationals in the 1950's and 1960's, European and Japanese governments subsidized their own global corporations and quickly began increasing their exports. By the mid-1970's, after Vietnam and the OPEC embargo, the percentage share of U.S. multinationals in total world investments dropped below 50 percent for the first time since World War II.[13] The resulting tensions were sharpened further by differences over the Middle East beginning in 1973 when the U.S. alone virtually supplied Israel in its war with Egypt. But the most fundamental factor in the widening fissure has been the ebbing of the first Cold War, the emergence of detente, and the weakening of America's global role. These events deprived the "Free World" of the glue holding it together—the perceived need for a united front under U.S. leadership against the Soviet threat. As the U.S.-Soviet rivalry became less confrontational than in the early Cold War, new power rivalries arose between Washington, Tokyo and Bonn. Henry Kissinger observed in the mid-1970's that "the biggest problem American foreign policy confronts right now is not to regulate competition with its enemies...but how to bring our friends to a realisation that there are greater common interests than simply self-assertiveness..."[14] And former Secretary of Commerce Peter Peterson broached the danger more seriously: "If we ignore it, we could drift further away from our European partners... Wars are rarely planned. Countries drift into them. Similarly, economic confrontations are rarely brought on by design. No one intended that the pair of wars in the 1930s take place, yet that happened and a devastating effect on world trade was not corrected until after World War II."[15]

Even if these seeds of rivalry do not grow into war, it is certain that "Western unity" is more and more a mirage, undermining the central basis of the Cold War foreign policy. In the 1970s, David Rockefeller, Zbigniew Brzezinski and others formed the Trilateral Commission, composed of European, American and Japanese opinion-leaders, partly to address the problems of declining unity. Since then, the Trilaterals have become the object of numerous articles, investigations and even conspiracy theories by those who see them as either a liberal "world government" (the right-wing analysis) or a "coordinating committee for the multinational corporations" (the left critique). While the latter notion is surely more accurate in view of the interwoven corporate and financial connections of the Trilateralists, there may be an even more significant analysis of them by future historians: for all their power, they do not seem able to overcome national rivalries, nor to agree on a unified approach to the issues posed by the Soviet Union, the Third World, or social and economic unrest in their own countries. As a power elite they are a failure because the realities of power have slipped beyond any traditional controls.

A foreign policy alternative to the Free World alliance structure will not be easy to define or accept, so wrenching is it for a majority of Americans. Perhaps the first response will be an American protectionism, or economic nationalism, including restrictions on foreign investment in U.S. industry, banking and agriculture, as well as federal subsidy and cooperation to shore up the capacity of American industry to export products. This approach is certainly preferable to an American economy gradually colonized and dominated by international bankers and millionaire foreign investors. No nation wants to lose its sense of economic sovereignty.

But such a strategy in the longer-run is chauvinistic and self-defeating. It is impossible to conceive of a walled-off American domestic economy enjoying access to foreign markets and resources. A better approach, though remote today because of national differences, is that of a common international front of workers and consumers against the policies of the multinationals which now drive them into competition for jobs and goods in a global factory. This would include joint agreements among labor organizations concerning runaway shops, policies aimed at uniform environmental and safety standards, inclusion of relevent national representatives on the boards of multinationals in their own countries, agreements to share resources with developing nations, and so on. Only by such a recognition of interdependency and equity can the old Cold War alliances be prevented from dissolution into trade wars or worse.

Such economic cooperation and unity would not seek to erase cultural and national differences as current governments tend to do. There would be a place for Irish independence, Quebec nationalism, Basque culture, and other identities to flourish rather than being buried under an Anglo-German-French "continentalism." Whereas the Cold War military doctrine and Trilateral economic theories would subordinate or suppress such differences for the sake of centralized "unity," an alternative policy would be to base a new kind of strength on the variety of cultural roots and identities by which people find meaning in their lives.

The Growing Impotence of Military Power

Now let us take a more serious example of where the new Cold War can lead—to war in the Persian Gulf. Even a brief survey of the "arc of crisis," which the new Carter Doctrine proposes to defend by force if necessary, reveals a feeble and counterproductive set of options for the United States.

The President's reborn Cold Warriors propose a Rapid Deployment Force, a kind of international SWAT team, able to move great distances quickly for an assortment of military emergencies. But just as the Green Berets made little headway in the jungles of Indochina, a recycled version is likely to accomplish even less in the sands of the Middle East. The physical terrain is forbidding—for example, one American soldier would need 12 gallons of water per day in the desert. And the more important "terrain" of warfare—political support from the local population—is no more existent than it was in Vietnam.

It is doubtful that the Soviets will be intimidated by news that 18-to-20 year old Americans are registering for the draft. Where will those recruits fight? No one even proposes sending American troops to Afghanistan, or into battle anywhere on the border of the Soviet Union. Using military force to free the hostages in Iran is impossible, as is the thought of invading there on the ground. Defending the Khyber Pass on the Pakistan-Afghan border is romantic lunacy. If our temporary new Pakistani friend, General Zia, gets substantial military aid from the U.S., it will only provoke an escalation from his bigger neighbors, Russia and India. In any case, we should hesitate before rushing weapons to a regime that is rotten to the core, whose president denounces democracy, will use our aid to further suppress its own population, may drive the oppressed region of Baluchistan into a separatist alliance with the Soviet Union, and which could become "the next Iran."[17]

That leaves only the Persian Gulf itself, where the military options are "limited" in the view of *New York Times* military writer Drew Middleton—and a majority of Arab nations fear the impact of our military presence. Assuming the limits of conventional warfare, what then do our strategic planners have in mind?

The answer is a return to Cold War nuclear brinksmanship and, if necessary, nuclear war itself. By their own deliberately-leaked admission in early 1980, U.S. officials were "thinking about the unthinkable."[18] A definitive Pentagon study recommended using nuclear weapons if the Soviets entered Iran, and the president declared himself ready to use "any means necessary" to protect the whole Persian Gulf, extending America's definition of its vital interests to a whole new region of the world.[19]

Seen this way, policies like the resumption of the draft and creation of a Rapid Deployment Force are only signals of toughness in a game of nuclear bluff. And if the bluff were to be called, Jimmy Carter would be compelled to either back down in disgrace or become the first world leader to drop the Bomb since Hiroshima and Nagasaki.

Let us remind ourselves of the effects of nuclear weapons to better understand what the president has implied a willingness to do. U.S. National Security Council studies show a strong possibility of 140 *million* American deaths in a nuclear war, 140 times the combined U.S. fatalities from the Civil War, World Wars I and II, Korea and Vietnam. A single 24-megaton H-bomb, according to Daniel Ellsberg, contains three times the total explosive force of all the bombs we dropped on Vietnam, and twelve times the force of all we dropped during World War II.[20]

Because of the magnitude of these figures, a generation of peace advocates have warned against even getting used to the concept of nuclear war. If nuclear weapons have any purpose, they must be strictly limited to deterrence until global nuclear disarmament is achieved.

President Carter was not engaged in nuclear deterrence in 1980, but in nuclear blackmail over an abrupt new definition of our vital interests. But there could be no interest so "vital" as to justify thermonuclear war, certainly not Afghanistan (never before listed as crucial to the Free World), nor Pakistan (or any other disintegrating dictatorship), nor the oilfields (which will produce their last affordable barrels in a generation or two).

Playing the China Card

There is a new, historical reason that the Cold Warriors believe they may be successful this time with Cold War II: the emergence of the full-blown rivalry between the Soviet Union and China. The new Cold Warriors are saying that America's relative decline in power from the first Cold War can be offset by the collapse of the unity on the part of "the Sino-Soviet bloc" (as it was known not so long ago). The conflict between the Chinese and Russians, especially if it becomes an open war, signals the existence of contradictions between "communist" states perhaps as great as those between capitalism and socialism. Since this is an unprecedented phenomenon in history, it is rather difficult to theorize upon its meaning or project its result on American foreign policy.

What the current Chinese leadership shares with Brzezinski and other Cold Warriors going back to U.S. Secretary of State John Foster Dulles is a view that the Soviet Union is the principle enemy of humanity. The elements of this Chinese view apparently lie in historic territorial and cultural differences with the Russians, in the Soviet attempt to subordinate China under its strategy direction, and in a Chinese theory that seems to define Western imperialism as a declining force and Soviet communism as the new hegemonic force in the world. At the same time, the Chinese have determined upon an "opening to the West" as an alliance against Soviet expansion, and a domestic strategy of industrial and technical development.

Naturally, American industries ranging from oil to aerospace to tourism are excited about drilling and computerizing China from their air-conditioned office buildings and Hilton hotels. But aside from this commercial self-interest, it is not clear what new strategic or historic analysis the U.S. is proceeding from.

Instead of a new analysis explaining why China and the U.S. are converging permanently, Brzezinski and others seem to see playing the "China card" as simply a new *tactic* in an old Cold War strategy. On his trips to China, Brzezinski has suggested that America and China have "parallel" interests in containing the Soviet Union. Parallel interests, however, are quite different than truly common or shared historical interests. China, for example, has changed its definition of its foreign policy interests several times since Mao's death; it now venerates the purged "running dogs" of a decade ago and castigates the "Gang of Four" who only recently held power. Its interests may yet shift back to an anti-U.S., if not pro-Soviet, perspective. Already in 1980, the Chinese have cancelled plans to allow U.S. aerospace corporations to supply them with ready-made jumbo jets; instead, China has taken the technology and intends to build its own planes.

Already, the tacit alliance with China has led the U.S. to disastrous policies in both Southwest and Southeast Asia. The problems of American involvement with General Zia in Pakistan have already been noted; but the Chinese would like to see such a U.S.-Pakistan military pact for reasons of their own: to play "the America card," as it were, against China's enemies in India and the Soviet Union.

In Southeast Asia, the U.S.-China pursuit of "parallel" interests led to an American acceptance of the barbaric Chinese satellite regime of Pol Pot in Cambodia. In a power struggle of uncertain nature after the Cambodian revolution of 1975, Pol Pot's group came to power and conducted a massacre on the model of Stalin's Russia in the 1930s. It was tragedy enough that American bombs had destroyed the neutrality of Prince Sihanouk's Cambodia from 1970 onwards, thus creating the conditions for the 1975 bloodbath, but official American silence afterwards was perhaps worse. The Carter Administration said little about Cambodia in the years of atrocities from 1976 to 1979. The apparent reason was our "parallel" interest with China. In a theory that could have been drawn from American Cold War ideology, the Chinese seemed to support Pol Pot's barbarism because he was their proxy in a Cold War against the Soviet Union's proxies in Hanoi. And like the East-West Cold War, the conflict soon led to bloodshed between the proxies. Pol Pot's forces staged military raids over the Vietnamese border in 1977 and 1978; they were met by a Vietnamese offensive that overthrew Pol Pot and installed the Heng Samrin government which was composed of Cambodians who had fought alongside Hanoi during the long Indochina war.* The Vietnamese occupation in turn set the stage for a Chinese invasion of the northern part of Vietnam in 1979, an assault that apparently was well known to the Carter Administration before it occurred. The tension between China and Vietnam led to the expulsion of Chinese nationals from Ho Chi Minh City as part of a larger exodus of Vietnamese, most of whom had lived or fought on the American side of the war. The flow of boat people, and the angry mood it generated in America, caused an eerie *deja vu* for historians of the Indochina conflict. Almost exactly the same sequence of events had happened in the heyday of the Cold War, when the French were defeated by the Vietminh in 1954. About 900,000 Vietnamese streamed by foot and boat out of the North to the South, as the two zones had been defined by the Geneva Agreements. Most of the refugees were Vietnamese who had lived under French colonialism, fought on the side of the

---

*The Hong Kong bureau chief of *Newsweek*, Andrew Nagorski, reached the same conclusion: "It is often forgotten that it was Pol Pot's Khmer Rouge, with full backing from Peking, who launched repeated raids into Vietnamese territory in 1977 and 1978." And he adds, "thanks to the Chinese re-supply effort through Thailand the (Pol Pot) guerillas are both well-fed and well-armed.' Nagorski instead proposes a cut-off of Western aid to the Khmer Rouge, an international aid program to Indochina, and U.S. diplomatic recognition of Vietnam. He accuses the West of deliberately making impossible demands on Hanoi "while allowing the Cambodian people to die," and concludes that "it seems short-sighted, both politically and strategically, to keep Vietnam isolated and totally dependent on the Soviet Union." (*Newsweek*, June 30, 1980)

French, and had ample reason to fear their earlier communist victims. They were encouraged, if not stampeded, by broadcasts from the Catholic Church promising protection from "godless communism" if they would come South. This migration, though rooted in the dynamics of colonialism, became the "moral" justification for U.S. intervention in 1956, beginning 20 years of bloody tragedy. At the end, a new swarm of refugees—much like the old, perhaps even their descendants—began to flee to the open seas, encouraged by "Voice of America" broadcasts from England. Many of the same Americans who lobbied for the *first* Indochina War were on hand again to exploit the refugee crisis for their Cold War goals.

In a replay of the 1950's, the Amercan government professes official agony over hunger, starvation and boat people, while seeming to take a perverse satisfaction from the new events in Indochina. The State Department disapproved of private, public and international attempts to get food and medicine to the majority of Cambodians under Heng Samrin (and Hanoi) control on the grounds that it would legitimize the Vietnamese invasion. But they lavished publicity and supplies on those starving Cambodians who had fled to the Thailand border as part of Pol Pot's constituency. Political expedience was a more important value to the U.S. than being against hunger. The exodus from Indochina *seemed* to confirm that the Vietnamese revolution had turned into a new Stalinism directing an oriental gulag archipelago. But while the Vietnamese deserved a share of serious responsibility for the tragedy, it was the U.S.-China rapprochement that lay at the root of the problem. And the war left Vietnam devastated. Having endured the most intense and concentrated bombing of military history, large parts of Vietnam were covered with craters resembling the moon more than once fertile countryside. Residual mines and munitions of all kinds continued to exact a heavy toll on innocent citizens. Infested, water-filled craters were a base for diseases of all kinds. And of course a large part of the economy and social infrastructure were destroyed while psychological scars would take decades to mend. Far from a gulag, Vietnam was a war ravaged, devastated homeland of a people richly deserving international assistance. And if after the war the U.S. had normalized relations with the new Vietnam and offered reconstruction assistance—as it did with Japan and Germany in the 1940's—it might have assisted in solving the problem of refugees before they became an exodus of thousands. Moreover, had the U.S. offered normalization, perhaps the Vietnamese could have better pursued their most desired policies of independence and non-alignment. The U.S. could have been a tacit ally balancing the Chinese to the North, allowing an independent Vietnam to remain in equilibrium with all three great powers. Instead, for Cold War reasons, the U.S. chose a path that contributed or led to further suffering in Indochina, a tightening of the Vietnam-Soviet alliance, and a danger of further wars between China and Vietnam. As with the first Cold War, this second one based on the "China card" has had no visible, weakening affect on the Soviet Union.

What the partnership with China *can* lead to, however, is the same danger as the first Cold War—a hot war between the U.S. and the Soviet Union. In fact, it is official Chinese doctrine that such a war is *inevitable*, a touchy subject which Brzezinski tends to downplay when he hosts and toasts the stream of Chinese visitors to Washington. The theory of an inevitable war between Washington and Moscow has been advanced before, in fact ever since 1917, by certain American interest groups and their allies abroad. That it has not occurred in 63 years, despite many dangerous showdowns, should be sufficient evidence for its lack of inevitability. In fact, the case can be made that those in America and the Soviet Union who believe a war *is* inevitable tend to promote views which could bring it on: paranoid visions of each other, calls for drawing the line in Pakistan or the east Caribbean, demands for a first-strike nuclear capability, and so forth. The Chinese have just this view of the Soviet Union (and, for that matter, the Soviets do of the Chinese). This being the case, it is plausible to assume that the Chinese look forward to fulfilling their analysis by helping provoke the war. They can do this, with our help, in any number of ways: destroying detente and the SALT treaty to de-stabilize the international climate, drawing the U.S. into making a "last stand" in Pakistan, employing U.S. military technology to provoke a clash with the Soviets in hopes of drawing the U.S. in. For the moment, this seems like madness that would be rejected by any American government. But as Soviet power and American frustration grows, there will be an increasing view among some U.S. policy-makers that military force is better used sooner than later.

The only question for them will be whether we should take on the Russians, or encourage the Chinese as our proxies. Where such a scenario leads is hard to imagine, but it cannot be the only way to "resolve" the Soviet-American relationship.

The Need For Political Struggle With the Soviets

There are in fact non-military approaches to the Soviet Union, even assuming the "worst case" model that the Soviets are intent on global expansion. There is no reason for America to be trapped between the twin futilities of nuclear brinksmanship or of passive isolationism. The United States should urge disarmament and affirm that its nuclear weapons policy is one of deterrence *alone*, and at the same time pursue an aggressive *political* competition with the Soviets instead of a military one. We have more than enough nuclear warheads to deter the Soviet Union from an attack, and while they may be maintained for deterrence they should never be looked upon as instruments with which to fashion a stable world order. The "order" of nuclear terror can only be temporary, not a lasting basis for resolving differences.

Americans often assume that the Soviet bureaucracy is too powerful or inhuman to be affected by dissent or political pressure from within. But perhaps we are too mesmerized by our own military mentality. There is no state so totalitarian that dissent, protest and resistance can be forever stifled or remain ineffective. In fact, the Soviet Union is rife with disputes within, and open conflicts in its foreign policy alliance have been apparent for years.

Any politically aware visitor to the Soviet Union—I have travelled there twice, once for six weeks—is struck by two general facts: the police apparatus is everywhere, but it cannot stop the spread of public and private criticism, including the adoption of "Western" notions of art and style. The government apparatus tries to maintain the appearance of total control, often by arbitrary crackdowns, but it also makes discreet adjustments to public pressure without always acknowledging them. Since Stalin, there has been a distinct, evolutionary "thaw" in Soviet society. Certain protests, like those of the Jewish dissidents or separatist groups, are basically frozen out as illegitimate and anti-Soviet activity by an intensely patriotic (and often anti-semitic) population. Any perceived pressure on the Soviet borders (from Germany, China or the U.S.) immediately reinforces patriotic support of their government by the Soviet people, most of whom recall the loss of 20 million kin during World War Two. Otherwise, there is a powerful trend which demands democratic reform and greater personal freedom within the structure of the Soviet state. How far this trend can evolve peacefully, and what level of intimidation it will confront, are difficult questions to answer. But there is no question that the Soviet bureaucracy is vulnerable to pressure from within.

Even from the inner gloom of detention in Gorky, the Soviet scientist and human rights activist Andrei Sakharov has written that the Soviet bureaucracy "cannot go against (the) dominant desire of the people" for peace, a popular desire which is "broad, profound, powerful and honest." Despite a police state apparatus, the needs for freedoms of information and the press, to travel abroad or emigrate, to have a multi-party system are "obvious to most people" in the USSR. And despite a resurgent Stalinism, Sakharov is convinced that what is needed is "a pure moral movement to plant in people's minds a basis for democratic and pluralistic transformation." While he calls on the West to remain militarily strong, and while his recommendation for more nuclear power seems outdated, Sakharov's main faith even from detention lies in building an essentially *political* movement: "Our only protection is the spotlight of public attention on our fate by friends around the world." [21]

Most Cold Warriors old or new have a vested interest in the totalitarian model of Soviet society because it justifies a purely military approach to the U.S.-Soviet relationship. If the people are helplessly enslaved, they reason, their liberation will only come from relentless, coercive pressure on the Soviet state. This view obviously serves the interests of those corporate leaders and their military allies who wish to sell the newest military weapons systems. But in fact, an opposite approach may be more reasoned even if less profitable: only in a relatively relaxed international climate can the political contradictions within the Soviet Union come to the surface without being smothered in patriotic appeals to support the beseiged government. At any rate, there are dissident and reformist trends in the Soviet Union which contain a ray of hope for change from within, and they need political allies more then NATO stockpiles in the outside world.

Furthermore, it is clear from the past 20 years that the Soviets have been unable to hold together their "international communist movement" despite all their military power and prestige. Objections to their bureaucratic centralism, national chauvinism, and even economic imperialism have led to constant ruptures within their "orbit." The Chinese broke away in 1960; small nations like Yugoslavia, Rumania, North Korea and Albania have become independent as well: heavy recipients of aid like Egypt, Sudan, Guinea, Somalia and Iraq have rejected Soviet technicians and troops; and an independent "euro-communism" tendency critical of the Soviet Union has emerged in Italy, Spain, France and other Western European countries in the 1970s.

In every case, it was not American bombs or assistance to internal guerillas that created the rupture; instead, it seemed inherent to Soviet policy that centrifugal forces would be set in motion. Because the U.S. has aligned itself with the "Free World's" corrupt dictators, our hands have never been clean enough to make an effective criticism of the Soviet state, and thus launch a political offensive in behalf of a better vision.

From Cold War to Interdependence

As the Soviets justify self-interested invasions of Czechoslovakia and Afghanistan by rhetoric about exaggerated CIA activity in those countries, likewise U.S. leaders rationalize their forays in defense of multinationals by exaggerated visions of a Soviet juggernaut. The right and the military on both sides are served by this "cold war" and reform is the chief casualty. If U.S. international policy were reassessed in light of an extension of the principles of economic democracy a better alternative could emerge. But as things stand, both the U.S. and USSR go against the flow of history where they attempt to dominate the world's economic, political and cultural systems. The age of single-nation empires is passing. "This is the first time in history," writes historian Barbara Ward, "that the ending of one imperial system has been attended not by an uneasy expectation of a successor, but by the passionate proclamation of the principle that imperialism itself is impermissible."[25] The world is at once too interdependent and too varied, and communication too instantaneous, for the imposition of any standardized and rigid set of controls. The Soviet Union can no more dictate the development of Latin America than the United States could the Asian subcontinent. The world is shifting from cold war competition for supremacy between two superpowers to a more volatile, complex and potentially more creative world of pluralism. The Western alliance will never again be dominated exclusively by the United States; indeed, Japan, West Germany and France are among our new competitors. Smaller European nations, like Ireland, will never accept full assimilation into an Anglo-Saxon or German continentalism; the republican motto, "Ireland, unfree, shall never be at peace," seems a realistic description of numerous nationalities seeking to preserve their own identities. The Third World nations will never again accept a form of colonial domination; the Group of 77 nations is now demanding a "New International Economic Order" and they have the economic power to force the attention of the rich nations. The once-unified "socialist bloc" is ancient history; more splits, fissures and rivalries are inevitable. The proliferation of nuclear energy at once makes military superiority harder to use, and turns small groups of terrorists into temporary superpowers.

When the U.S. does employ "political" criticism, it usually is through support of dissidents who want to overthrow, rather than democratically reform, the Soviet State. The most famous of these is Alexander Solzhenitsyn, the noble literary exile whose works are broadcast by Voice of America into Soviet society. Solzhenitsyn, unfortunately, believes the Soviet people would be better off under a return of the Czars, a view that is not shared by most people on the street. While they may criticize their leaders, and maintain cultural attitudes tracing back to the pre-revolutionary period, most Russians are loyal to their government and proud of the scientific and military achievements of the past six decades. The flaw of Solzhenitsyn's criticism, and the root flaw of the Cold War thinking, is to assume that communism is only a "ploy" imposed on a billion or so people who would prefer the old ways to the new. Communism, say the anti-communists, can *never* be

better than the past—meaning *their* past. Above all, according to
the anti-communist dogma, communism can never be chosen
freely and where there is even a possibility of the democratic election of communists, the U.S. reacts curiously.

In the case of Italy's independent Communist Party in the
mid-1970s, for example, rather than endorsing its anti-Stalinism
and acceptance of democratic processes, the U.S. poured CIA
agents and slush funds into a secret campaign to subvert their
chances of success at the polls.[23] America acts as the mirror opposite of the Soviet Union; we too act as an invisible authoritarian
force interfering with free elections, and acting as if power over
history could only be entrusted to reliable and subservient elites.

Americans forget at their peril that nationalism, religion and
the desire for freedom have been more powerful than military
weapons in Vietnam, Iran, and with regard to the rise of OPEC—
just as they were in the American Revolution against British rule.
American forces were not frustrated in Indochina and the Shah
was not overthrown in Iran for a lack of material strength. In those
two crises which illustrate our time, hardware was defeated by
human commitment. A former Turkish official, now teaching at
Princeton, wrote of the coming world order in early 1980:
"Superpower hegemony is bound to shrink as we go into the
third millenium. Micro-states will crowd the future world map. *We
shall move from the monolithic to the minilithic, from blocs to
mosaics.*"[24]

Seen this way, the Soviet Union is actually declining while it
appears to be expanding. It cannot go against the flow of history
by an outmoded interventionism which weakens its economy,
over-extends its military and meets with the cold disapproval of the
world's people.

But neither can we. Are Americans ready to live in a "planetary mosaic" instead of a superpower rivalry? The basic question of
the coming decade is whether we can realize that being Number
One is an intoxicating illusion that produces no final victories, but
insures inevitable decline. Can we move from arms sales to
enlightened economic assistance for the Third World? Can we
regard the Soviets politically and not militarily long enough to
perceive our real national interests? Or will the narrower interests
of multinationals and private corporations afraid of nationalism

and peace forever cloud our vision? We have been jolted through the 1970s with this message, first by the Vietnamese, then by OPEC, and in 1979 by a tiny handful of unknown Iranian students. The question for Americans is whether there is life after Empire.

The Resource Crisis: True Threat to National Security

The key to understanding the world future, and America's role, is the worldwide resource crisis. Military power can temporarily reinforce corrupt regimes, but it cannot end hunger and the growing anger that hungry nations feel toward the West. Nuclear arsenals can instill a temporary confidence in national elites but it can not stop irrational terrorists from kidnapping children of executives, seizing nuclear plants, or building bombs of their own. Nor can it stop revolutionaries from organizing to change their countries so development becomes possible and starvation a thing of the past. Must they do this by violence and terror because we oppose the process, or can they accomplish advance more peacefully and with our support even against the monetary interests of certain U.S. corporations?

The resource crisis in the relatively long run is one of coming to terms with the absolute limits to affordable raw materials, fossil fuels, and even clean water and grazable or arable land as world population and human aspirations grow. In the urgent short-run, the crisis is one of *distribution*, however. As President John Kennedy once declared, "If a free society cannot help the many who are poor, it cannot save the few who are rich." [25]

It is here in the issue of allocation of resources and opportunities that the functioning of the multinational corporations becomes a malignant and dangerous force rather than the instrument of global progress its admirers proclaim. Without repeating the analysis of Barnet and Mueller in *Global Reach*, one news item from Santiago, Chile, dated October 4, 1979, is sufficient to illustrate the role of the multi-nationals.

The story, reported in the *New York Times*, began with the following "paradox":

While Chile's Supreme Court was refusing to extradite to

the United States this week three army officers accused of planning a political assassination in Washington, Anaconda was signing a contract to invest up to $1.5 billion in a new copper mine here.[26]

The assassination was of Orlando Letelier, former official in the government of Salvadore Allende, overthrown by force in 1973. Letelier was murdered by right wing terrorists who fastened a bomb to his automobile in Washington, D.C. Also killed in the explosion was Ronnie Moffett, an American active in human rights organizations in the U.S. An investigation led to evidence that the Chilean secret police were operating inside the United States. It was an embarassing blow to a U.S. government officially dedicated to "human rights" while also maintaining relations with Chile. But no such contradiction seemed to bother the American companies, some of whom were nationalized by Allende, as they rushed into the "new Chile"of lower wages and repressive violent rule.

Human rights violations, to which American liberals attach so much significance, are not a factor in corporate decision-making, businessmen here say.

"I don't think we spent five minutes talking about human rights when the board made the decision to invest in Chile," said Jack Carter, manager of Goodyear's $34 million tire, battery and rubber products plant.

Reflecting the general enthusiasm of American businessmen here for the government of President Augusto Pinochet, Robert Smith who runs Dow's operations in Chile, said that business conditions were "excellent."

Chile's foreign debt of $6 billion has been refinanced recently on more comfortable terms, with longer amortization periods and relatively more favorable interest rates.[27]

Though American citizens and an exiled foreign leader were murdered in Washington, the U.S. government was not charging "aggression" but attempting a mild rebuke of the Chilean dictatorship. Why? Because though the environment in Chile has been deadly for trade unionists, students, socialists and priests, it is also "excellent" for the multinationals. While American workers lost jobs to runaway plants in Ohio and Pennsylvania, those factories were rushing to a Chile which provided workers without unions and plenty of air to pollute. While small American entre-preneurs could barely afford rising interest rates, the international banks were arranging "comfortable" financing for a government of torturers. The public relations rhetoric of the multinationals can do little to beautify a close examination of their policies' actual results on working people in America and the Third World. Their processes of production worsen the world economic situation for billions of people, and perpetually lead the U.S. into alliances with unpopular governments which, sooner or later, are overthrown. The only way out of this destructive cycle is through serious negotiations towards a new, *international standard of conduct for corporate behavior*, consistent with our domestic aims of economic democracy. To begin with, the President of the United States should declare his executive authority to appoint public representatives to the boards of every major multinational to report back to the President and American people whether the firms are operating in the public's interest and how they might be re-directed to do so. More important, the principles of economic democracy must be extended. As a steel plant in Ohio is responsible to community residents to not despoil their environ-ment nor disrupt their economic or social lives, so a multinational must be responsible to its "foreign" workers and all citizens in its host country. As a Ford plant in Detroit should be guided by social criteria and not just profit, likewise if the plant is in Brazil. And to ensure this, in Brazil and host countries all over the world, as in the U.S., decision-making must come under the sway of those who are most directly affected. "There is an answer," as the historian Barbara Ward has concluded in *Progress for a Small Planet,*

> to introduce at the planetary level a principle essential to understanding and good will *within* domestic societies. Call it participation. Call it co-determination. Call it the application of democratic principles....
> It was one of the many acts of imagination in the preparations for the Marshall Plan that the Europeans themselves were invited to help to frame the policies from which they were so greatly to benefit... It was, in short, a genuinely co-operative venture." [28]

The Mineral Riches of Southern Africa
as percent of total world production in 1976

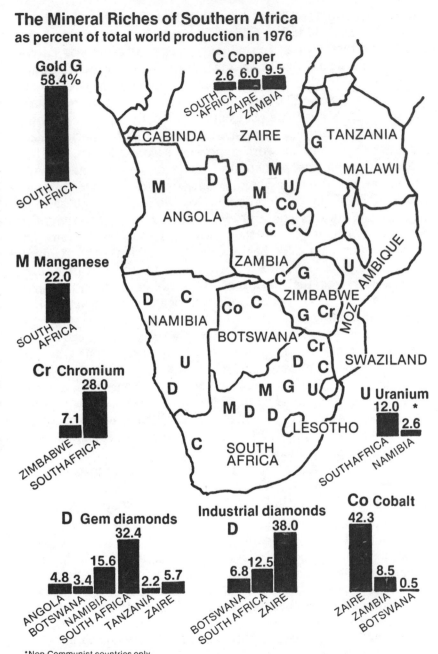

Gold G
58.4%
SOUTH AFRICA

M Manganese
22.0
SOUTH AFRICA

Cr Chromium
28.0
7.1
ZIMBABWE
SOUTHAFRICA

C Copper
2.6 6.0 9.5
SOUTH AFRICA ZAIRE ZAMBIA

U Uranium
12.0 *
2.6
SOUTHAFRICA NAMIBIA

D Gem diamonds
32.4
15.6
4.8 3.4
2.2 5.7
ANGOLA BOTSWANA NAMIBIA SOUTH AFRICA TANZANIA ZAIRE

Industrial diamonds D
38.0
12.5
6.8
BOTSWANA SOUTH AFRICA ZAIRE

Co Cobalt
42.3
8.5
0.5
ZAIRE ZAMBIA BOTSWANA

*Non-Communist countries only.
Source: U.S. Bureau of Mines.

Military Conscription Versus Energy Conservation

The most dangerous arena where the resource crisis could turn to war if the imperatives of the multinationals are permitted to dominate policy is, of course, the Persian Gulf. There one can observe a dangerous dynamic leading to war that is caused, not by Soviet aggressors or outrageous Iranian militants, but by the very economic process of the petro-chemical age. Put simply, American institutions have massive—and wasteful—energy requirements that make brinksmanship and force ever more likely in a world of diminishing supplies.

Long before a single hostage was seized in Teheran or a Soviet tank rolled into Kabúl, there was growing talk of war over the oilfields in American business and military circles. In its May 7, 1979 issue, *Fortune* printed no less than five maps of possible invasions of the Middle East. *Business Week,* in its November 19, 1979 cover article, "The Petro-Crash of the 80s," concluded that "as OPEC pushes the West toward the edge of economic survival, the option of a military response becomes more and more justifiable." [29] Secretary of Defense Harold Brown had been on record with the same message for six months.

The most apocalyptic scenario of the energy-economic crisis was sketched by *Business Week*. The U.S. will pay out $70-80 billion for imported oil yearly. National monetary authorities then create more money to make up for what is lost. The declining value of the dollar gives OPEC further reason to raise prices. The petro-dollars are recycled mostly to U.S. banks like Chase Manhattan, on short-term, 30-day deposits. Billions are then lent out to underdeveloped countries to pay their rising oil bills. The debt becomes staggering, tripling since 1974. In the meantime, countries like the U.S., Germany and Japan attempt to make up their balance-of-payments deficits by greater borrowing and competitive exporting. This results in greater deficits, and in trade wars among the advanced nations that lessen export opportunities for the underdeveloped. Lacking a way to overcome debt through exports, the underdeveloped nations become unable to pay back their loans. The non-oil-producing nations increased their external debt from $142 billion in 1974 to $315 billion in 1978, primarily to finance energy costs and keep up with inflation. American banks in 1979 were owed $57 billion by the non-OPEC developing nations, or about 130 percent of their total equity capital and loan-loss reserves. Claims on 128 U.S. banks by Brazil and the Phillipines, for example, alone were almost 40 percent of the equity capital and loss reserves of those banks. Argentina, Turkey, Thailand and South Korea were also in critical debtor condition. The Salomon Brothers investment firm predicted that 1981 would be the watershed year in rescheduling debt payment. A stringent demand by U.S. banks for repayment would almost certainly bring drastic reductions in living standards in the developing nations, and possibly revolutionary upheaval as a result. The other alternative, a rescheduling (or extension) of loans to the debtor nations would dangerously over-extend U.S. financial institutions, even threatening their collapse. The banks would have so many "non-paying assets" on their hands that oil-producing depositors will change from dollars to a new, more secure "basket currency." At that point, as the Western economy became a house of cards in a rising wind, *Business Week* would apparently recommend war.[29]

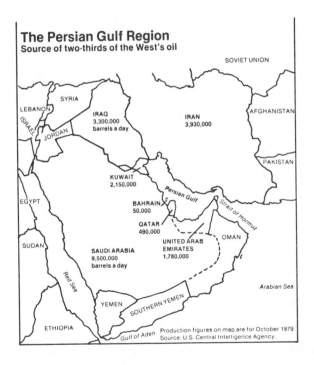

The Persian Gulf Region
Source of two-thirds of the West's oil

SOVIET UNION

SYRIA
LEBANON
ISRAEL
JORDAN

IRAQ
3,300,000
barrels a day

IRAN
3,930,000

AFGHANISTAN

PAKISTAN

KUWAIT
2,150,000

Persian Gulf

Strait of Hormuz

EGYPT

BAHRAIN
50,000

QATAR
490,000

OMAN

SUDAN

UNITED ARAB
EMIRATES
1,780,000

SAUDI ARABIA
9,500,000
barrels a day

Red Sea

Arabian Sea

YEMEN

SOUTHERN YEMEN

ETHIOPIA

Gulf of Aden

Production figures on map are for October 1979.
Source: U.S. Central Intelligence Agency.

The scramble for oil is only the most obvious resource crisis which threatens American national security. The racist and unstable regime of South Africa has 86 percent of the world's platinum reserves, 83 percent of the chrome, 64 percent of the vanadium, 40 percent of the gold, 48 percent of the manganese, and one third of the world's uranium supply.[30] Will the U.S. side with black African liberation movements who threaten to nationalize control of them, or will the U.S. bind itself in an immoral and virtual suicide pact with South African racism to maintain easier access to minerals?

Or to take another example of the resource crisis: there is enough grain and other food to provide sustenance to every person on earth, but because of inequitable distribution there are currently 450 million human beings starving to death, half of them children under five years of age. There are another one billion persons who are under-nourished.[31] Massive famine and hunger seem to be ignored except in the case of Indochina where Communist regimes can be blamed; in India, sub-Sahara Africa, Ethiopia, parts of Latin America and elsewhere millions of people have died of hunger in the past decade. Will the U.S. continue to identify with international grain monopolies and opulent police states, or will we make a commitment to end world hunger by any practical means? The answer to that question will have to do with the amount of strife, human dislocation, revolution, and warfare which will occur by the year 2000—but still more important, it will determine whether millions and perhaps even a billion souls will unnecessarily die or instead live to prosper and contribute their energies to the human legacy.

The alternatives to these fatal scenarios are neither easy nor simple, but they certainly are preferable to a new generation of young Americans dying in the desert for the oil industry, or being used as pawns in a global game of nuclear chicken. And, no matter the loss in profits to big multinationals, we can no longer support dictators and consign other countries to perpetual poverty.

A serious program of energy conservation is far more important than military conscription. And a crash investment in renewable resources like solar, wind, hydro and biomass, or in mass transit, is far more vital to national security than increased billions for an MX missile system.

It is madness that American oil imports keep increasing yearly. From 1970 to 1978, the imports rose from 3.4 million barrels per day, or 24 percent of total consumption, to 8.2 million barrels per day, or *50 percent* of consumption; that is, our imports doubled during the very years that every president preached "independence."[32] One reason for this paradox is that by holding on to domestic reserves while OPEC prices rose, the American oil companies were inflating the value of their oil and gas holdings from $200 billion in 1973 to $2 trillion in 1980. Meanwhile as our imported oil bill rose to over $80 billion, the combined conservation and solar program of the federal government was a pitiful $2.5 billion.[33]

Perhaps the greatest irony of going to war for oil is that the American military-industrial complex might well burn up more fuel in fighting than it could obtain in the case of "victory." The Pentagon is America's largest consumer of energy, using more alone in a given year than Sweden. The Pentagon and its top contractors devour more energy yearly than does India with 600 million people.

If the Harvard Energy Report is correct, America could reduce energy consumption by over 30 percent—through technical adjustments that would in no way reduce our standard of living.[34] That would radically reduce our Middle East dependency, and thus the dynamic towards war, *while making energy supplies available where they are vitally needed in the poorer countries.* If America were to reduce its annual air-conditioning budget by half, for example, it would provide an equivalent of *all* the energy needs of China for six months.[35] The same is true of conserving other crucial resources. If Americans followed the one-third reduction in meat-eating the AMA recommends to prevent heart attacks, it would provide the grain equivalent to meet the needs of millions of starving people.[36] If Americans even saved the food which is thrown away annually, it would feed 50 million people.[37] Or take the global maldistribution of water, which Richard Barnet says is "even more pronounced than the maldistribution of energy or food."[38] The U.S. loses 110 billion gallons of water per day because of contaminants, or inefficiencies. We use 1200 gallons daily for the alfalfa and water it takes to fatten one cow; we use up

100,000 gallons for every automobile produced.[39] Yet there are between 1 and 2 billion human beings without adequate water in the world.[40] Only one gallon provides the minimum requirements for five people. With the water lost in America each day, we could provide the minimum needs of 550 billion people or five hundred times the number of thirsting people. This is not to blame world hunger on personal habits. The structure of the world economy is far more to blame than individual customers at McDonalds. The essential point, however, is that there is enough waste in the bloated American economy to redistribute vital resources to those in need while not cutting back essential goods for the average American family. If anything, a redistribution would improve the diet, personal health, and family budget of many overfed Americans.

We urgently need, to quote an earlier Jimmy Carter, "the moral equivalent of war" to begin to solve the interrelated crises of energy, food and water. But where is the draft for the war on waste and overconsumption? Why does Washington threaten stern measures abroad, and plan the mobilization of young Americans for war, but adopt such feeble initiatives to conserve at home? Has the country become so callous that it would actually send its sons and daughters to kill and die in Saudi Arabia to preserve the right to gas-guzzling cars, heated swimming pools, year-round air conditioning and garbage cans of wasted food?

In addition to the need for an alternative energy focus at home, there is an exciting possibility of American participation in a global solar energy program. While President Eisenhower's "Atoms for Peace" program has resulted in a rising nuclear menace, the "Solar for Peace" program proposed by Denis Hayes could have the reverse impact. Hayes, founder of Earth Day in 1970 and Sun Day in 1978, is director of the Solar Energy Research Institute (SERI). In *Energy for Development*, a 1977 Worldwatch pamphlet, he sketched in outline form how the energy and economic needs of the poor countries could be met by solar applications.[41] The possibilities include passive solar systems for space heating in buildings, solar cookers and baking ovens, solar absorption cooling systems for homes, hotels or refrigeration, solar dryers for grain and fruit, solar (photovoltaic) cells for irrigation pumps or powering radio and television transmitters. Already there are a number of demonstration projects in the Third World, a major solar water heating program in Israel, as well as ethanol programs in Brazil and biogas plants in China based on the power of the sun.

The crucial point to understand is that current conventional energy systems are not working for the Third World, and rising price and safety problems will probably put such options even farther out of reach. Rural electrification programs, for instance, had reached only 12 percent of the rural Third World by 1971, and only half of those villagers could afford to purchase power. The second crucial fact is that the impossible prices of building new power plants and transmission lines in the rural Third World makes solar energy even more *cost-competitive* than it is in the United States. Therefore a *solar program aimed at the villages of the Third World would be a constructive solution to the energy and economic crisis of the world's poorest people.*

The decentralized, flexible nature of solar energy makes it specially suitable for global economic development. The failure of many such development programs lies in their being imposed from above in alien ways on cultures with their own traditional character. The "modernization" process often defaces cultural identity, destroys village and community life and sweeps the rural poor towards the unemployment lines and acquisitive atmosphere of urban society. There is another path to development, however, and that is through local self-reliance and community improvement. Called the kibbutz tradition in Israel, Ujamaa in Tanzania, or cooperativas among farmworkers in California, this movement substitutes labor for capital and energy, and defines progress as land reform rather than migration to the city. A major problem for the self-reliance movement, however, has been the centralized systems of production and energy transmission that have dominated the last several decades. Solar energy promises the possibility of decentralized manufacturing and distribution, however, creating a possibility of production complementary to the character of the self-reliance movement.

A Transition From Oil Imperialism

This scenario will undoubtedly seem fanciful unless it faces the more immediate issue of the *transition* from overdependency on Persian Gulf oil to a new age of conservation and solar. Even during a crash solar transition, the U.S. and other nations will need considerable amounts of oil, natural gas, coal and other supplies of energy derived from fossil fuels. The oil-producing nations will need a planned transition as well, investing their new wealth prudently in meaningful development projects and alternative sources of energy for the future. A global planning process is long overdue and tragically missing in the stormy area of international politics.

Short of such global planning, there are steps the U.S. can take to ease the transition. But it is only possible with a new diplomatic definition of allies and enemies going beyond the Cold War categories. This does not mean a supine foreign policy of courting the oil-producers at any price, as when certain corporate advocates like John Connally propose Mid-East policies premised only on greed for oil. But is does mean a comprehensive shift in foreign policy towards respect and understanding for the basic aspirations of nations we have long treated as marginal, expendable, even inferior. This includes the Islamic world, the Palestinian people, African states like Nigeria and Zimbabwe, Latin American nations like Mexico and Venezuela and the Asian powers of China and Vietnam. Without ignoring the differences of principle, the U.S. has to appreciate the *interdependence* of the world rather than dividing it into Number One and the also-rans. The potentials and the pitfalls in making such a transition are perhaps best illustrated by two case studies, those of Mexico and the Middle East.

Mexico: Not An Oilfield But A Nation

Perhaps the case of Mexico best highlights the lack of American global vision in the new era, and the void which must be filled by a new policy towards the developing world. Mexico is different from the Soviet Union, Saudi Arabia or other nations considered top priority in the power politics of American diplomacy in an obvious and overlooked way. With Mexico, there is a permanent, interlocking relationship that reaches deeply into the life of both countries. These links are historical, cultural, economic and geographic; taken together, they are a microcosm of the American relationship to the Third World. Mexico was an early victim of the expansion of the American frontier. Texas was lost to the U.S. in

1836; Arizona, Utah, Nevada, California and part of Colorado in 1848; and New Mexico in 1853. Periodic violence between the two countries continued until the 1920's, including the bombing, shelling and occupation of Veracruz in 1913, and violence nearly broke out again in the late 1930's when Mexican President Lazaro Cardenas nationalized the British and U.S. oil companies, creating Petroleo Mexicanos (PEMEX).

On another level, that of immigration, tension and violence never ceased. The promise of jobs in America pushed millions of Mexicans towards the border, and the desire of American businessmen for cheap unorganized labor pulled them across. When the economy during upswings needed them, they were housed in perhaps the worst conditions in American society, worked harsh hours for little pay, and since they had no political rights or power, were treated more like serfs than citizens. When the economy during its downswing no longer needed them they were deported by the hundreds of thousands, often with force and violence. Those millions of people still move back and forth with the seasons, rubbing a festering sore on both cultures and suffering perpetual indignities themselves. Mexico views the mistreatment of the migrants as a racial and national insult, while most Americans are hostile to what they perceive as a "floodtide" of aliens. The employers profit, and so the exploitation continues. The condition of Mexican-Americans in the U.S. deepens the problem: the discrimination against them in the Southwest is seen as further evidence of Yankee racism by Mexico, while the flow of migrants takes jobs from Americans of Mexican descent already here, and causes harassment by "La Migra"—the Immigration and Naturalization Service—towards anyone with brown skin, be they citizens or not. The relationship with Mexico illustrates how American "domestic" and "foreign" policy are inseparable and how nations are becoming interdependent.

Relations with Mexico could well be the most explosive issue for America in the next two decades. The U.S.-Mexican border is already the longest line between the greatest extremes of wealth and poverty in the world, stretching some 2000 miles from San Ysidro, California to Brownsville, Texas. The Mexican population, 60 million in 1975, will more than double to 132 million by the year 2000, while the Mexican-American community in the Southwest reaches as much as 40 percent of the total population and California may have a Third World majority by the year 2000.[42] The extremes of wealth and poverty within Mexico are the widest in the Western Hemisphere, fostering a time bomb of immense proportions. Revolution on its southern flank in Central America is sending new immigrants northward to Mexico, bringing added unrest as they join the migrant trail towards Los Angeles, El Paso and points north.

The U.S. is deeply implicated in Mexico's simmering economic crisis. We are Mexico's principle trading partner, supplying 62 percent of their imports and 60 percent of their exports in the mid-1970's. Mexico is indebted to American banks more than any nation in the developing world; their external debt was over $30 billion in 1976, more than 60 percent of it to U.S. banks. U.S. private investment is calcuated at nearly $3 billion, and multinationals mostly from the U.S. control 35 percent of the 200 largest Mexican firms.[47] Their investment policies move jobs and plants out of America to take advantage of the tariff and tax advantages, as well as the cheap labor (which they wish to maintain) on the Mexico side of the border, where the combined unemployment and under-employment rate is a staggering 50 percent.[44] If the fragile stability of Mexico's governing coalition ever sharply declines or collapses, the U.S. could be faced with millions of economic refugees on the doorstep.

And yet, staggering as these prospects are, it is more shocking to contemplate the profound callousness of U.S. foreign policy towards Mexico in the past generation. To say the least, Mexico has been taken for granted, shunted to a "second-class priority" and neglected in the priorities of the Cold War. By comparison, Cuba—a nation of 7 million people 90 miles further away from us than Mexico—has been an absolute obsession of U.S. foreign policy for 20 years because it happens to be revolutionary and allied with the Soviet Union. Cuban refugees to America, unlike the daily Mexican migrant, are saluted as heroes, given eased immigration requirements, and provided greater economic assistance that any generation of immigrants in American history.

Suddenly in 1978 Mexico learned how to become an important factor in American eyes—it discovered oil, more oil than it knew what to do with. Awash in the dream and reality of oil wealth, the government drew charts of the Mexican continent that showed 90 percent of the land is a sedimentary basin.[45] Now a new dynamic in U.S.-Mexico relations developed. On the one hand, Mexican nationalism became euphoric. They had discovered the modern key to power and respect. It could provide wealth which, *if properly reinvested*, would create economic growth and jobs to a desperate country. And with power would come independence, a chance to become a respected nation in the world, no longer an overshadowed dependent of the U.S. Reversing the past, Mexico would become a new Colossus of the South. Above all, they wanted to become "an oil *power* but not an oil *country*," in the words of President Lopez-Portillo. That is, Mexico wanted to exploit its national treasure of oil to raise capital for a balanced economic development instead of becoming an inflation-ridden and insecure Western colony like the Shah's Iran or contemporary Saudi Arabia. Here was a chance at last to correct the historic imbalance between the two countries while also easing the U.S. energy crisis. Mexico had the possibility of power and independence, setting the stage for a relationship of *respect* based on equality and interdependence. The U.S. could have made a decision to see in the new nationalism an opportunity to wash away the mutual superiority-inferiority complex and start anew. If a new respect had been forthcoming from the U.S., even though prompted by the oil discovery, it could have led in time to a comprehensive new relationship including a Mexican supply of oil to ease the U.S. transition to conservation.[46]

But instead, into this complex forest of nationalism built on the soil of anti-Americanism strode the U.S. Energy Secretary James Schlesinger and planeloads of corporate attorneys with briefcases from New York, Washington, Houston and Los Angeles. They saw only oil, not Mexico. They had no sensitivity to the fact that oil in Mexico was not an energy question but a *national* question. They did not realize that President Lopez-Portillo was risking his authority by even *considering* selling the "national patrimony," as oil was referred to by Mexicans. And so the U.S. Energy Secretary undermined a tentative agreement for gas sales in 1977, apparently on the grounds that Mexico wanted too high a price (though it would have been an excellent bargain by 1980 prices). President Lopez-Portillo angrily described himself as "hanging by a paintbrush" after the U.S. pullout.⁴⁷ The break-down could not be limited to the subject of energy, according to one U.S. official there; "it released a poison that infected the whole relationship."⁴⁸ This diplomatic failure, along with other follies of the 1970s ("Operation Intercept," a militaristic drug enforcement program run by Watergate spy G. Gordon Liddy; the "Tortilla Curtain," an ill-conceived and ineffective border fence complete with glass spikes on top; and President Carter's remarking in Mexico City that he got "Montezuma's revenge"—diarrhea—on his one previous visit) may have effectively damaged the relationship for years to come.

But because of the permanence of the relationship, it is never too late to improve U.S. policies toward Mexico. The chief difficulty lies in moving away from opportunistic Cold War policies to a profound realization of America's connectedness with other countries, a humbling process that could replace traditional arrogance with a sincere new respect. As with any relationship deeply damaged by a past dominance, it is easier to turn away than to work at overcoming old wounds with trust. But there cannot be even a separation, much less a divorce, in this case. America must deal with its historic relationships with the developing world, starting with Mexico, or be swamped with insurmountable crises in the near future.

Only a policy based on respect could move toward a comprehensive transformation of the current negatives of U.S.-Mexico relations into positives. Extending the principle of economic democracy beyond domestic corporate reorganization to international policy would make initiatives such as these, if connected in a single vision, viable possibilities:

1) Establishment of a prestigious joint U.S.-Mexico planning commission, with direct access to the two presidents, to emphasize the "special" new relationship, promote public awareness, and anticipate problems before they erupt.⁴⁹

2) An urgent dialogue between the two presidents and the leaders of U.S. multinationals about a responsible job-creating investment strategy for the region plus inclusion of American labor and Mexican government and labor representatives on the corporate boards;

3) Joint commissions in the arts and education to create

binational universities and cultural centers, one of them at the Alamo, to reverse the cultural imperialist premises of the past;

4) A requirement of Mexican history and language in American schools; a requirement of American history and language in Mexican schools, at least in the border region;

5) a joint development of guayule (a natural rubber plant used in World War II and afterwards destroyed), jojoba (an oil-producing plant), mesquite (for biomass applications), to create viable jobs and self-sufficient communities on both sides of the border.[50]

6) creation of binational "industrial zones" for production of geothermal energy, solar technology, and new information technologies;

7) support of Mexican tomato exports and other "winter crops" to the U.S.;

8) joint mutually respectful agreements on controlling narcotics and weapons traffic, and other forms of corruption thriving in the vacuum between the two nations aimed not only at traffickers over the border but at the more genteel syndicate leaders directing the flow as well;

9) binational cooperation in decisions on common problems facing the ten governors and numerous other officials in the states and cities separated by the border;[51]

10) a new immigration policy based on either a) a "regulated" border with enlarged and humanized entry possibilities combined with more job creation in Mexico, or b) an "open" border for people, goods and services with strict enforcement of the rights to join unions, make minimum wages, and receive health and safety protection in America and Mexico;

11) a much-diminished, or phased-out, military presence on the part of the Border Patrol;

12) the long-range creation of a binational, bilingual "Mex-American" state or entity in the border region, recognizing the equal realities of nationalism and interdependence.[52]

13) an "energy trade" agreement which would respect Mexico's right to preserve its depletable resources, especially should U.S. reserves prove larger than current public petro-chemical rhetoric lets on, but also guarantee the U.S. a long-term assured supply of gas which, even at cartel prices that would

greatly benefit Mexican development, would still be cheaper than LNG transported thousands of miles from Indonesia or Algeria.

It is important to stress that while America must take the first step towards respect and recognition of new realities, this new policy would be in the *common interest* of the people of the two countries. The alternative is to rapidly drift apart, risking a polarization that would threaten both nations. At the end of the frontier era, after the illusions of conquest, after a generation of the Cold War mentality, it is necessary to accept the fact that foreign policy begins at our border, and our border actually begins with our inner vision.

The Mideast: Trading Israel for Oil?

The Custer politics of actually scrambling for resources while claiming to fight for democratic principles is nowhere more dangerous than in the Middle East. By making oil and anti-communism paramount, the U.S. has redefined the meaning of Israel from a model of democracy to an outpost on the most dangerous frontier, an outpost whose destiny is governed by great power bargaining in the global oil sweepstakes.

When Israel came into the world as a new nation in the 1940s, its global strength was moral and political in character. Though weapons were necessary in the fight, though the Zionists employed terrorism to achieve their ends, and though the Palestinian Arabs were largely driven off their land, the world generally approved the creation of the new nation for two distinct reasons. First, global sympathy and guilt for the victims of the Nazi holocaust was extremely strong. In the face of that genocidal assault, the demand for a Jewish homeland seemed eminently justified to most nations, including both the U.S. and the Soviet Union. Second, Israel's own idealistic self-conception—to become a democratic nation, with a cooperative economy and transformative institutions like the kibbutzim—seemed a great step forward from the doldrums of British rule. Even Professor Edward Said, a member of the Palestinian National Council, the "legislature" of the Palestinian Liberation Organization (PLO), notes that "Israel has some remarkable political and cultural achievements to its credit".* This general view of Israel as a *progressive* nation provided powerful additional justification for its establishment.

Israel's moral power contributed to its security until the Six Day War in 1967 when the Israelis suddenly changed in public image from victims to occupiers—of the West Bank, the Gaza Strip and the Sinai. However justified the Israeli security fears, however benign their occupation by comparative standards, Israel's stature in the world began to be tarnished. The occupation, as with all conquests of frontiers inhabited by others, would take its inner toll, placing Israeli soldiers in dehumanizing roles, promoting racial chauvinism, dividing Israeli society to a point approaching civil strife between those favoring a permanent annexation of the territories and those supporting negotiated withdrawal, and even creating unprecedented fissures between Israeli and American Jewish leaders.** Moreover, in the same period, the Israelis supported the U.S. aggression in Vietnam and engaged in arms sales to dictators like Somoza in Nicaragua and Vorster in South Africa, which further isolated them from progressives throughout the world. Increasingly, as Israel was linked to American imperial designs, its existence and purpose was defended by the U.S. as a "strategic asset" in the Cold War and as a gendarme of the Mideast, and less and less on either moral or historic grounds.

At the same time, the Palestinian cause acquired a growing moral persuasiveness. Their use of terror and threats against Israel's existence became balanced by a global perception that they had a reasonable grievance. They were a dispossessed people, up-

---

* The quote is from Edward Said, *The Question of Palestine,* Times Books (New York City) April 1980, p. 72. Said, a Palestinian-American author and member of the PLO's National Security Council, is a moderate representative of Palestinian views in this country. I draw heavily on his work as a reflection of the Palestinian position.

** See, for example, the statement criticizing "extremists in the public and within the government, guided by secular and religious chauvinism, (who) distort Zionism and threaten its realization," and who "advance the vicious cycle of extremism and violence which nurture each other," signed by more than 50 influential American Jewish leaders in June 1980. The names included three past chairs of the Conference of Presidents of Major American Jewish Organizations, and more than ten leaders of the United Jewish Appeal. Their names were added to a statement drafted by the Peace Now movement and signed by 250 Israelis, including five former generals (UPI, July 2, 1980).

rooted by and for the Israeli presence. The images of Palestinian refugee camps, the Israeli use of American napalm to bomb southern Lebanon, and discrimination against Arabs within Israel itself, became the basis for a new sympathy towards the Palestinian position in the arena of world opinion.*

After 1973, the "oil factor" began shifting the orientation of the U.S. government. America's "moral" and strategic support for Israel's existence was now partly counter-balanced by its greed for hydrocarbons. The Saudis in particular became explicit seducers in offering oil supplies in exchange for a Palestinian state. The oil blackmail was augmented by economic pressure in the form of Arab petrodollar investments, purchases and deposits. Standard Oil of California (Chevron) became the most flagrant corporate advocate of a new sympathy towards the Arab cause. Undersecretary of State and leading "Arabist" Harold H. Saunders subtly argued that "a definition of U.S. interests in the Middle East must take serious account of the new dimensions of U.S. economic relations with the area."** This was only a cultured version of the repeated message of Billy Carter, agent of Libya, that there are a

---

*The following excerpt is from an interview with General Gur, Chief of Staff of the Israeli Army and appeared in Al-Hamishmar, May 10, 1978:

Q—Is it true that you bombarded agglomerations [of people] without distinction [during the March 1978 Israeli invasion of Lebanon]?

A—I am not one of those people who have a selective memory. Do you think that I pretend not to know what we have done all these years? What did we do to the entire length of the Suez Canal? A million and a half refugees! Really: where do you live?...We bombarded Ismailia, Suez, Port Said, and Port Faud. A million and a half refugees... Since when has the population of South Lebanon become so sacred? They knew perfectly well what the terrorists were doing. After the massacre at Avivim, I had four villages in South Lebanon bombed without authorization.

Q—Without making distinctions between civilians and non-civilians?

A—What distinction? What had the inhabitants of Irbid [a large town in northern Jordon] done to deserve bombing by us?

Q—But military communiques always spoke of returning fire and of counterstrikes against terrorist objectives?

A—Please be serious. Did you not know that the entire valley of the Jordon had been emptied of its inhabitants as a result of the war of attrition?

**The Saunders quote is from official testimony on June 12, 1978 (Said, p. 188)

lot more Arabs in the world than Jews. At any rate, whether stated in Ivy League or down-home rhetoric, the Carter Administration began applying diplomatic pressure on Israel to withdraw from the occupied territories and negotiate a new arrangement with its neighbors in the Middle East.

At this point, it might be said that the Palestinians became strategic pawns in a larger conflict over regional stability, oil and petrodollars. From the 1940s to the 1970s, the Palestinians were never the key "cause" of the Arab world against Israel, but only a submerged part. Only since the late 60s have the Palestinians become an independent, organized, volatile force which no party could ignore. Even then, "Arab solidarity" with the Palestinians has never been profound. In the 70s, for example, both Jordan and Syria have unleashed fierce attacks against Palestinian forces (in Jordan and Lebanon, respectively), ironically killing more Palestinians than the Israeli army has. Relations between Egypt and the PLO are frequently hostile or frozen, and between the Saudis and the PLO there are gulfs that Arab solidarity cannot always bridge. Palestinian factions, sponsored by different Arab countries, have even fought each other. Why, then, have the Arab nations recognized the PLO as the sole, legitimate representative of the Palestinian people? Why have they made improved relations with the U.S. conditional on a Palestinian state?

There are, of course, many reasons, not the least of which is an Arab hostility to Zionism and what it has created in Palestine. However, the military attacks on the PLO by Jordan's King Hussein and Syria's President Assad suggest that the Palestinians are also an independent power center causing revolutionary ferment that poses a challenge to royalty, opulence and traditional relationships within the existing Arab countries. For the stability of the feudal regimes, then, what better answer than revolutionary anti-Israeli rhetoric, conditional support for the PLO, and the eventual creation of a "Palestinian homeland" in the West Bank or the area of Israel itself? Anywhere, at least, where the Pales-

Saunders is viewed with suspicion on both sides of the Israeli-Palestinian conflict. The Israelis suspect him of pushing negotiations with the PLO. Said, on the other hand, sees him as trying to guarantee access to Middle East oil and consumer markets without accepting the radical change in power relations implied in recognizing the Palestinians.

tinians will be preoccupied with the problems of economic survival and development rather than the internal politics of existent Arab states. On at least this point, ridding the Middle East of independent radical ferment, the Arab nations' interests converge with those of the U.S. As the State Department's Saunders puts it, the "moderate Arab leaders have turned to the U.S. for cooperation in achieving peace and development. Their success will limit the role of radical forces.... "[53]

The kind of "peace and development" referred to, of course, is within the context of monarchies, feudal states, and military dictatorships, hardly the sort of governments where one would expect to find a passionate concern for the poor and disadvantaged. From an economic standpoint, none of the Arab governments can be considered as progressive as Israel's. And none of them, presumably, want militant Palestinians incorporated into their "electorates." Such governments pursue "development" only as marketed by Western oil companies, bankers, arms merchants, and purveyors of the consumer culture. This development is not likely to create "peace" or moral advance, but a dangerous involvement of the U.S. in deepening tensions. For example, after the Shah of Iran's collapse (brought on partly by a U.S. military build-up), the search for new outlets for American arms sales became almost frantic. As the Pentagon looked for new military purchasers, American multinationals like Bechtel and Fluor kept developing a Western-style infrastructure in Arab deserts. The value of Arab arms jumped from $5 billion in 1973 to $50 billion in 1980, and threatened to reverse the military balance of power away from Israel in the next several years. Equally portentous is the fact that the Americans will be integrally employed in the Arab build-up. Tens of thousands of Americans, for example, have already been involved in creating the infrastructure, and supplying the equipment, to make the Saudi army operational. According to Dan Bawly, an Israeli military information officer, "the most worrying aspect of the deepening American involvement in the Arab states is the presence of American personnel on Arab soil. These are no less than latter-day mercenaries. They have signed on for extended periods of service with West Coast corporations such as Vinyl and Bechtel in Saudi Arabia and the Gulf Emirates. Their influence is already felt on the governments of the Saudi Arabian peninsula.''*

Thus, the scramble for oil tipped the American geopolitical calculations away from Israel's priorities, while necessitating the drive for arms exports to recapture the oil-producers' new wealth and bending U.S. foreign policy significantly towards the needs of greater oil consumption and weapons manufacture. In turn, this has raised the level of Israeli insecurity and increased their commitment to dominate the West Bank, a course causing their further diplomatic isolation and lending great legitimacy to the Palestinians. The latter, however, found themselves no closer to a homeland, but instead were becoming radical pawns in a very conservative game of economic chess. The Palestinians were, as Said puts it, an example of "the tendency of modern politics to rule over masses of people as transferable, silent, and politically neutral populations."[54]

The further militarizing of the Israeli-Palestinian conflict seems to lead nowhere, and its contamination by oil geo-politics only makes the dispute more difficult to resolve. As long as the U.S. depends on feudal regimes for imported oil, it will continue the immorality of weighing Israeli security against barrels of oil, militarizing the Middle East to a frightening degree, supporting the repression of dissidents in the Arab world, ignoring the human plight of the Palestinians, turning the desert into a shopping center for consumer goods, and enriching a few multinationals without developing the conditions for a lasting peace.

A visitor to Israel is struck by the fact that all paths to peace seem closed. Israel can never be secure without safe borders, the diplomats argue, but neither can it be secure by means of military power alone. A Jewish state whose indigenous Arab population might become a near-majority by the year 2000 cannot remain stable in the long-run, however militarized its borders may be. An indefinite continuance of the present tension, terrorism and military-related inflation is hardly a workable vision. The Palestinians

---

* I interviewed and spent a day with Bawly visiting the Golan Heights in 1980. For more of his analysis, see the article "The U.S. Is Dependent Upon the Arab Arms Purchasing and Development Programs," August 15, 1977, from Bawly-Millner Co., Ahuzat Bait St, Tel-Aviv 6100.)

claim a right to self-determination just like any other dispossessed people.* Accepting a Palestinian state described by the PLO as a "transition" towards a "secular, democratic state" located where Israel is today is unacceptable to anyone supporting the maintenance of the current Israeli state. But if the Israelis and Palestinians themselves cannot arrive at a new understanding of mutual respect and coexistence, it is possible that an artificial settlement will be imposed by outside powers, including the U.S. and the Soviets, who would carve up the Middle East into "spheres of interest" as happened in the wake of World War II to Western Europe and Asia.

In looking for an alternative to this depressing scenario, perhaps one must begin with the personal, with the consciousness that keeps Jew and Palestinian apart, untrusting, and what it might take for the perception to change. Jane Fonda and I visited the kibbutz of Amos Oz, perhaps Israel's greatest living novelist, a committed student of consciousness, and an advocate of the Peace Now movement in Israel, in June 1980. Kibbutz Hulda, where Oz lives with his wife Nily and three children, is about four miles from the old Jordanian border. In a world where borders are always changing, I wondered, how does one find personal or national security without either reducing the importance of the border itself or fighting for its maximum expansion into other people's lands? Oz has spent 25 years on this same kibbutz, and Nily her whole life. Oz fought in the 1967 and 1973 wars without finding increased security as a result (the tank battle he fought on the Golan Heights, he says, was the one event in his life too shocking to describe in words later).

---

*Although he cursorily dismisses Zionists as a "remnant of European Jews" who displaced the Palestinian people, Said is eloquent in presenting the case for self-determination: "We were on the land called Palestine; were our dispossession and our effacement, by which almost a million of us were made to leave Palestine and our society made nonexistent, justified even to save the remnant of European Jews that had survived Nazism? By what moral or political standard are we expected to lay aside our claims to our national existence, our land, our human rights? In what world is there no argument when an entire people is told that it is juridically absent, even as armies are led against it, campaigns conducted against even its name, history changed so as to "prove" its nonexistence?" (*The Question of Palestine*, Edward W. Said, Times Books, 1980, pp. xvi-xvii)

As we talked in the modest Oz home so surrounded by borders old and new, I realized that the purely diplomatic, economic and geo-political definitions of the conflict were ultimately inappropriate to the search for a solution. What looks like a contested area from the U.S. is, pure and simple, *home* for millions of Israeli and Palestinian people with competing claims to a place for themselves. They cannot be thought of as pawns when you meet them; they are active human beings living through a transition from ancestral religious notions to a workable contemporary philosophy. They cannot be easily reconciled, but neither can they achieve their human aims on the edge of annihilation. Coexistence, perhaps, is the only near-term possibility.

I recalled to the Oz family a meeting that afternoon with a well-known Palestinian human rights lawyer, Aziz Shehadeh. The conversation was in Jerusalem, within moments of the Old City, and we talked about the West Bank crisis raging just outside the windows of our quiet and elegant restaurant. If we could meet here and talk, I naively wondered, why couldn't everyone? My acquaintance described how until recently it was "an offense in the Arab world even to talk to a Jew." But persons like himself had evolved from being "rejectionists" to a position of "seeking a peaceful settlement." A dialogue between Arab and Jew, he noted, was "not welcomed by certain people" on both sides. As long as the Begin government continued its rigid, theologically dogmatic policies on the West Bank, he said, the possibilities of a dialogue would decline to zero. Under these conditions, he added, raising his arms in a weary so-be-it gesture, "We are all PLO."

When I related this conversation to Amos Oz, he began talking about the personal, cultural dimension of the conflict which must be broken before real peace becomes possible. He felt that the 1977 visit of President Sadat of Egypt to Jerusalem, the first by an Arab leader, was most successful on this psychological level:

> Sadat's genius has been in understanding our emotions. The worst thing for Jews is perhaps not even the history of our extermination but our sense of *exclusion*. As a boy, I used to hear Cairo Radio speaking of the "so-called government" of the "so-called state of Israel." We always felt excluded from the family of nations. Then Sadat came here, and spoke in the Knesset to our

so-called government, and recognized this as a real country. He affected my emotions, and people go to war for
their emotions, not their more rational interests.

Then pausing to reflect on Sadat's example, Oz went on:
*Sometimes I think we should simply do the same towards
the Palestinians. They too are excluded. They are becoming the Jews of the Jews.*

Like the Israeli's being ridiculed on Cairo Radio, the
Palestinians have been defined as a virtual non-people for a generation. Israeli officials, academics and military officials have
described them as "so-called Palestinians," identifying them as
Arab refugees of Syrian or Jordanian origin. To define them as a
"national" grouping would open to question the legitimacy of the
Israelis having built a state upon their lands. In one sense, the
Israelis have a point: the Palestinians were not historically a
"nation"; Said notes that "Palestine had been part of the Otto-
man Empire until the end of World War I" and that "in any
accepted sense it had not been independent."[55]

But the Palestinians are more than refugees. They are at least a
distinct *people* with identity, character, customs, a definable history, and lands where they have lived, worked, and been buried.
While their demand for statehood is relatively recent (not taking
on large-scale dimensions until the late 1960s), their *national* identity has been formed mostly in response to Zionism. While drawing
important distinctions between themselves and Syrians, Lebanese
and Jordanians, "much of what we can call Palestinian self-assertion was articulated in response to the flow of Jewish immigrants
into Palestine since the 1880's."[56] This "self-assertion" is
unlikely to disappear by being ignored, ridiculed, academically
refuted, or physically attacked. On the contrary, such are the conditions in which the aspiration for separate national identity
grows.

Morally and practically, it is becoming untenable for Israel to be
the occupying government of the West Bank and Gaza, and an
occasional invader of Lebanon, supported, armed and financed by
the American government. But what is a solution compatible with
Israeli security needs?

The short-range *negotiable* answer probably lies somewhere between Israel's 1977-80 version of "autonomy" in the occupied

territories and the PLO concept of a Palestinian state. What may be needed is a structural and stable means of co-existence that can support human interaction on a broad scale for the next decade or longer. During this transition, the parties who have denied each other's existence may come to accept one another as legitimate. At that point, a later generation may be able to move from coexistence to cooperation.

On the West Bank, this would mean that the Israelis would have to withdraw from all but those few military bases serving legitimate and essential security needs. They would have to relax the doctrinaire insistence that Judea and Samaria are theirs by biblical right regardless of the several hundred thousand Palestinians living there. Moreover, they would have to change their view that the Palestinians of the West Bank are simply and forever "Jordanian."

The Palestinians, on the other hand, would have to defer the idea of a genuine nation-state bordering Israel—at least in the foreseeable future. It is totally impractical to envision an armed state dominated by the PLO being accepted by Israel or the U.S., nor should it be. The PLO version of a Palestinian state is only a step towards a "secular, democratic state" which would require the dismantling of Israel as it now exists. And this is a relatively moderate demand, according to Said, which is denounced as a "sellout to Zionism" by other Palestinian nationalists. The only other version of a Palestinian state is a de-militarized one in which security would be kept on the borders by an international force specifically including U.S. troops. Besides extending the Cold War directly into the Middle East and intruding on the sovereignty of the real parties involved, such a solution would do little or nothing about violence between Israelis and Palestinian "rejectionists," not to mention violence between Palestinian factions themselves.

The remaining possibility—aside from the dread but very real option of war—is a *geo-politically* autonomous West Bank and Gaza. Israeli troops would remain in scattered bases, designed not for occupation but only for security against outer attack. The citizens of the territories might have a special dual status, the West Bankers "confederated" with Jordan and Gaza residents with Egypt. But they would be recognized as *Palestinians* with maximum civil liberties. They would be free of the current military government, able to raise their children with a concept of identity and place and under conditions of local self-government. The achievement of economic self-sufficiency, not to mention possible statehood, would be an elusive goal but not forever prohibited by law or force. Within this framework, the Palestinians would struggle politically for recognition of their claims with Israel.

The crucial problem in evolving towards a world of genuine interdependence is the balance between struggling for a rich cultural identity while not denying the same right to others. If war is to be avoided, this balance will have to be achieved across the globe, between Vietnamese and Chinese, Irish and English, native Americans and "settler Americans," on many levels in many places. In some instances, it may be too late. But the Middle East does not have to be one more case of such historic antagonisms leading to cycle after cycle of war. It is the critical case of West confronting the East, of the white European world colonizing a place for itself in the non-white traditional world, to be sure; but in this case with the irony that the occupiers have been persecuted themselves. More poignantly Jews represent a test case of whether a religious-cultural-political minority can survive and keep its values in a world of powerful nation-state antagonisms. It is commonplace now for the world "left"—the United Nations majority, the Third World, the Socialist states—to deny diplomatic recognition of Israel while pressing support for the PLO. Israelis have good reason to believe that if their security was indeed threatened, no one would come fully to their aid. But if the preservation of Israel cannot be taken for granted, what other political-cultural-national minority can expect to be more secure?

To take an exaggerated example of how power alone often defines legitimacy, compare the case of Israel with that of the United States. By most standards, Israel has a greater rationale for existence than the U.S. does, yet one rarely hears calls for the placing of Americans under another structure of government. Israel, after all, has a religious-cultural heritage tying them to the Mideast, whereas American settlers in the "New World" had none. The Jews were victims of a Nazi terror that made Old World persecution mild by comparison. The Zionist treatment of the Palestinians in 1948 was not as cruel or extensive as the U.S. policies towards the Indians. The founders of Israel had far greater revolutionary dreams than our "founding fathers", and Israel's social programs even today far outstrip what America offers its disadvantaged. And the wrongs committed today against the West Bank inhabitants cannot be corrected by dismantling Israel, any more than those committed against the Native Americans can be balanced by dismantling the current structure of the U.S.

The point for Palestinians and oppressed people is not to forget cruelties, but to adjust to new historical conditions rather than attempting to roll them back, for example, to pre-1948 Palestine. And for the Israelis and all Western powers, what can be learned is that those who create their national existence by force against others will sooner or later find it threatened unless they extend their cause— for America, democracy, for Israel, human transformation—to the others whose existence they have threatened. The method of the bomb always seems to be in order, but rarely the apology, the offer of respect, the promise of a new attitude of live and let live. But without this change—from America to the developing world, from Israel to the Palestinians—the possibilities of peaceful pluralism are rapidly being replaced by the rise of passion without conscience, bloodshed without remorse, the stereotyping required for merciless hate. A Palestinian national poem cited by Said, titled "Identity Card," demonstrates the sociology of this hate very clearly:

> Record!
> I am an Arab
> without a name—without title...
>
> Therefore!
> Record on top of the first page:
> I do not hate man
> Nor do I encroach
> But if I become hungry
> The usurper's flesh will be my food
> Beware—beware—of my hunger
> And my anger.

This is the heart of the matter, dangerously ignored by those who would exploit Israel as a strategic battering ram against Soviet influence, or bargain over whole cultures in pursuit of oil, or try to preserve a regional status quo by international agreements. By making the human factor secondary, millions of individuals are turned into fuses of hate. Such will be the case until America and other countries conduct their foreign policies as if human beings mattered.

Empire Versus Democracy

Summing up the global task of the new era: America has to turn away from the frontier of military anti-Communism, the rapacious conquest of the world resource base, the futile attempt to homogenize the world for the multinationals, and instead turn towards an inner frontier of peaceful pluralistic interdependence. We now turn to a final issue, the connection of foreign policy to the basic values and institutions within American society. Foreign policy, it is truly said, begins at home, as a reflection of the dominant world view and interests of those making national decisions. To put the matter simply, if the corporate, Cold War elite holds sway at home, we can anticipate continued crisis abroad and authoritarianism in America; but if citizens have a say in the American future, there is hope for peace abroad and a richer democracy at home.

There have been rather long periods in American history with little domestic opposition to the main lines of foreign policy, because it was perceived to be in the economic, national and religious or cultural interest of the country. For example, the years from 1945 to 1960 were a time when it was an accepted cliche that foreign policy was "bipartisan" and that American political differences stopped at the water's edge. The Eisenhower era saw little or no dissent from the broad consensus favoring the Cold War, based as it was on satisfaction with life at home and, it must be admitted, enforced public ignorance about such activities as the support of the Shah, etc., abroad.

There was another reason as well for the lack of dissent in the 1950's: the repression during the "McCarthy period" in the beginning of the decade. Present, former, and suspected members of the rather small U.S. Communist Party, trade unionists, and many plain New Deal liberals became the sudden objects of a political witchhunt that derived its passion from the growth of a perceived foreign threat: the Soviet achievement of the hydrogen bomb, the Chinese Revolution, the Korean War. Through suspension of certain civil liberties, spy trials, blacklisting, and innuendo campaigns, what there was of an American left was crippled and destroyed. The populist, progressive movements that had loomed as quite powerful in the 1930's because of domestic economic crisis were now eliminated as a serious factor in postwar politics. More than that, the very possibility of protest was chilled for years.

The climate of war or perception of dangerous enemies abroad has always been a useful cure for the ills of the state. A key dynamic of American history, accidental or not, has been the emergence of war or foreign threats as a "solution" to rising domestic pressures. The international tension unites the nation in patriotism, isolates critics and reform movements, diverts attention away from pressing social or economic issues, and often ameliorates domestic problems by creating jobs (through the draft or in military production).* During the American Revolution, the impoverished and often-rebellious lower classes were united with the upper by the external threat of the Indian and the promise of settlements. In the Civil War South, the white poor united with the plantation hierarchy against the poor black slaves. World War I was closely connected with the repression and even deportation of radicals, socialists, wobblies, and union leaders. World War II "solved" the economic and political crisis of the Depression. The McCarthyism associated with Korea did not fade until the 1960's.

The 1960's period probably constituted the most powerful challenge to the domestic base of foreign policy in American history. The civil rights movement of 1960-63, along with the student movement, broke the silence of the 1950's and the double illusion that all was well at home and our only enemies were beyond our borders. The domestic pressure was not only a factor in the election of John F. Kennedy over Richard Nixon (who had been a key member of the HUAC during the McCarthy period); but civil rights concerns coupled with the rediscovery of an "other

---

*It is quite reasonable, though no apology, to note that this purgative function of war is not confined to the U.S. nor even to the West. Indeed, the idea has been broached, with some telling evidence and argument, that the Soviet invasion of Afghanistan was more important to the resolution of Soviet domestic problems than the extension of Soviet international aims.

America" of serious poverty, were certainly responsible for forcing President Kennedy to seek a thaw in Cold War rhetoric, the first nuclear arms limitation treaty, and new idealistic initiatives like the Peace Corps, even if he also created the Green Berets.

But Kennedy would not keep us out of Vietnam, and so the domestic protest soon became an opposition to the draft, to the killing in Vietnam and to foreign policy in general. So unpopular was the war that it was never legally declared by Congress, never funded by tax increases, and only continued by a rising deception of the public and even the press. When the polarization became extreme enough in the late 1960's, the government deployed the FBI to "neutralize" the new left with "counter-intelligence" programs that later became the heart of Watergate. The contradiction between pursuit of empire abroad and maintenence of democracy at home now came out into the open. The recent publicity attending the release of G. Gordon Liddy's autobiography shows the degree to which the threat to democracy grew. Apparently "what goes round, comes round." From murder of dissenters in Brazil we see a coming home of immoral ideology until the murder of a new columnist, Jack Anderson is frankly contemplated by Liddy for implementation in New York. One wonders how far Nixon might have gone in undermining political democracy had not the Watergate burglars bungled their assignment, thereby destroying his opportunity.

But mercifully, for the first time in American history the forces of war and repression did not prevail against dissent. Instead, President Nixon was driven from office for his transgressions, and the war ended with the collapse of America's allies in Indochina. A new domestic climate was in the making. Those who had been denounced as "un-American" and subversive were suddenly considered to have been right about the war; those who were thought to represent "law and order" were discovered committing crimes in the White House. This new turnabout was reflected in the comparative results in 1967 and 1973 of an annual poll asking Americans who represented a "threat" to the country.

In 1967, the poll showed that the public feared black militants, student demonstrators, atheists, prostitutes and homosexuals. But in 1973, it was generals who conduct secret bombing raids (67 percent), politicians who engage in secret wiretapping (71 percent), businessmen who make illegal contributions (81 percent), and politicians who use the CIA and FBI for political purposes (88 percent) that people feared.[57]

After Vietnam, a distinctly domestic focus returned to American politics. Energy and economic trouble became paramount concerns. A new populism emerged. Labor unions like the United Auto Workers and International Association of Machinists became bitterly dissatisfied with corporate management and made new political alliances with consumer organizations. The anti-nuclear movement arose, along with citizens groups fighting high utility rates. Clerical workers began to fight for equal pay and the struggle for the Equal Rights Amendment intensified. Gray Panthers began to organize among irate senior citizens. Even Jimmy Carter saw fit to run for president in 1976 as an "outsider," and avowed "populist." His later appointment of Andrew Young, known as a symbol of the domestic concerns of the 1960's, as United Nations ambassador, signalled a potentially sharp turnaround in the blueblood style and corporate content of American foreign policy.

But all that began to change in 1979, and by 1980 we were sliding back to the Cold War. The President claimed that an international crisis required he remain in the White House, a ploy quickly named the "Rose garden" strategy. The Vice President questioned the patriotism of Senator Edward Kennedy. Angry Americans beat up Iranians in a few cities, and the President made plans to deport the new "foreign menace." Talk of war enveloped the Capitol, and a majority of Americans in a poll said they expected to be at war in five years. The oil companies were replaced as popular villians in Americann life by mysterious ayatollahs. Instead of boycotting Exxon, America was boycotting the Soviet Olympics. The greatest national thrill of the year was the American hockey triumph over the Communist threat at Lake Placid.

Was it all necessary, caused by the Iranians seizing hostages and the Russians seizing Afghanistan? Or was it contrived by the likes of David Rockefeller and Henry Kissinger, plotting the return of the Shah to the U.S. on "flawed and incomplete" medical grounds while knowing the possible consequences in Teheran?[58] Or by a Jimmy Carter whose inability to handle the burning issues of inflation and energy made him appear to be weak and incompetent to a majority of voters? Did someone in the White House re-election campaign suddenly see that the nightly televised "hate Carter" demonstrations in Teheran were better than any commercials by Gerald Rafshoon? Did they discover that brandishing the U.S. sword deflected attention away from economic issues, and buried the charge of "weak leadership" under a new podium-pounding image of Presidential toughness? Was the "guiding spirit" of Carter's Iran strategy domestic politics, as columnist Joseph Kraft has suggested?[59]

The answer may not be knowable, it may be a mix of these and other factors, or it may only be the non-conspiratorial drift of events. Those who emphasize the Soviet role are not simply inventing false images of Soviet expansionism, but given all we have learned about government manipulation from the Pentagon Papers and the Watergate tapes, neither are those who look for the cause among domestic factors. What we can tell for certain, without knowing the cause, is the answer to the question: *who benefits and who loses from a new Cold War?*

The temporary winners are those whose vision and interests are hopelessly connected with restoring America's former role. The restored Cold Warriors in the White House are the new Custers of America. Occasionally we can glimpse behind the diplomatic curtain and observe their pathetic and outmoded derring-do:

SWAGGER, FARCE AT KHYBER PASS
Bursts From Jammed Rifle
Give Brzezinski a Start

IN THE KHYBER PASS, PAKISTAN—Against a backdrop in the legend of vanished empires, national security adviser Zbigniew Brzezknski toured Sunday a frontier of the crisis that is threatening this rugged corner of the world.

At times within rifle shot of Afghan territory, Brzezinski inspected a forward post of Pakistan's legendary Khyber Rifles, exhorted an encampment of Afghan refugees to fight on against the Soviet invaders "with God on your side," and received the symbolic gifts of a huge mound of floral necklaces and two goats from tribal chieftains.

In the outpost, barely two miles from the border crossing point of Torkum clearly visible in the valley below, Brzezinski climbed through the obsolete stone and rubble fortification, which, in modern warfare, would be flattened in the first enemy artillery barrage.

He inspected a Chinese-made AK-47 automatic rifle, caressed the trigger, thought better of it and then handed it to a nearby rifleman, who squeezed off a single shot in the general direction of Afghanistan.

The rifle jammed, then unexpectedly fired again, spraying fully 20 rounds out into the empty countryside while the startled soldier staggered backward.

It was that kind of day, part swagger, part farce, part deadly serious. Brzezinski, wearing a battered Army parka, heavy rubber-cleated boots and wire-rimmed tank commanders' sunglasses, was in his element: by turn eloquent, flamboyant, inquisitive but throughout playing the part of President Carter's special emissary to a nation that appreciates a theatrical display.[60]

Down through history the appeal of the Custers has been to the patriotic and economic interests of a majority of Americans. Stay with our leaders and our party, they imply, because the defense of *our* interests is a defense of the flag and system which really are *your* interests. They have not been entirely wrong. The economic and political elite has won a certain popular respect for defending the patriotic interest through the experience of the American Revolution, the Civil War and World War II. In addition, the system of an expanding frontier has *delivered* at least a flow of commodities and this has often been enough to win a broad measure of popular confidence. But much more would be possible if economic democracy reorganized corporate priorities. Will the American people be led back down the treadmill of the Cold War, and away from democracy, or will the protest which began in the 1960's mature into a prevailing common sense of the future?

There are two historical reasons for believing that a positive change will take place instead of a tragic regression.

The first is that the system of expansion itself is stagnating as it collides with the era of limits. The mutinational corporation does not protect "us" (American prosperity) against "them" (less-developed foreign countries). Instead, the multinationals have a net negative effect on the American economy and democracy, while they abuse the environment and block development abroad. A low-paid South Korean electronics worker living under a police state has a common problem with the American worker whose plant has shut down in St. Louis. As the world grows more hostile to the multinationals, there may come a time when the corporation has nowhere to go to hide its responsibility and protect its privileges. At that time a new global "social contract" will be possible, a set of ground rules which can turn the international economic environment from a checkerboard of privilege and poverty to a fertile ground for human development.

The second new historical fact that makes regression unlikely is that the multinationals are losing the banner of patriotism which has been the source of their authority in the past. It cannot any longer be said, as it was in the prosperous 1950's, that what is "good for General Motors is good for America." The rise of a global economy headquartered more in multinational banks than national capitals has meant that American national interests are sacrificed on an international altar. The critics who call for democratic control of corporate behavior are standing on the ground of patriotism. The "foreign menace" is a global economic structure, led by American multinationals, that places its immediate interests before the best interests of individual countries.

Thus the historic rationale of the Custers is ebbing, and a new concept beyond the old poles of isolationism and imperialism—the concept of inter-dependence, drawn from ecology and applied to economic and foreign policy—is growing. The coming generation of Americans can find life beyond empire. Instead of a vain dream of American military dominance, the vision must shift to finding a new niche for humanity in the world, from Number One-ism to a sense of oneness.

Such an agenda is a worthy challenge for a new generation of Americans who have outgrown the culture of the physical frontier, Manifest Destiny and the Cold War.

Whether such an agenda is a possibility, however, depends on whether the Cold War generation now in power casts a final, fatal curse on a future not its own.

SEVEN
POSSIBILITIES FOR THE EIGHTIES

Cast your whole vote, not a strip of paper merely, but your whole influence.

Thoreau

Most individuals, even those who desire social change, feel powerless today. They often minimize their own role, thinking that either a well-known leader, an impersonal force of history, or new objective conditions will bring the improvements they want. But the changes proposed in this book—the enrichment of the inner frontier, the democratization of economy and government—cannot be achieved without the individual taking personal responsibility for his or her life. The personal change makes the historical change possible.

The Role of Common Vision in History

The great movements to expand democracy in America have all shown this lesson. In each case, a few individuals had to feel a desire for recognition, a need for self-determination going against the grain of current opinion. When a sufficient number of them resolved to pursue their vision together, they became a movement. When their message and their commitment became contagious, they could affect history. As Samuel Adams wrote on the eve of the American Revolution, "When it appears beyond contradiction that we are *united in sentiment*, there will be a confidence in each other, and a plan of opposition will be easily formed and executed with spirit." [1]

Just as there was a "unity of sentiment" before there was a Revolution, there were countless unknown Americans taking charge of their lives before there was a George Washington who could become the first President of a new democratic government. Similarly, there was an anti-slavery movement including an underground railroad before there was an Emancipation Proclamation and an Abraham Lincoln; a women's suffrage movement before there was a Nineteenth Amendment; a labor movement before there was a New Deal; and in the 1960's, wave after wave of movements preceded such achievements as civil rights and equal opportunities legislation, consumer and environmental protection, the abolition of the draft, the peace candidacies of Robert Kennedy, Eugene McCarthy and George McGovern, and the end of the Vietnam War.

At the outset of the seventies a nuclear future was assumed inevitable. Now, after postcards and marches, petitions, teach-ins, and civil disobedience, solar has come into its own as a viable alternative and the cry "No Nukes" echoes even on Wall Street. Perhaps even more significant has been the steady expansion of a woman's movement seeking not only equal rights but also a redefinition of American values. The percolation of women's militance from the streets into official policy circles is evident for all to see. The seventies were not at all "quiet."

Despite the oft reported stability of American history, there has actually been a continuous and rich legacy of struggle for democratic rights. Rarely has even a decade passed without the presence of at least one challenging and unpredicted social movement led by individuals who chose to make their own history.

There is a consistent pattern in these movements which we might call the "laws of change," at least for American society. First, fundamental change is never initiated by the established economic or political elites. Our system is quite conservative, designed to prevent the restoration of monarchs or the dominance of militant factions. Its behavior is regulated by a forest of law which limits change to a marginal or incremental pace, confining innovation to that which already has precedent in legal tradition. The governmental structure is deliberately fragmented into executive, legislative and judicial branches, again to provide a check against rapid change.

Inevitably, so conservative a structure is slow to anticipate emerging trends or act on over-ripened crises. There is a "cultural lag" between the vision of those with vested interests in the status quo and those individuals or small groups who begin to feel impatience at contradictions between certain realities—racial discrimination, for example—and the lofty ideals professed by the elites. Where the abuse is flagrant, and where it is neglected or perpetuated by those in authority for long periods, organizers of protest begin to appear. At first, the organizers are ridiculed or ignored, and their attempts to raise consciousness and motivate people against the injustice are without visible success.

But then a provocation occurs—a police shooting, an oil spill, an unjust arrest or firing, a near nuclear meltdown—and suddenly a mass movement arises. The once-marginal voices of protest have lifted consciousness enough so that people will no longer accept what previously they would have borne with an apathetic shrug of the shoulders.

The newborn movement first seeks to resolve its grievance through the system, by petitioning or voting. There are disputes between radicals and pragmatists over whether conventional tactics will work, but the more moderate voices usually prevail. They remain in leadership, however, only so long as the movement is progressing. But the existing establishment is usually rigid and resistant to the demand for change. When conflict becomes serious, official repression is a common response.

At this point, if the movement isn't destroyed it acquires both a more radical edge as well as a broader public sympathy with its original goals. The elites come under pressure to make concessions or lose a degree of their legitimacy and public confidence. If they continue to harden and refuse, the movement becomes more militant, and the cycle of repression-and-resistance can reach the point of violence or even revolutionary conflict. In American history, it has usually been at this point—somewhere after the collapse of polite protest and the beginning of revolutionary struggle—that a breakthrough typically occurs. The elites make concessions—allowing women the right to vote, accepting a minimum wage, withdrawing from war, even relinquishing the Presidency in the face of popular scorn. At the same time, the more radical elements of the movement, those who had come to want more than the original demands—are repressed, discredited or isolated. The result is a new version of the traditional order which incorporates some change while trying to contain its impact as much as possible. The masses of people who fought for the change are temporarily satisfied with their victory, and take up living within the new and expanded definition of the rights of normal life.

Does the System Work?

Two false conclusions are usually drawn from this progression. The first, heard most recently after Watergate, is "See? The system works." The second, a lament of many radicals, is that the system "co-opts" dissent, that is, creates the cosmetic appearance of change but not the real thing.

The argument that Watergate and Vietnam prove the system works is a bit strained on the face of it. America was, after all, defeated in a war which was illegal in origin, immoral in practice and ended with secret police operating inside the White House. Street confrontations, bombings and the forced resignation of an incumbent president were not what the Founding Fathers envisioned as the routine remedies available to the electorate.

Nevertheless, it is crucial to note that crises are historically resolved in large measure through existing institutions (presidential primaries, court cases, media criticism) and without the right-wing military take-over that is common response to popular challenges in other countries. A basic demand for change among millions of people is eventually channeled through the system. In fact, the "outside" pressure is exactly what opens the system up from within. The system does not bend until the people make it bend. Credit should go to the people who made total commitments of their lives to ending the Vietnam War, not to the wondrous flexibility which too many political scientists see inherent in the checks-and-balances built into the American government.

But was the anti-war movement co-opted? In one sense, yes. If, for example, the movement's leaders and organizations wanted to end not only the war but also imperialism, racism and the military-industrial complex, then we failed. If we wanted to dissolve the over-centralized Executive Branch instead of merely getting rid of Nixon, then we failed. But if those were anyone's primary objectives, they were illusory to begin with. The broad popular support on which the movement rested primarily wanted to end the war and rid the White House of Johnson and then Nixon. Those were the original outrages that aroused people, and they remained the goals that millions shared at the end. A movement of millions could not then have been built against imperialism or the imperial presidency, but only against the Vietnam War and Richard Nixon. To believe that the movement failed because the war ended and Nixon fell while Wall Street and the Pentagon still remained intact is to snatch defeat from the jaws of victory. It trivializes a historic achievement.

The warning against co-optation also includes the notion that activists of today will wind up tomorrow in the snares of the system, gain respectibility and sell out their ideals. This has happened historically and it is a constant danger in any process. But does one guard against it by abstention, by refusing on principle to run for office, do social work, teach, establish small businesses, work in the corporate media, serve in government? Where is the line drawn? Must one function only on the farthest periphery? This too is a way of redefining victory as defeat. In fact, only through *grassroots movements* is it possible for ideas to become respectable, for one-time radicals to become electable, and for change to be ratified by people perched within the system. It is not so much a question of being "inside" or "outside." One goal is to get inside, but only in a way that is principled, accountable and feeds back into the larger and more important grassroots movement.

Does this mean the system itself can be changed from within?—another famous question which has long plagued reformers and radicals, and which has no provable answer. Certainly it is hard to imagine the corporate leadership peacefully or politically accepting the loss of their power to a new coalition for economic democracy. Repression has been used again and again against movements which threatened to become too powerful. On the other hand, privilege has been surrendered peacefully many times after bitter battles. Just as none of our present rights, beginning with the Declaration of Independence and First

Amendment, have been gained without struggle, none have been gained without forcing powerful groups to unwillingly concede, but they have conceded.

The struggle against bureaucratic and corporate power could evolve in stages, each of them bitter, but not totally convulsive, until the balance of political and economic power shifts in democracy's favor.

This is indeed a key lesson of American history—that successive movements have implemented the full vision of democracy only in stages. The American Revolution basically empowered white, male property-owners. It took a further cycle of movements to enfranchise women and minorities, and to end property qualifications in voting. The rights of labor were achieved in the same step-by-step process, brought about by successive waves of unionism. Each movement fell short of its most radical visions but nevertheless achieved a new plateau of rights from which the next struggles could be more powerfully launched.

Step-by-Step Reform as Strategy

This suggests an argument, based on history, for a *strategy of reform*. But it is for a very special *kind* of reform. It must focus on the symptoms of crisis as the way to the root. By pulling up the symptoms, the roots are exposed and weakened. If curing the symptoms is all that can be achieved in a current confrontation, then a later movement will find it still more necessary and—more important—less difficult to get to the roots. The key to an effective reform is whether it empowers people in some way—through change in both consciousness and structure—to take greater control over their lives, and then to make still greater advances. Then the reform is an achievement in its own terms and also a platform for the future, an aid to the living generation and to the unborn.

Three facts stand out in this pattern of American history: first, rights we now take for granted were matters of endless dispute and polarization before national consciousness was raised and related battles were engaged and won. It is helpful to recall, for example, that the very first social and economic legislation of the industrial revolution was passed in 1832, when England limited the allowable amount of child labor to 84 hours per week.[2] Unthinkable today, that issue was resolved only 150 years ago. It was the same for slavery, women's rights, the opportunity to join unions and civil rights. There is no change without a conflict in which people choose to live lives of danger and controversy rather than ones of safety and conformity.

Second, the individuals who actually stood up and began these great movements personally created a shift in the winds to a climate in which millions of other citizens looked at their rights and responsibilities differently. In every case, these movements were initiated by individuals who were unknown at the time, and remain less known than those who later rode the final crest of success to power. Suffragette or abolitionist, labor leader or anti-war activist, they were all at one point in their lives feeling helpless and powerless, but they reckoned to do something about it.

Third, each of these movements was an expansion of democracy, both in terms of the climate they created and the later laws they won. The path of American history is littered with the threats of tyranny but it leads forward slowly to greater and greater recognition of the rights of individuals and disenfranchised groups. At each point along the way the philosophical conservatives prophesy a collapse of culture, a disintegration of government into mob rule, and even the loss of individual motivation—and each time they are revealed to be protecting only *their* own notions of elite culture, government of the propertied few and inherited privilege. Democracy being only a process, it has not solved certain of America's overwhelming problems, but there are at least no visible groups of Americans at this point who believe in giving up their democratic rights for the good of the country. The idea of democracy for the past 200 years has typically expanded and almost never contracted.

New values linked to an era of limits—finding a simpler lifestyle than conspicuous consumption, placing the quality of life over the quantity of things, enriching the dignity of the individual at work—will require yet another expansion of the American tradition of citizenship and democracy. This will occur only if enough people are willing to live their lives differently to become a "critical mass" for change, and if the economic and political system can be reformed enough to provide new possibilities for citizen participation and control.

A New Climate of Values

There is ample evidence of millions of Americans beginning to adapt and align themselves with new visions for the age of limits. A 1977 Louis Harris Survey titled "Quality Wins over Quantity," for example, concluded that "significant majorities place a higher priority on improving human and social relationships and the quality of American life than on simply raising the standard of living." Among Harris' findings were these:

—by 77-15 percent, the public favored "spending more time getting to know each other better as human beings on a person to person basis" instead of "improving and speeding up our ability to communicate with each other through better technology";

—by 59-26 percent a majority felt that inflation could better be controlled by "buying much less of those products short in supply and high in price" than by "producing more goods to satisfy demand";

—by 64-26 percent, most people felt that "finding more inner and personal rewards from the work people do" was more important than "increasing the productivity of our work force";[3]

These findings were consistent with an earlier 1975 poll in which Harris found that 92 percent of Americans were willing to eliminate annual model changes in automobiles, 91 percent were willing to eat meat one less day per week, 90 percent were willing to do away with annual fashion changes in clothing, 73 percent were willing to wear old clothes until they wear out, 82 percent were willing to reduce the amount of advertising, and even 57 percent were willing to see a policy making it cheaper to live in multi-family units than individual homes.[4]

Some of these popular views, Harris noted, reflected the energy crunch and the realization that raw materials are not boundlessly available; others were "a legacy of all those ideas that young people pressed for in the 1960's that have now begun to take root in the 1970's." Altogether the poll results convinced Harris that a "quiet revolution may be taking place in our national values and aspirations."[5]

A 1975 Hart Poll specifically addressed the concept of economic democracy, and discovered extremely positive public attitudes. Thirty-three percent of those polled believed that "our capitalist economic system has already reached its peak in terms of performance" while only 22 percent believed it "has not yet reached its peak." A majority of 58 percent believed that America's major corporations "tend to dominate" the national government. More significantly, 66 percent agreed that people don't work as hard as they could "because they aren't given enough say in decisions which affect their jobs." Seventy-four percent supported a plan in which consumers in local communities "are represented on the boards of companies that operate in their local regions"; 52 percent supported a plan "in which employees determine broad company policy," and 66 percent favored working for an employee-owned and -controlled firm.[6]

Another sign of coming changes is the growth of the movement for "voluntary simplicity," a phrase of the writer Richard Gregg who in 1936 spoke of a life that would be outwardly resistant to consumption while inwardly rich in growth.[7] Studied and championed by writers like Schumacher, social scientists at the Stanford Research Institute, and journals like *Co-Evolution Quarterly*, the philosophy of voluntary simplicity has seen a major upsurge in the 1970s. Writer/researchers Duane Elgin and Arnold Mitchell estimated in 1977 that 4-5 million Americans lead lives of "full Voluntary Simplicity," and over one-third live in some way sympathetic with the goals of material simplicity, human scale, self-determination, ecological awareness and personal growth.[8]

A signal of gloom from the business world appeared in a survey done by the Harvard *Business Review* in late 1975. The editors pitted two ideologies against each other, and asked their readers which they preferred and which they expected to prevail in the U.S. by 1990. "Ideology I" was based on traditional values of rugged individualism and marketplace free enterprise, while "Ideology II" was based on emphasizing the public interest and common good over the rights of the individual. While the readers preferred the first framework over the second by 70 percent to 29 percent, a full 73 percent thought that the second ideology would be dominant in the U.S. by 1985.[9]

Of course, the polls do not measure readiness of a commitment to act. But what is interesting is the *breadth* of the majorities at least interested in new values and priorities.

If sufficient numbers of Americans are interested in an alternative, what are the "points of entry" where their feelings can start having an effect on the status quo?

One that has been the subject of this book and needs no further elaboration is the avenue towards *economic democracy*. The conception of American citizenship should be extended by law to the economic domain with the empowerment of workers, consumers and community representatives in the decision-making that is now left to a privileged handful. There can never be truly effective political democracy in America if economic decisions that affect the many are made by the few.

The second avenue for achieving an alternative vision is through the effective *decentralization of government*. The monolithic nation-state has become a lethal and expensive bureaucracy enjoying less and less public confidence and denying meaningful opportunities for participation to millions of people. We should learn that in diversity there lies strength, rather than continuing with the Madisonian fear of factions and mobs. The trend toward decentralization is exemplified in the widespread adoption of "district elections," which favor the power of neighborhood groups over "downtown" interests, and the growing use of initiatives and referendums as the leading political reforms of the 1970s. The shift from a one-dimensional centralized system to a "multi-dimensional" political culture can only increase with the focus on inner frontiers. The new separatism and localism is a reversal of the old theory of the "melting pot."

A third crucial element in expanding democracy would be through a "participatory media," *breaking the standardizing hold of corporate television on American political life*. It is almost forgotten that the commentators' medium belongs to the public, and that networks—more than other corporations—are licensed in the public interest. While the news and prime-time features are boringly interchangeable on the three major networks, the technology of mass communications lends itself to what might be called an "electronic democracy." Helped by "citizen computer terminals," the average citizen could discover information, question candidates, observe government hearings, vote or express an opinion by pushing a button, perform certain kinds of work at home instead of the office, "attend" school in the mornings or evenings. As the old political parties based on traditional patronage machines crumble, the television networks have begun to replace them as the arena of American politics and civic dialogue. There is little chance of going back to a pre-electronic era, as Jerry Mander has quite seriously suggested in *Four Arguments for the Elimination of Television*.[10] The only real choices are either letting the corporate monopolization of television continue, or effectively demanding that the networks become a new electronic equivalent of the ancient Greek *agora*, the marketplace where thousands of people communicated, bargained and argued over ideas throughout the day.

Options in the Eighties

As the 1980's begin to unfold, the shape of American politics seems to reflect three trends:

1. A shift to the classic conservative authoritarianism, symbolized by the Ronald Reagan candidacy, based on a stubborn and futile attempt to retain the balance of privilege and consumption at home and abroad.

2. Growth of a progressive populism at local levels, reflecting the demands of many unrepresented groups of women, minorities, consumers, progressive unions, seniors, the disabled, tending in its direction towards economic democracy and political decentralization.

3. The decline of the liberal-conservative center, formerly based on the New Deal-Cold War consensus and now represented by a growing void filled in part by various personalities.

In past eras when "the center did not hold," prophets of Left and Right have predicted radicalization of one kind or another, only to be surprised by the reappearance of a new consensus, some kind of "New Deal," patched together but nonetheless offering enough to stabilize American society for another generation. Let us therefore examine what might fill the current empty center before examining the prospects for either corporate authoritarianism or economic democracy.

The proposal most likely to become the new center of American political thought is *economic planning*. As the energy crisis worsens and foreign economic competition grows, the logic of planning will become more attractive to government, business and labor. At present and for the immediate future, the idea will be abhorrent to those absorbed by a free market perspective. But in fact, the American economy is already "planned"—privately and separately by the corporations whose production and profit projections run years into the future. The only question, therefore, is whether American society benefits from this strange combination of private planning and public anarchy, a status quo that few will find comforting in the face of one crisis after another in the 1980s. In a process like the New Deal, a majority of Chambers of Commerce are likely to be pulled against their will into planning as the only economic arrangement with even a chance of protecting their interests.

"Reindustrialization of America" is the current banner of those favoring a planned corporate economy. The White House, *Business Week*, the AFL-CIO, and politicians as disparate as Governor Jerry Brown and Senator Lloyd Bentsen have begun using this awkward new phrase, often with different emphasis, to describe a scenario for recovery.

The *Business Week* version, carried in a special issue on June 30, 1980, recounts the familiar problems of American decline in the face of economic competition, rising energy shortages, failing productivity, and a lost entrepreneurship ("...resistance to change seems to be endemic in corporate America." [11]). Their proposed solutions contain many familiar and self-serving complaints against government intrusion. Among the roadblocks to improving exports they cite the Foreign Corrupt Practices Act (which prevents them from bribing officials in other lands), trade embargoes (which curb their ability to sell wheat to the Soviets at will), nuclear proliferation policies (which block them from sending reactor and bomb-grade materials abroad), anti-trust laws (which prohibit merging into joint trading companies), and health and safety laws (which reduce workplace and environmental hazards).[12] It is as if the world would be all better again if suddenly American multinationals could merge into larger, government-protected conglomerates free to bribe, pollute and contaminate on an equal basis with their competition. The message is that America has to abandon human rights concerns, support a nuclear arms race, and ignore social and environmental horrors of all kinds to assure economic stability. This, of course, is no trade-off at all, merely a formula for maintaining short-term privilege on the way to a global nightmare.

However, in other respects, these *Business Week* editors are more enlightened than in their previous 1974 calls for a majority of Americans to accept less so that big business could have more. The editors realize, for example, that unimaginative "dollar-oriented specialists" are becoming the corporate leaders of tomorrow,[13] that "top management has become insulated from its employees,"[14] that more capital is expended on corporate acquisitions, which create no new value, than on research and development programs,[15] and that the multinationals will resist investing at home instead of overseas.[16] Perhaps more important than their criticism of corporate attitudes, however, is their realization that a "new social contract" must take into account the views of labor, minorities and public interest groups, not simply the business community. They observe the danger that "businessmen, fully absorbed in the problems of the economy, will push social problems into the background"[17] . . . whereas "reaching out to minorities is the price that will have to be paid to achieve any new social consensus."[18] Enlightened as these views are by traditional business standards, and difficult as it will be to win business support for them, they still suffer from the absolute priority placed on the growth of corporate profit over every other interest, and the continued sanctity of private and exclusive corporate decision-making processes.

The "reindustrialization" program, then, would rest on a type of economic planning that would reflect the interests and participation of the large corporations, government bureaucrats, and perhaps representatives of the major unions. In its mildest form, as proposed already by a number of national leaders, this planning would be "indicative" and voluntary; that is, it would concentrate on forecasting shortages and other trends, gathering data about other nations' economies, and proposing investment priorities with only voluntary compliance expected. A more thoroughgoing form of planning, however, is a rising possibility as the struggle over markets and resources intensifies. Like Japanese and Western European regimes, the U.S. government could enter into virtual partnerships with certain key industries, providing massive subsidies to improve their advantages in the global sweepstakes. This would go well beyond voluntarism to a new social contract.

Whatever the kind of planning, any form emanating from anxious corporate and government bureaucrats is bound to leave out the public interest, not to mention public participation, to a considerable degree. They are the same planners and forecasters, after all, who predicted victory in Vietnam, engineered the Great Society, missed the emergence of the energy crisis, and left us with congestion on freeways, deteriorating cities, "health planning" organizations, and as a measure of progress a GNP that "grows" with every expensive catastrophe that occurs. They do not necessarily lack expertise, but they are blinded by the desire to preserve their own values and profits as a higher priority than maintaining a human scale, protecting the environment, keeping costs down, and making institutions liveable.

Their kind of economic planning threatens local democratic processes. It imposes on communities and on the American people as a whole as the only way to break the stalemate over energy policy, or prevent escalating wage demands, or create a climate of certainty for major investors. For such planning, grass-roots participation would be seen as an obstruction, not a source of necessary feedback or wisdom.

It would be far better to create a form of *democratic and participatory economic planning,* with direction and ideas flowing from the workplace and community upwards instead of down. This would be possible if major corporations had labor, consumer and community representation on their boards, if government was decentralized in its approach to decisions, and if the media were an accessible channel of information, debate and communications for the public. In this manner a national plan of investment could be decided with popular participation and consent to guarantee protection of worker, regional, and community interests. Such popular involvement would be critical to the plan itself, adding to morale and productivity in the workforce and creating a higher sense of commitment to a common mission in the society as a whole.

The least preferable scenario would be an authoritarian expansion of the present system in which corporations make their own private plans for the future and seek to dominate or stifle government whenever it seeks to represent the public interest. This would be a sure harbinger of war abroad, inflation at home, a reduction of democracy, and a general decay for the human fabric of society.

Towards a New Coalition

Since the immediate prospects for achieving full economic democracy on a nationwide basis are non-existent, the best path in that direction in the 1980s will probably fork in two complementary directions: towards a "new majority governing coalition" on the one hand, and a more populist movement for direct democracy, community control, and self-sufficiency at regional levels.

A "new majority governing coalition" would be based on an urgent recognition that the strategies of the "Custerites" on the right are a disaster, and that practical, winnable short-term solutions have to be found to the problems of energy, inflation, recession and global military tension. Its leadership would be based on the joining of several forces: however many enlightened bankers and industrialists as can be enlisted, labor leaders (and especially the rank-and-file), minorities and women constituencies, many liberal politicians of both parties, and of course an energetic base of representatives of the newer movements for social change. This coalition would be distinguished by its agreement to curtail short-term self-interest in behalf of mobilizing for a sane investment strategy. Sacrifice would begin at the top with capitalists, but organized labor might also be asked to defer certain demands in exchange for a voice in the process. The coalition's planning emphasis would be on determining how rapidly, and with what compromises, a transition to conservation and renewable resources could be achieved; on what to do with the burdensome U.S. military budget without making destabilizing cuts; on ways to massively re-invest in crucial American technology while de-emphasizing the frills of the opulent past; on what to do about the explosive gaps between poverty and wealth here and abroad. In short, it would be a reformist, mainstream coalition, the most far-reaching of its kind since the New Deal.

This coalition would be pushed by, and in turn exercise a restraining influence over, the newer, progressive movements for further change. To continue the analogy with the 1930's, these grassroots movements would be the contemporary counterparts of the 1930's industrial union movement, the agrarian populists, and the political campaigns of such men as Upton Sinclair and perhaps Huey Long. They would stress a redistribution of power via economic democracy, a crash program towards renewables, and a range of tactics from electoral campaigns to strikes, boycotts and civil disobedience to achieve their goals. They would be opposed by the likes of Howard Jarvis and Anita Bryant, the modern parallels of the reactionary populists of the 1930's, Father Charles Coughlin and Robert Townsend. In the center would be the "new majority coalition," like the New Deal, leaning to the left but seeking a greater consensus to calm the sea of treacherous political currents.

The 1930's resulted in progressive improvements for working men and women, for the poor and elderly, and created a new legitimacy for government intervention in the economy. But the era did not resolve our economic and racial problems before World War II, and at various moments it subordinated itself to corporate priorities and even moved dangerously to the right. While in the end it left a progressive legacy, it also stabilized and even saved the corporate economic system.

But who can deny that the men and women who fought for the rights of labor, for the 8-hour day, for an end to the breadlines, who developed an authentic folk culture with heroes like Woody Guthrie and Paul Robeson, were not the driving force that made the best of the New Deal possible? And if that were not honor enough, who can tell how far the progressives of the 1930's would have carried their campaigns were it not for World War II?

A similar coalition in the 1980s could come to power nationally, with representatives of the "majority coalition" in the White House and Congress, the movement for economic democracy coming to power in local and state governments, as well as certain unions, and their outlook becoming influential among rank-and-file workers in the professions, in educational institutions, among small business and farmers, and even in some rational corporate circles. Through the progress of such a coalition, the "economic Democrats" could conceivably move towards national power in the 1990s, making America an economic democracy and a solar society by the year 2000.

Whether this happens at all is an open question. But so is the future of humanity. What lurks between us and the year 2000 is a greater series of threats than ever were faced in so short a time by any previous American generation.

But there is no outlook worth having except optimism. An old Quaker saying pledges "to light the candle rather than curse the darkness." It is the same when viewing the transition before us: we will either believe in our ability to make it, believe that our greatness lies always before us, that our potential still is infinite, or we will join the chorus of doom orchestrated by those who are willing to destroy humanity if necessary to protect their investments in yesteryear.

The crisis is one of will, imagination and faith. Ours is a great and young nation, living in a yet richer and older world. It is not too late for a new beginning, no longer based on a hostile assessment of nature and others. When physical frontiers close, hope and love still know no boundaries.

APPENDIX: FOUNDING STATEMENT OF THE CAMPAIGN FOR ECONOMIC DEMOCRACY

(This declaration was adopted by a conference of one thousand California activists in February 1977.)

We are gathering in Santa Barbara to affirm a new vision of California.

We already see pursuit of individual wealth, status and power has left us with three of our five air basins permanently polluted, cancer from industrial causes multiplying like a scourge, water and food quality inferior, rich land being paved over, one million people indefinitely out of work, prices tripling for natural gas that supplies half our wasteful energy needs, most families unable to buy a house, poor people and senior citizens barely able to live on services about to be cut back, crime mounting dangerously as economic tensions increase.

Once again we see long lines of people queuing up for the necessities of life—with the breadlines of the past being replaced by gasoline lines, job lines as thousands appear at 5 a.m. to compete for a handful of openings in Santa Clara or Los Angeles, even house lines—as thousands congregate when a few dozen new homes appear on the Southern California market.

The old ways of organizing social and economic life have failed. Not even their supporters proclaim their virtues very loudly. The corporate leaders who once supplied the economic stimulus to California's dream—from the Gold Rush, to oil, to Hollywood, to aerospace—today can only grumble about environmentalists, labor costs, and business taxes. Instead of hope, they propose only greater burdens and sacrifices for the majority—a program of prosperity for the few and austerity for the rest of us.

The time has come for the people of California to create a new dream. Whole new industries are waiting to be born in California, thousands of jobs to be created from producing solar and other clean energy, developing transit, and cleaning up the environment. Tremendous energies are waiting to be unleashed, as workers,

303

small businesses and consumers begin to participate in making basic decisions about their lives.

This dream has a name: ECONOMIC DEMOCRACY. We want the quality of life and the public interest to be more important than the individual pursuit of profit. This is the final California frontier: *we can achieve it* by letting the public have a real voice in economic decisions, by controlling giant corporations by directing investment to productive and human ends.

Economic Democracy means that a few hundred corporate leaders will no longer make basic economic decisions that affect all of our lives. It means that ownership and control will be spread among a wide variety of public bodies: city, state and federal governments; churches, trade unions, cooperatives, and community groups; small business people, workers and consumers.

This is not a new dream, of course. But it may be that its time has finally come. For California's economic boom time has clearly ended. The only question is whether those who favor Economic Democracy can muster the political skill, and sustain the political and social effort, to make it a reality.

We need to build a grass-roots citizens' campaign to take back power over our lives—and create healthy individuals, families, communities and workplaces.

The Corporate Alternative

We have often tried to change our priorities in California—by protest, by demonstrations, by the vote, by simply crying out. And we have made gains—in consumer and labor protection, political reform, women's and minority rights, environmental regulations.

But what we have accomplished is only a beginning. We are consistently working against the pressure of permanent lobbies and uncaring bureaucracies. Most of our economic and environmental problems are actually worsening. Now with national economic stagnation, even the modest gains of the past generation may be wiped out.

We have learned that an unchosen corporate elite has more power than even the leaders we elect.

They *circumvent political reform*. Two years after passage of Proposition 9, California's progressive campaign reform act, new real estate lobbies are emerging in Sacramento and we hear more than ever about corporate bribery by aerospace giants.

They *win elections* with Orwellian propaganda and huge sums of money. Oil companies, private utilities and agribusiness financed the defeat of the nuclear safeguards and farm labor initiatives in 1976. Their dollars sudsidized the scare talk about electricity shutdowns and private property being trampled if the initiatives had passed.

They *defy regulatory agencies*. "Dealing with ARCO is like dealing with a foreign power," one Public Utilities Commissioner said last year. He and another new appointee had voted to give ARCO millions of dollars to explore for natural gas though he felt "blackmailed."

They arbitrarily *lay off workers and raise prices*. California corporations like Del Monte and Fairchild move to Mexico and South Korea in search of cheap labor, with our legislators unable to protect the workers in their districts. They raise our gas bills, phone bills, food bills throughout 1976, even as they recorded the greatest profits that year since 1955.

It all adds up to a problem of overwhelming corporate power, in which a few corporate heads are more powerful than the Governor or Legislature of California. And when government does step in, it is often to shore up an indifferent and inefficient corporate structure.

Our Alternative: Economic Democracy

We do not need to destroy California to "save" it. We only need a new dream, a new economic direction which puts people first, creates meaningful work, saves energy and preserves resources. We need to headquarter a *new economic experiment* in California, producing everything from conservation devices to mass transit vehicles, planning the restoration of cities, searching for new answers to the world's food, health and energy crises. But to do any of this, we will have to find ways to take control of our economic destiny.

Economic Democracy is our alternative to both the corporate nightmare and the twin peril of big government bureaucracy. In order to build a safe, sane and personally fulfilling world for ourselves, we must break the power of economic and bureaucratic elites. We must *transfer power* back to the people—in the neighborhoods where we live, the offices or plants where we work, the stores where we shop, the schools where we study, the whole political arena in which we are endlessly abused.

Economic Democracy will be a new process of economic decision-making emerging from the current stage of corporate monopoly. It will be an evolving system in which economic decisions are made with the involvement and consent of the people affected, rather than on a criterion of private profit for a remote few.

Economic Democracy would end the arbitrary power of the absentee managers on our lives. It would encourage a shift to productive, job-producing, non-inflationary investment.

An enterprise where workers have a voice is far less likely to become a runaway shop than one owned by a giant multinational. A plant in which community people have a say is more likely to find an alternative to poisoning the town water supply than a giant oil company which can relocate at will.

Consumer-directors of an enterprise are more likely to push for increased efficiency rather than raising prices in times of slack demand. Worker-directors are more likely to improve health and safety standards, find ways to increase morale and job productivity, than a distant corporate elite whose principal concern is profits on a balance sheet.

Economic Democracy and Government Spending

Our privately-dominated economic and energy system has depended on a world of unlimited expansion and resources. With that world coming to an end, we face new choices. Our "Trickle-down" welfare state can no longer provide both more for the many and more for the few. More for the U.S. means less for the Third World. *More for U.S. corporations means less for the rest of us.* In this era of limits, we will be thrown into dangerous competition over less and less resources—unless we can change our vision and priorities.

The only "answer" to this crisis so far has been to cut spending, with liberals everywhere hiding from the label "big spender." Of course, big government spending has created wasteful bureaucracies without reducing social ills. But it is also true that *most* government welfare goes to sudsidize the private sector directly, or indirectly by supporting the millions the corporations will not employ. As government spending is cut, the increased austerity will only set a fuse to more explosive social tensions.

Economic Democracy is the only viable alternative to wasteful bureaucratic spending or tight-fisted fiscal conservatism. By basing investment on *public needs* rather than *private greed*, Economic Democracy *reduces* wasteful spending by:

—increasing investment in healthy, *job-producing* sectors like mass transit and low-cost housing, rather than for wasteful priorities like the B-1 bomber which absorb our scientific establishment in a war economy at the expense of other needs.

—revamping our unjust tax system to produce more tax *revenues* instead of loopholes.

—shifting from expensive energy sources to *cheap* and *renewable* ones.

Reducing prices by giving consumers more direct power over prices and products.

Principles of Economic Democracy

The vision of Economic Democracy includes these general principles:

1. An *Economic Bill of Rights* which recognizes that every citizen is assured the rights to work, health, housing, education, personal safety and environmental sanity.

2. *Participation in economic decision-making.* The private pinnacles of financial and corporate power must be opened to the people. Employees have human rights on the job, and a democratic right to a voice in corporate and government decision-making. So do consumers and representatives of the general public. And communities must be assured the right to referendums on the crucial decisions affecting them.

3. *Democratic economic planning and public enterprises.* We must create public bodies, tied to the grass-roots level, which enable citizens' groups to shape their economic and environmental destiny in a time of diminishing resources.

4. An *energy policy* stressing solar energy and conservation. We need conservation-minded public control of offshore drilling, land use, and water decisions which for too long have been geared to the priorities of wasteful consumption and greed.

5. An *agricultural policy* which promotes family farms and cooperatives, decent conditions for farmworkers, organic and nutritious food, and consumer control of prices.

6. *Decentralized, community-based social services* with maximum power in the hands of those people directly affected.

7. An *employment policy* which taps the immense energy of our people to do *meaningful work*, instead of forcing every group into ugly competition with others. We should turn towards labor-intensive, rather than capital or energy-intensive, production; towards the maintenance of quality goods rather than production for waste; and we should expand rather than reduce the numbers employed in services such as health and education.

8. A real *equality of opportunity* in a framework of expanding jobs, rather than turning back the clock for minorities and women.

9. *Progressive tax reform.* Instead of shifting the burden to small businesses and middle- to lower-income people, the giant corporations ought to pay their fair share.

10. We need a *foreign policy that serves our human needs* over corporate profit.

The Strategy for Winning Economic Democracy

We believe it necessary to begin a long process of political change—first, to make these objectives part of public life and debate and, second, to achieve them step-by-step in our lifetime.

Our strategy must rest on the power of people united for a cause. We will not be able to whisper our ideas, or mask them or cleverly package them, to persuade the powerful of our case. We will only make an impact at all by inspiring and mobilizing thousands of Californians to the cause.

We believe Californians must use *political organization* and *votes* to affect public policy. We can resist threatened cutbacks in services, higher burdens for consumers and taxpayers, and rollbacks of environmental safeguards. We can force discussion of corporate power, and begin to achieve reforms which empower consumers and local communities. We can elect or defeat politicians.

We need to create a *Campaign for Economic Democracy.* This will be a movement of activists, community organizations and concerned citizens. Its unity will flow from vision and program. Its structure will be flexible, open, allowing various levels of commitment and participation. It will be a campaign designed for outreach of the *largest number of Californians possible.*

We need regularly to come together in conference form to decide on a *Legislative Agenda* of proposals to be made in a particular period. We need to formulate a program which grows from the needs of local community groups and can have impact on statewide politics.

We need to use our strength to demand support from elected officials for our Legislative Agenda, to form a *coordinated statewide network* to bring pressure to bear for the priorities we have chosen. Such a network might require a *steering committee* of local activist groups, constituency representatives, and elected officials, from this conference to ensure our future communications, conferences, lobbying efforts, and organizational training.

We need to *support candidates* for local, state and federal office who support our goals, to oppose candidates who do not. We are realists, but willing to consider support for candidates of our own, to avoid being forever trapped in the "lesser evil" choices we find today.

Democratic and independent voters in particular represent a majority of the people who want change. We will engage in struggle to reform the Democratic Party, but never become a mere "loyal opposition" trapped within the confines set by its leaders.

Towards a new Coalition for Economic Democracy

With Thoreau, we also believe it necessary to *"vote with your whole life,"* not just once a year at the ballot box. There must be *permanent citizens' action* at the grass-roots level—to make sure that laws are enforced, to make elected officials accountable, to make real the dream of community self-government.

Therefore, we need to encourage the growth of single-issue, community, labor, cultural and educational groups outside the immediate electoral process as well as within.

We seek a coalition comprising as many strands as possible. This is not only right but necessary, because in the coming economic crunch we will either destroy ourselves in competition or learn to live together under new rules of harmony and justice. Each constituency of the coalition will make its own urgent demands, while having to find ways to understand and unite with the needs of all.

We do not invite opportunists or the faint-hearted on this journey, but only those for whom the potentiality of the dream is worth the difficulty of transforming unconventional and unpopular ideas into a new common sense.

We expect no quick victories and many painful defeats—but also that we will lead richer and more joyful lives along the way.

We are confident that millions of California citizens are ready to join in making this dream a reality. We have the determination, patience and willingness to work to achieve them.

We believe the human spirit can overcome any obstacle to its freedom.

In our time, it must.

And it will.

(Adopted by the planning committee for the Santa Barbara Conference)

FOOTNOTES—AMERICAN IDENTITY: THE FRONTIERS OF CUSTER AND THOREAU

1. *Time Magazine*, January 7, 1980.
2. *Ibid.*
3. Sampson, Anthony. *The Seven Sisters*, New York: Bantam Books, 1976, p. 140.
4. Blair, John M. *The Control of Oil*, New York: Vintage Books, 1978, p. 78.
5. Official White House Transcript, December 31, 1977.
6. Rostow, W.W. *The Stages of Economic Growth*, Cambridge: Cambridge University Press, 1960, pp. 151, 162.
7. Council on Environmental Quality. *Solar Energy: Progress and Promise*. Washington, D.C., April 1978, p. 1.
8. *RIO, Reshaping the International Order: A Report to the Club of Rome*, Tinbergen, Jan, coordinator. New York: New American Library, 1976, pp. 129-30.
9. *Ibid.*, p. 29.
10. Associated Press, July 21, 1980.
11. Sale, Kirkpatrick. *Human Scale*, New York: Coward, McCann & Geoghegian, 1980, pp. 22-23.
12. Weber, Max. *The Protestant Ethic and the Spirit of Capitalism*. New York: Charles Scribner's & Sons, 1958, p. 121.
13. Beck, Warren A. and Haase, Yniz D. *Historical Atlas of California*, Norman, Oklahoma: University of Oklahoma Press, 1974, p. 1.
14. Watkins, T.H. *California, An Illustrated History*, Palo Alto: American West Publishing Co., 1973, p. 102.
15. *Ibid.*, p. 249.
16. Williams, William Appleman. *The Tragedy of American Diplomacy*, New York: Dell Publishing Co., 1972, pp. 32-8.
17. Zinn, Howard. *A People's History of the United States*, New York: Harper & Row, 1980, p. 149.
18. *Ibid.*, p. 161.
19. *Ibid.*, p. 139.
20. *op. cit.*, Williams, p. 63.

21. *op. cit.*, Zinn, p. 412.
22. Lynd, Staughton and Hayden, Tom. *The Other Side*, New York: New American Library, p. xx.
23. *Ibid.*, p. xx.
24. Hayden, Tom. *The Love of Possession is a Disease with Them*, Chicago: Holt, Rinehart & Winston, 1972, pp. 99-100.
25. *op. cit.*, Williams, p. 27.
26. *Ibid.*, p. 48.
27. *Ibid.*, pp. 310-11.
28. *Ibid.*, pp. 21, 72, 127.
29. *op. cit.*, Zinn, pp. 96-7 and *Federalist Paper #10*.
30. *Ibid.*, p. 79, 96.
31. *Ibid.*, p. 96.
32. *Ibid.*
33. Kinsley, D.A. *Favor the Bold*, New York: Holt, Rinehart & Winston, 1967, p. 154.
34. *Ibid.*, p. 164.
35. Brown, Dee. *Bury My Heart at Wounded Knee*, New York: Holt, Rinehart & Winston, 1970, p. 277.
36. Berry Wendell. *The Unsettling of America*: Culture and Agriculture, San Francisco: Sierra Club Books, 1977, p. 4.
37. *Ibid.*, p. 5.
38. Chief Luther Standing Bear.
39. *Less is More*, VandenBroeck, Goldian, editor. New York: Harper and Row, 1978, p. 282.
40. *The Portable Thoreau*. Bode, Carl, editor. New York: Penguin Books, 1975, pp. 258-308.
41. *op. cit.*, Watkins, p. 169.
42. *Ibid.*, p. 199.
43. *Ibid.*, p. 279.
44. Heilbroner, Robert L. *The Economic Problem*, Englewood Cliffs, New Jersey: Prentice-Hall, 1968, p. 60.
45. *op. cit.*, Williams, p. 310.
46. E.F. Schumacher in *op. cit., Less is More*, p. 236.
47. Silberman, Charles E. "Identity Crisis in the Consumer Markets," *Fortune*, March 10, 1971.
48. Margolis, Diane Rothbard. *The Managers*, New York: William Morrow & Co., 1979, p. 116.
49. Twain, Mark in *op. cit., Less is More*, p. 21.
50. Galbraith, John Kenneth. *The New Industrial State*, New York: New American Library, 1967, p. 19.
51. Maccoby, Michael. *The Gamesman*, New York: Bantam Books, 1978, p. 108.
52. *Ibid.*, pp. 106, 331.
53. Henderson, Hazel. *Creating Alternative Futures*, New York: Berkeley Publishing Corp., 1978, p. 310.

54. Meeting with the author, 1980.
55. Maslow, Abraham. "The Need to Know and the Fear of Knowing," *Toward a Psychology of Being*, New York: Van Nostrand Reinhold, 1962, pp. 60-61.
56. Toffler, Alvin. *The Third Wave*, New York: William Morrow & Co., Inc., 1980, pp. 381.
57. *op. cit.*, Henderson, p. 349.
58. Jung, Carl. Cited in *Changing Images of Man*, Menlo Park, California: SRI International, April 1978, p. 96.
59. Tawney, R.H. Cited in E.F. Schumacher, *Small is Beautiful*, New York: Harper & Row, 1973, introduction.
60. Ferguson, Marilyn. *The Aquarian Conspiracy*, Los Angeles: J.P. Tarcher, Inc., 1980, p. 302.
61. *Co-Evolution Quarterly*, Summer, 1977.
62. Veblen, Thorsten. *The Theory of the Leisure Class*, New York: New American Library, 1953.
63. Rifkin, Jeremy. *Entropy: A New World View* (manuscript), to be published by Viking Press, New York, September 1980, p. 121.
64. *Business Week*, October 1974 editorial.
65. Schell, Orville. *The Town That Fought to Save Itself*, New York: Pantheon Books, 1976, p. 125.

FOOTNOTES—ECONOMY: HUMAN SOLUTIONS TO INFLATION AND RECESSION

1. Los Angeles *Times*, Jan. 29, 1980.
2. *Ibid.*
3. *Newsweek,* May 19, 1980.
4. Henderson, Hazel. *Creating Alternative Futures,* New York: Berkeley Publishing Corp., 1978, p. 151.
5. Exploratory Project for Economic Alternatives, "The Costs of Continued Unemployment," Washington, D.C., 1977, pp. xv-vii.
6. Harrington, Michael. *Decade of Decision*, New York: Simon and Schuster, 1980, pp. 34-35.
7. Edward, Reich, and Weiskopf. *The Capitalist System*, New York: Prentice Hall, 1979; *op. cit.*, Harrington, pp. 83-84.
8. *op. cit.*, Harrington, pp. 96-106.
9. *Ibid.*
10. *Ibid.*
11. *Ibid.*, pp. 184-88.
12. *op. cit.*, Exploratory Project, p. xii.
13. McGovern, George. *Full Employment for an America at Peace*, Statement before the Subcommittee on Priorities and Economy in Government, the Joint Committee, U.S. Congress, June 16, 1972, p. xi.
14. *South African Roulette*, California Public Policy Center, Los Angeles, 1978.

15. Fuller, Robert. "Inflation: The Rising Cost of Living on a Small Phamphlet," *Worldwatch Paper 34*, January 1980.

16. Barnet, Richard J., *The Lean Years,* New York: Simon & Schuster, 1980, p.

17. Heilbroner, Robert. *Beyond Boom and Crash,* New York: W.W Norton & Co., 1978, p. 12.

18. *op. cit.,* Fuller, pp. 28-29.

19. *op. cit.,* Henderson, p. 179.

20. *op. cit.,* Fuller, p. 28.

21. *Ibid.,* p. 29.

22. Proxmire, William. *Uncle Sam, Last of the Bigtime Spenders.* New York: Simon & Schuster, 1972, p. 82.

23. *op. cit.,* Fuller, p. 40.

24. Nulty, Leslie Ellen. "Understanding the New Inflation: The Importance of the Basic Necessities," Exploratory Project for Economic Alternatives, Washington, D.C., 1977.

25. *Ibid.,* p. 8.

26. COIN (Consumers Opposed to Inflation in the Necessities) Report, adapted and reprinted in *CED News*, December 1978.

27. *Ibid.*

28. *Ibid.*

29. *op. cit.,* Nulty, p. 34.

30. *op. cit.,* COIN.

31. *Ibid.*

32. *Ibid.*

33. Los Angeles *Times*, April 23-24, 1980.

34. Sherrill, Robert. "Big Oil, Big Banks, Big Trouble," *Penthouse Magazine*, June 1980 and *Paying More for Less: The Gass Crisis,* California Public Policy Center, Los Angeles, May 1979, pp. 33-34.

35. *Ibid.*

36. Harrington, Michael. *Decade of Decision,* New York: Simon & Schuster, 1980, p. 304.

37. *Ibid.*

38. *op. cit,* COIN.

39. *op. cit.,* Heilbroner, pp. 38-39.

40. Compiled by Fred Branfman, California Public Policy Center, Los Angeles.

41. *U.S. News and World Report*, March 12, 1979.

42. *Ibid.*

43. *Ibid.*

44. *op. cit, Heilbroner, p. 53.*

45. *Business Week Team, The Decline of U.S. Power,* Boston: Houghton Mifflin Co., 1980, p. 203.

46. Stobaugh, Robert and Yergin, Daniel, editors. *Energy Future*, New York: Random House, 1979, pp. 202-07.

47. Illich, Ivan. *Medical Nemesis: The Expropriation of Health.* New York: Bantam Books, 1977, pp. 41-70.

48. *op. cit., Henderson, p. 83.*

49. *Ibid., p. 84.*

50. *op. cit.,* Fuller, p. 38.

51. *op. cit.,* Stobaugh, p. 327.

52. Toffler, Alvin. *The Third Wave,* New York: William Morrow & Co., 1980, p. 285.

53. Thoreau, Henry David. *The Portable Thoreau,* New York: Penguin Books, 1977, p. 109.

54. de Tocqueville, Alexis. *Democracy in America.* New York: A. S. Barnes & Co., 1862, Vol. 2, pp. 114-18.

FOOTNOTES—ENERGY: TOWARD A SOLAR SOCIETY

1. Washington *Post,* April 15, 1979.

2. *Paying More for Less: The Gas Crisis,* A California Public Policy Center Study, Los Angeles, May 1979, p. 33.

3. Business Week Team. *The Decline of U.S. Power, Boston: Houghton Mifflin, 1980, p. 33.*

4. *Hayes, Denis. Rays of Hope,* New York: W.W. Norton & Co., 1977, p. 47.

5. Stobaugh, Robert and Yergin, Daniel, editors. New York: Random House, 1979, p. 216.See also their article in *Foreign Affairs, January 1980.*

6. *Business Week,* November 11, 1979; *Newsweek,* April 9, 1979.

7. *Decade of the Sun,* Staff report of the California Energy Commission, Sacramento, April 1980, p. 8.

8. Available from the office of Commissioner Emilio Varanini, California Energy Commission, 1111 Howe Ave., Sacramento, California 95825.

9. "Distributed Energy Systems in California's Future," Interim Report, Volumes 1 and 2, May 1978 reprint, prepared for U.S. Department of Energy, Office of Technology Impacts, Washington, D.C. 20545, Introduction by James L. Liverman. See also Lovins, Amory, *Soft Energy Paths,* San Francisco: Friends of the Earth, 1977.

10. *op. cit.,* "Distributed Energy Systems...," Vol. 1, p. 154.

11. *Ibid,* Foreword.

12. *Ibid.,* p. 191.

13. Bienniel Report of the California Energy Commission, *California Trends and Choices,* "Status of Alternative Energy Technologies," Vol. V, p. 4.

14. *op. cit,* Stobaugh, p. 149.

15. Commoner, Barry. *The Politics of Energy,* New York: Alfred A. Knopf, 1979, p. 29.

16. *op. cit.,* "Distributed Energy Systems...," p. 63.

17. *Ibid.*

18. *Solar Energy: Progress and Promise,* Council on Environmental Quality, Washington, D.C., April 1978, p. 2.

19. *Jobs From the Sun,* A California Public Policy Center Study, Los Angeles, February 1978, Abstract, p. 92.

20. *op. cit., Decade of the Sun,* p. 66.

21. Clark, Wilson. *Energy for Survival*, Garden City, New York: Doubleday, 1975, p. 576.

22. *Ibid.*, p. 486-7.

23. *op. cit., Decade of the Sun*, p. 49.

24. *op. cit.*, Stobaugh, p. 170.

25. *Ibid.*

26. O'Connor, Rory. "Can We Live Without Nuclear Power?" Boston *Real Paper,* July 7, 1979.

27. *op. cit.*, Council on Environmental Quality, pp. iv-vi.

28. Domestic Policy Review, Department of Energy, Washington, D.C., 1979.

29. *op. cit.*, Stobaugh, p. 227.

30. *Ibid.*, p. 212.

31. Melman, Seymour. *Permanent War Economy,* New York: Simon & Schuster, 1974.

32. *Make the Future Ours,* Draft Program of the Tom Hayden for U.S. Senate Campaign, Los Angeles, 1976, p. 42.

33. New Hampshire League of Women Voters pamphlet, 1979.

34. *op. cit.*, O'Connor.

35. Gyorgy, Anna and Friends. *No Nukes,* Boston: South End Press, 1979, p. 260.

36. *op cit.,* Business Week Team, p. 81.

37. *op. cit., Paying More for Less,* p. 66.

38. Henderson, Hazel. *Creating Alternative Futures*, New York: Berkeley Publishing Corp., 1978, p. 130.

39. *op. cit., Paying More for Less,* p. 6.

40. Associated Press, April 23, 1979.

41. *op. cit., Paying More for Less,* p. 58.

42. *op. cit.*, Commoner, p. 59.

43. *op. cit.*, Council on Environmental Quality, p. 4.

44. For more information contact SolarCal Council, 1111 Howe Ave., Sacramento, California 95825.

45. *op. cit., Decade of the Sun.* p. 7.

46. *Ibid.*

47. *Financing the Solar Transition: A Report to the California Legislature*, California Public Utilities Commission, San Francisco, January 2, 1980.

48. Memo by Laura King, Natural Resources Defense Council, 25 Kearny St., San Francisco, California 94108.

49. *op. cit.*, Stobaugh, pp. 148-9.

50. *op. cit.*, Commoner, p. 36.

51. *op. cit.*, Council on Environmental Quality, p. 35.

52. *Ibid.*

53. Los Angeles *Times,* May 24, 1980.

54. *op. cit.*, Lovins, p. 23.

55. *Ibid.*

56. *Ibid.*

57. *op. cit.*, "Distributed Energy Systems...," p. 62.

58. *Ibid.*, p. 195.

59. *op. cit.*, Stobaugh, p. 225.

60. *Ibid.*, p. 185.

61. Testimony by Fred Branfman to Domestic Policy Review hearings, Los Angeles, 1979.

62. *op. cit.*, Commoner, p. 75.

63. *Ibid.*, p. 82.

64. Butti, Ken and Perlin, John. *The Golden Thread: 2500 Years of Solar Architecture,* New York: Cheshire Books/Van Nostrand Reinhold, 1980, p. 13.

FOOTNOTES—HEALTH: PREVENTING CORPORATE CANCER

1. Brown, Michael. *Laying Waste: The Poisoning of America by Toxic Chemicals,* New York: Pantheon, 1979, p. 278.

2. *Ibid.*, p. 297.

3. Agran, Larry. *The Cancer Connection,* Boston: Houghton Mifflin, 1977, p. xv.

4. Epstein, Samuel S., M.D. *The Politics of Cancer,* New York: Doubleday, 1979, pp. 4, 19.

5. *Ibid.*, p. 18. See also HEW Report, "Estimates of the Fraction of Cancer in the United States Related to Occupational Factors," September 15, 1978.

6. Los Angeles *Times*, May 18, 1980.

7. Uhl, Michael and Ensign, Tod. *GI Guinea Pigs,* New York: Playboy Press (Harper & Row), 1980.

8. Page, Joseph A. and O'Brien, Mary-Win. *Bitter Wages,* New York: Grossman Publishers, 1973, pp. 17-30.

9. "Testicular Function in DBCP Exposed Workers," *Journal of Occupational Medicine*, March 1979, Vol. 21, No. 3, pp. 161-66.

10. Stellman, Jeanne and Daum, Susan. *Work is Dangerous to Your Health,* New York: Random House, 1973.

11. *op. cit.*, Brown, p. 294.

12. Chicago *Sun-Times*, June 8, 1980.

13. Environmental Defense Fund and Boyce, Robert H. *Malignant Neglect,* New York: Alfred A. Knopf, 1979, pp. 82-101.

14. *Ibid.*, p. 83.

15. Corbett, Thomas H. *Cancer and Chemicals*, Chicago: Nelson-Hall, 1979, pp. 179-81.

16. *op. cit.*, Brown.

17. *op. cit.*, Uhl, pp. 3-108.

18. Los Angeles *Times*, December 30, 1979; *Business Week*, March 24, 1980.

19. New York *Times,* May 31, 1980.

20. Singer, Charles et al., editors. *A History of Technology.* Forbes, R.J., "Petroleum," Oxford at the Clarendon Press, 1958, Vol. V, pp. 102-22.

21. *Ibid.*, Holmyard, E.J., "Dyestuffs in the 19th Century," Vol. V, pp. 271-2.
22. *Ibid.*, Greenaway, Frank et al., "The Chemical Industry," Vol. VI, p. 552.
23. *Ibid.*, Forbes, R.J., "Petroleum," Vol. V, p. 115.
24. *op. cit.*, Brown, p. 293.
25. Hamilton, Alice. "Exploring the Dangerous Trades," 1945, reprinted by Kelley Publishing Co., New York.
26. Sontag, Susan. *Illness as Metaphor,* New York: Farrar Straus Giroux, 1979.
27. *Ibid.*, p. 86.
28. *Ibid.*, p. 67.
29. *Ibid.*, pp. 69-70.
30. *Ibid.*, pp. 60-61.
31. *Ibid.*, p. 69.
32. *op. cit.*, Epstein, p. 331.
33. Leavitt, Judith Walzer and Numbers, Ronald L. *Sickness and Health in America: Readings in the History of Medicine and Public Health,* Madison, Wisconsin: University of Wisconsin Press, 1978, p. 6.
34. Israel, Lucien, M.D. *Conquering Cancer,* New York: Random House, 1979.
35. *Ibid.*, pp. 52-3.
36. Thomas, Lewis. *The Lives of a Cell,* New York: Viking Press, 1975.
37. Moss, Ralph. *The Cancer Syndrome,* New York: Grove Press, 1980.
38. Katz, Michael; Marsh, William P.; Thompson, Gail Gordon, editors. *Earth's Answer,* New York: Harper and Row, 1977, p. 164.
39. *op. cit.*, Thomas, p. 1.
40. *Ibid.*
41. *op. cit.*, Katz, p. 165.
42. Sontag, Susan on back cover of Lucien's *Conquering Cancer.*
43. *op. cit.* Sontag, pp. 60-61.
44. Thomas, Lewis, quoted on the back cover of Lucien's *Conquering Cancer.*
45. Carson, Rachel. *Silent Spring,* New York: Fawcett Crest, 1962.
46. Jewes, John; Sawers, David; Stillerman, Richard. *The Sources of Invention.*
47. *Ibid.*, p. 77.
48. *op. cit.*, Epstein, p. 331.
49. *Ibid.*
50. *Ibid.*, pp. 331-2.
51. *op. cit.*, Leavitt, p. 241-52.
52. *op. cit.*, Singer. Fleck, Sir Alexander, "Technology and Its Social Consequences," Vol. V, p. 834.
53. Harris, Leon. *Upton Sinclair, American Rebel,* New York: Thomas Y. Crowell, 1975, pp. 78-90.
54. *op. cit.*, Singer. Bruce, F.E., "Water Supply," Vol. V, pp. 566-67.
55. *op. cit.*, Leavitt. Shafel, Norman, "History of Purification of Milk in New York," p. 277.
56. Jordan, P.D. *The People's Health: A History of Public Health in Minnesota to 1948,* Minnesota Historical Society, 1953, pp. 165-66.
57. *Wall Street Journal,* May 9, 1980.

58. Center for Law in the Public Interest. "Criminal Enforcement of California's Occupational Health Laws," 1979, p. 18.

59. "An Interim Report to the Congress on Occupational Disease," U.S. Department of Labor, December 1979.

60. "Report on the Environmental Assessment of Pesticide Regulatory Program," California Department of Food and Agriculture, 1978, Summary Volume.

61. *op. cit.,* Brown, pp. 330-5.

62. *Ibid.,* p. 331.

63. *Ibid.,* p. 334.

FOOTNOTES—POWER ECONOMIC DEMOCRACY OR A CORPORATE STATE

1. Silk,, Leonard and Vogel, David. *Ethics and Profits,* New York: Simon & Schuster, 1976, p. 122.

2. Zinn, Howard. *A People's History of the United States,* New York: Harper & Row, 1980, p. 256.

3. *Ibid.,* p. 255.

4. *Ibid.*

5. *Make the Future Ours,* Draft Program of the Tom Hayden for U.S. Senate Campaign, Los Angeles, 1976, p. 11.

6. Nader, Ralph; Green, Mark; Seligman, Joel. *Taming the Giant Corporation,* New York: W.W. Norton & Co., 1976, p. 16.

7. *op. cit.,* Silk, p. 176.

8. *op. cit., Make the Future Ours,* pp. 11-12.

9. *Ibid.,* p. 12.

10. Business Week Team. *The Decline of U.S. Power,* Boston: Houghton Mifflin, 1980, p. 122.

11. *op. cit.,* Silk, p. 154.

12. Business Week Team, *The Decline of U.S. Power,* Boston: Houghton Mifflin Co., 1980, p. 168.

13. Rifkin, Jeremy. *Own Your Own Job,* New York: Bantam Books, 1977, p. 6.

14. Shonfield, Andrew. "The World Economy in 1979," *Foreign Affairs: America and the World, 1979,* Vol. 58, No. 3, Council on Foreign Relations, 1980, pp. 596-8.

15. Crowe, Kenneth C. *America For Sale,* Garden City, New York: Doubleday & Co., 1978, p. 45. See also Fry, Earl H. *Financial Invasion of the USA,* New York: McGraw-Hill Book Co., 1980.

16. *op. cit., Make the Future Ours,* p. 12.

17. Green, Mark and Massie, Robert, Jr., editors. *Big Business Reader,* New York: Pilgrim Press, 1980, p. 301.

18. *op. cit.,* Silk, p. 75.

19. *Ibid.,* p. 190.

20. Brill, Steve. "Connally: Coming on Tough," New York *Times Magazine,* November 18, 1979.

21. Blair, John M. *The Control of Oil,* New York: Vintage Books, 1978, pp. 148-51.
22. *Ibid.,* pp. 129-48.
23. Barnet, Richard J. *The Lean Years,* New York: Simon & Schuster, 1980, p.
24. *op. cit.,* "The Promise and Perils of Petrochemicals," p. 352.
25. *Paying More for Less: The Gas Crisis,* A California Public Policy Center Study, Los Angeles, May 1979, p. viii.
26. New York Times, January 26, 1980.
27. *op. cit.,* Barnet, p. 27.
28. Gyorgy, Anna and Friends, *No Nukes,* Boston: South End Press, 1979, p. 148.
29. *op. cit.* Blair, p. 134.
30. *Business Week,* April 28, 1980.
31. *op. cit.,* Commoner article, p. 347.
32. Howard, Ted and Rifkin, Jeremy. *Who Should Play God?,* New York: Dell Publishing Co., 1977, p. 190.
33. *Ibid.*
34. *Ibid.,* p. 197.
35. *New Age,* April 1980, p. 32.
36. *Business Week,* October 1974 editorial.
37. *op. cit.,* Green, Mark, "The Road to Monopoly," p. 509.
38. *op. cit.,* Silk, p. 187.
39. New York *Times,* October 12, 1972.
40. *op. cit.,* p. 251.
41. Branfman, Fred. *Public Control of Corporate Managers: Focal Point for the 1980s,* manuscript, 1979, California Public Policy Center, pp. 16-17.
42. *Fortune,* May 27, 1978.
43. *op. cit.,* Nader, p. 16.
44. *op. cit.,* Green. Ewing, David, "Free Speech Within the Corporation," p. 296.
45. *op. cit.,* Nader, p. 27.
46. *op. cit.,* Green, p. 385.
47. *op. cit.,* Nader, p. 30.
48. *Ibid.,* p. 28.
49. *op. cit., Make The Future Ours,* p. 12.
50. *Jobs From the Sun,* A California Public Policy Center Study, Los Angeles, February 1978, p. 1. See also *Decade of the Sun,* Staff report of the California Energy Commission, Sacramento, April 1980.
51. *op. cit.,* Business Week Team, pp. 121-2.
52. Associated Press, May 6, 1980.
53. *op. cit, Make the Future Ours,* p. 14.
54. *op. cit.,* Nader, p. 19.
55. Commoner, Barry, *The Closing Circle,* New York: Bantam Books, 1974, p. 138. See also *op. cit.,* Nader, p. 18.

56. Agran, Larry, *The Cancer Connection,* Boston: Houghton Mifflin, 1977, p. xv and Epstein, Samuel, S., M.D. *The Politics of Cancer,* New York: Doubleday, 1979, pp. 23-35.

57. Green, Mark et al. *A Case for a Corporate Democracy Act of 1980.* Washington, D.C.: Americans Concerned About Corporate Power, 1979, p. 61.

58. *op. cit.,* Nader, pp. 25-6.

59. *op. cit.,* Green, "A Case for...," p. 104.

60. *Ibid.,* p. 106.

61. *op. cit.,* Nader, pp. 31-2.

62. *Ibid.,* pp. 24-5.

63. *op. cit.,* Green. *Big Business Reader.* Green, Mark, "Big Business as Neighbor," p. 215.

64. *op. cit.,* Silk, p. 65.

65. Harrington, Michael. *Decade of Decision,* New York: Simon & Schuster, 1980, p. 304.

66. *op. cit., Make the Future Ours,* p. 39.

67. *op. cit.,* Harrington, p. 59.

68. Boggs, Carl and Plotke, Davie. *The Politics of Eurocommunism,* Boston: South End Press, 1980.

69. *op. cit.,* Barnet, pp. 300-301.

70. *op. cit.,* Green, *Big Business Reader,* Staff of the Committee on Small Business, House of Representatives, "On the Importance of Small Business," p. 587.

71. *Ibid.,* p. 588.

72. *Ibid.,* p. 589.

73. *Ibid.,* pp. 589-90.

74. Toffler, Alvin, *The Third Wave,* New York: William Morrow & Co., 1980.

75. *Ibid.,* pp. 221, 281.

76. *Ibid.,* p. 289.

77. Sale, Kirkpatrick. *Human Scale,* New York: Coward, McCann & Geoghian, 1980, p. 47.

78. *op. cit.,* Green, *Big Business Reader. op. cit.,* Commoner, p. 350.

79. Interview with Fred Branfman, California Public Policy Center, 1977.

80. *op. cit.,* Green, *Big Business Reader. op. cit.,* Committee on Small Business, p. 591.

81. *op. cit.,* Green, *Big Business Reader.* Rofsky, Mitch and Thompson, David, "Cooperatives Deserve Credit," pp. 539-41.
Deserve Credit," pp. 539-41.

82. *op. cit.*Sale, p. 46.

83. Ferguson, Marilyn. *The Aquarian Conspiracy,* Los Angeles: J.P. Tracher Inc., 1980, p. 332.

84. *op. cit.,* Sale, pp. 45-6.

85. *op. cit., Make the Future Ours,* p. 44.

86. *op. cit.,* Toffler, p. 253-5.

87. SRI International, *Changing Images of Man,* Menlo Park, April 1978, pp. 253-58.

88. *Ibid.*, pp. 229-30.

89. Tinbergen, Jan, Coordinator. *RIO, Reshaping the International Order: A Report to the Club of Rome.* New York: New American Library, 1976, pp. 193-5.

90. Hayden, Tom. Testimony at hearings of the Securities and Exchange Commission, Los Angeles, October 11, 1977.

91. Stone, Christopher, D. *Where the Law Ends,* New York: Harper and Rown, 1975.

92. *op. cit.*, Green, "A Case for...," p. 78.

93. For full details, write Ohio Public Interest Campaign (OPIC), 340 Chester 12th Bldg., Cleveland, Ohio 44114.

94. Woodcock, Georege. *Pierre-Joseph Proudhon.* New York: The MacMillan Co., 1956, p. 45.

95. "Criminal Enforcement of California's Occupational Health Laws," Center for Law in the Public Interest, Los Angeles, 1979, p. 18.

96. *op. cit.*, Green, "A Case for...," p. 107.

97. *op. cit.*, Nader, p. 123.

98. *op. cit.*, Hayden SEC testimony.

99. *Fortune Magazine*, April 1977.

100. New York *Times*, October 27, 1979.

101. Interview with author, 1980.

102. *op. cit., Paying More for Less*, Chapter 3: "Oil Company Non-Oil Operations.

103. *op. cit.*, Green, *Big Business Reader*. Green, Mark, "The Road to Monopoly," p. 507.

104. *Ibid.*

105. *op. cit.*, Branfman, p. 44.

106. *Ibid.*, p. 46.

107. *Ibid.*, p. 48.

108. *Ibid.*, p. 49.

109. Burger, Chester, *The Chief Executive,* Boston: CBI Publishing Co., Inc., 1978, p. 143-4.

110. *op. cit.*, Green, *Big Business Reader*. Ewing, David, "Free Speech With the Corporation," p. 291.

111. Zwerdling, Daniel. *Democracy at Work,* Self-published, Washington, D.C., 1978.

112. Henderson, Hazel. *Creating Alternative Futures*. New York: Berkeley Publishig Corp., 1978, pp. 6-7.

113. For more detailed information, write: United Auto Workers, Solidarity House, 8000 E. Jefferson Ave., Detroit, Michigan 48214.

114. Ogilvy, James. *Many Dimensional Man*. New York: Harper & Row, 1979, p. 35.

FOOTNOTES—GLOBAL VIEW:
THE FRONTIER OF PEACE

1. Interview with George Ball and William Simon on "The Kissinger-Shah Connection," *Sixty Minutes*, May 4, 1980.

2. Chomsky, Noam and Herman, Edward. *The Political Economy of Human Rights, Vol. I,* Boston: South End Press, 1979, pp. 13, 14, 19, 45, 64, 68, 292-293.

3. Business Week Team, *The Decline of U.S. Power.* Boston: Houghton Mifflin, 1980.

4. Ibid.

5. Shawcross, William. *Sideshow.* New York: Simon & Schuster, 1979, p. 90.

6. *Paying More for Less.* A California Public Policy Center Report, Los Angeles, May 1979, p. 11.

7. Duncan, Andrew. *Money Rush.* Garden City, New Jersey: Doubleday & Co., Inc., 1979, p. 113. See also New York *Times,* February 22 and 25, 1980.

8. Zinn, Howard. *A People's History of the United States.* New York: Harper & Row, 1980, p. 548.

9. Business Week Team. *The Decline of U.S. Power.* Boston: Houghton Mifflin, 1980, p. 125.

10. New York *Times,* January 25, 1980.

11. *Newsweek,* March 31, 1980.

12. *Ibid.*

13. *op. cit.,* Business Week Team, p. 142.

14. Kaldor, Mary. *The Disintegrating West.* New York: Hill and Wang, 1978, p. 25.

15. *Ibid.,* p. 105.

16. Ward, Barbara. *Progress for a Small Planet.* New York: W.W. Norton & Co., 1979, p. 95.

17. New York *Times,* January 25, 1980.

18. Los Angeles *Times,* January 18, 1980.

19. New York *Times,* February 2, 1980.

20. Daniel Ellsberg interview, Sierra Club Newsletter, January 1980.

21. New York *Times Magazine,* June 8, 1980.

22. *op. cit.,* Ward, p. 3.

23.

24. Halman, Talat Sait. "Islam Tomorrow," New York *Times,* January 15, 1980.

25. Inaugural address, January 20, 1961.

26. New York *Times,* October 20, 1979.

27. *Ibid.*

28. *op. cit.* Ward, pp. 262-3.

29. *Business Week,* November 19, 1979; see also New York *Times,* April 14, 1980 and *Wall Street Journal,* February 20, 1980.

30. Barnet, Richard J. *The Lean Years.* New York: Simon & Schuster, 1980, p. 126.

31. *Ibid.,* p. 152.

32. New York *Times,* January 21, 1980.

33. *op. cit.,* Yergin, p. 592.

34. Stobaugh, Robert and Yergin, Daniel, editors. *Energy Future.* New York: Random House, 1979, p. 136.

35. Hayes, Denis. *Rays of Hope*. New Yo .: W.W. Norton & Co., 1977, p. 139.
36. *op. cit.*, Ward, p. 95.
37. *Ibid.*, p. 93.
38. *op. cit.*, Barnet, p. 193.
39. *Ibid.*, pp. 191-198.
40. *Ibid.*, p. 19ᶜ
41. Ha᷅ , ᴠenis. "Energy for Development," *Worldwatch Paper 15*, December 1ᶠ ⸳/.
42. Clement, Norris, Professor of Economics, San Diego State University. "ᴠnited States-Mexico Economic Relations" working paper, November 1977.
43. *Ibid.*
44. *Ibid.*
45. President Lopez-Portillo quoted by U.S. Ambassador to Mexico, Patrick Lucey in personal interview with author, July 14, 1979.
46. *Ibid.*
47. *Ibid.*
48. *Ibid.*
49. Suggested by Mexican author Carlos Fuentes, personal interview with author, May 25, 1980.
50. See *Guayule: An Alternative Source of Natural Rubber*, National Academy of Sciences report, Washington, D.C., 1977.
51. This began to occur June 26-27, 1980 at the occasion of the first meeting of the border governors in Juarez-El Paso.
52. Suggested by Mario Obledo, California Secretary of Health and Welfare in remarks made at meeting May 2, 1980.
53. Said, Edward, *The Question of Palestine,* Times Books, 1980, p. 189.
54. Ibid. p. 125.
55. Ibid. p. 115.
56. Ibid. p. 115.
57. *op. cit., Make the Future Ours*, p. 8.
58. "The Pahlavi Problem: A Superficial Diagnosis Brought the Shah to the United States," *Science Magazine*, January 18, 1980.
59. ABC interview, May 21, 1980.
60. Los Angeles *Times*, February 4, 1980.

FOOTNOTES— POSSIBILITIES FOR THE EIGHTIES

1. Rifkin, Jeremy. *Own Your Own Job*. New York: Bantam Books, 1977, p. 60.
2. Ward, Barbara. *Progress for a Small Planet*. New York: W.W. Norton & Co., 1979, p. 117.
3. Harris, Louis. Louis Harris and Associates, 1637 K St., N.W., Washington, D.C. 20006.
4. *Ibid.*
5. *Ibid.*

6. *Make the Future Ours*, Draft Program of the Tom Hayden for U.S. Senate Campaign, Los Angeles, 1976, p. 44.

7. Ferguson, Marilyn. *The Aquarian Conspiracy*, Los Angeles: J.P. Tarcher, Inc., 1980, p. 338.

8. Schumacher, E.F. *Small Is Beautiful*, New York: Harper & Row, 1973; *Changing Images of Man*, Menlo Park, California: SRI International, March 1974; *Co-Evolution Quarterly*, Summer 1977.

9. *Ibid., Co-Evolution Quarterly*.

10. Mander, Jerry. *Four Arguments for the Elimination of Television*, New York: William Morrow & Co., 1978.

11. *Business Week*, June 30, 1980, p. 82.

12. *Ibid.*, p. 68.

13. *Ibid.*, p. 13.

14. *Ibid.*, p. 81.

15. *Ibid.*, p. 78.

16. *Ibid.*, p. 70.

17. *Ibid.*, p. 87.

18. *Ibid.*, p. 87.